INTRODUCTION TO COMPUTATION THEORY

INTRODUCTION TO COMPUTATION THEORY

RICHARD G. HAMLET
University of Maryland

INTEXT EDUCATIONAL PUBLISHERS
New York and London

Copyright © 1974 by Intext, Inc.

All rights reserved. No part of this book may be reprinted, reproduced, or utilized in any form or by any electronic, mechanical, or other means, now known or hereafter invented, including photocopying and recording, or in any information storage and retrieval system, without permission in writing from the Publisher.

Library of Congress Cataloging in Publication Data

Hamlet, Richard G
  Introduction to computation theory.

  Bibliography: p.
  1. Machine theory. I. Title.
QA267.H33   519.4   74–6071
ISBN 0–7002–2458–0

Intext Educational Publishers
257 Park Avenue South
New York, New York 10010

CONTENTS

List of Displays ix
Preface xiii

Chapter 1 Introduction

    1.1 Formal Theory and Intuition 1
    1.2 Finite Procedures 2
    1.3 Effective Procedures 4
    1.4 Digital Computers 7
    1.5 Plan of the Text 8

Chapter 2 Finite Automata

    2.1 "Black-box" Input/Output Behavior 11
    2.2 Formal Finite Transducers 13
    2.3 The Relation of Formal to Real Objects 17
    2.4 Recognition Behavior 20
    2.5 Formal Finite Acceptors 21
    2.6 Finite-State Languages 24
    2.7 Equivalence of Deterministic and Nondeterministic Finite Acceptors 25
    2.8 Regular Sets and Regular Expressions 29
    2.9 Closure Properties of Finite-State Languages 30
    2.10 Equivalence of Finite-State Languages and Regular Sets 35
    2.11 Non-Finite-State Languages. Multiplication 37
    2.12 Equivalence Problem for Finite Acceptors 39

Chapter 3 Number-Theoretic Functions

    3.1 The Natural Numbers $\mathbb{N}$. Functions from $\mathbb{N}^n$ into $\mathbb{N}$. 45
    3.2 Primitive Recursive Functions 46
    3.3 Examples. Explicit Transformations 47
    3.4 Primitive Recursive Derivations, Totality of Primitive Recursive Functions 49
    3.5 Enumeration of Derivations. Diagonalization. Non-Primitive-Recursive Functions 51
    3.6 (Total, General) Recursive Functions 52
    3.7 Partial Recursive Functions 54

vi Contents

Chapter 4 Turing Computability

    4.1 Partial-Recursive-Function-Derivation "Programs" 59
    4.2 Turing Machines 60
    4.3 Turing Computability 65
    4.4 Graphical Representation of Turing Programs. Examples 66
    4.5 Turing Computability of Each Partial Recursive Function 74
    4.6 Arithmetization. Gödel Numbering. Syntax and Semantics of Languages ...79
    4.7 "Predicates" and Functions 84
    4.8 The Syntax Predicate $TM(z)$ 87
    4.9 The Semantic Predicates $T_n(z,x_1,...,x_n,y)$ 90
    4.10 Partial Recursiveness of Each Turing-Computable Function 93
    4.11 Total Partial Recursive Functions. Effective Enumerations 95
    4.12 Church's Thesis 96
    4.13 Parametrization $(S\text{-}m\text{-}n)$ Theorem 97
    4.14 Syntactic Combination of Programs for Composition 99
    4.15 A Partial Recursive Function with No Total Recursive Extension 100

Chapter 5 Sets of Natural Numbers

    5.1 Recursive, Recursively Enumerable Sets 107
    5.2 Relationships between Recursive Enumerability and Recursiveness 109
    5.3 Post Canonical Systems 110
    5.4 Nonrecursive Sets. The Turing Halting Problem 115
    5.5 Further Reductions of K. Non-Recursively-Enumerable Sets 116
    5.6 Rice's Decision Theorem 118

Chapter 6 Argument Counts: Computable Numbers

    6.1 Pairing Functions 123
    6.2 Equivalence of One- and Multi-Argument Partial Recursive
          Function Theories 125
    6.3 Equivalence of Parametrization and Syntactic Composition in the
          Presence of Enumeration 125
    6.4 Computable Numbers 127
    6.5 Uncomputable Reals 128

Chapter 7 Register Machines

    7.1 An Idealized Computer and Its Assembly Language 130
    7.2 Formal Register Machines 131
    7.3 Compilation of Turing Programs to Register Programs 134
    7.4 Compilation of Register Programs to Turing Programs 139

Chapter 8 Abstract Programming Languages

    8.1 Partial Recursive Function Characterizations 144
    8.2 Numberings (Abstract Programming Languages) 145
    8.3 Acceptable Numberings (Abstract Programming Languages with
          Interpreters and Composers) 145

Contents vii

    8.4   Compilers. Rogers' Translation Theorem 147
    8.5   Separation of Syntax and Semantics 149

Chapter 9   Random-Access Machines

    9.1   Further Idealizations of Single-Address Computers 152
    9.2   Random-Access Machines (RAMs). Index Registers 153
    9.3   Random-Access Stored-Program Machines (RASPs). Program
           Modification 158

Chapter 10   Beyond the Partial Recursive Functions

    10.1   Program Complexity 167
    10.2   Abstract Program Complexity 168
    10.3   Concrete Program Complexity.................................170
    10.4   Formal Computations 173

    Solutions and Hints for Exercises 178

    References 191

    Index 193

LIST OF DISPLAYS

Universal flowchart for solving any problem 3
Flowchart to decide if any input chain has a weakest link 4
Useless multiplication flowchart 5
A data sheet for a finite transducer experiment 12
Prototype state diagram of a finite transducer 15
Transition table for the finite transducer experiment 15
State diagram for the finite transducer experiment 16
State diagram for a two-symbol code converter 16
State diagram for binary adders (serial in reverse) 16, 17
Moore code converter state diagram 20
State diagram for acceptors for the empty set, and for $\{a\}* - \{\Lambda\}$ 22
A state diagram for a deterministic acceptor which extends easily to a nondeterministic acceptor for a larger set 23
State diagram for $\{aba\}$ acceptor 24
State diagram for $\{a^k \mid k \geq 0\}$ acceptor 25
State diagram for an acceptor for (almost) ALGOL 60 identifiers 25
A natural nondeterministic acceptor converted to an unnatural deterministic acceptor 28
Schematic state diagram of an acceptor for the union of the languages accepted by two given acceptors 32
Schematic state diagram of an acceptor for the set product of the languages accepted by two given acceptors 33
State diagram of an acceptor for a particular finite set of strings 35
Definition of the sets R_{ij}^k related to finite acceptor behavior 36
State diagram of an acceptor to be reduced to standard minimum-state form 40
Table showing the acceptor reduction example 40
State diagram of the resulting minimum-state acceptor 41
Primitive recursive definition formats 46
Primitive recursive function derivation examples (sloppy) 47, 48
A primitive recursive derivation (less sloppy) 50
Primitive recursive derivation of the addition function and an implied computation of $3 + 2$ 51
Function which decides whether or not Fermat's last theorem is 51
A diagonalization question 52

ix

List of Displays

Recursive definition format 52
Sloppy recursive derivation of the division-by-two function 53
Partial recursive definition format 54
The Poor Richard Turing machine 60, 61
Yield operations permitted a Turing machine 62
Sample computation by the Poor Richard Turing machine 63
Exploded view of a Turing machine quadruple 63
Quadruples of a Turing machine which accepts $\{0^n1^n \mid n \geq 0\}$ ...64
Appearance of a numerical computation 65
Quadruples of a blanking-out Turing machine 66
Quadruples of a blankity-blanking-out Turing machine 68
Conventional diagrams for combining Turing machines using
"test and branch" 68
Turing machine for shifting over number code groups 69
Turing machine for computing the successor function 69
Turing machine for computing the projection functions 70
Comment diagram for the projection-function Turing machine 71
Turing machine for marking a tape at the left and shifting the original
contents to the right 72
Turing machine and comment diagram for repositioning a computed value
to the left on tape 73
Turing machine for copying a code group across an intervening collection
of code groups 75
Summary of the capabilities of component Turing machines used to prove
that all partial recursive functions are Turing computable 75
Turing machine which handles closure under composition 76
Turing machine which handles closure under primitive recursion 77
Comment diagram for primitive recursion Turing machine 78
Turing machine which handles closure under minimalization 78
Comment diagram for minimalization Turing machine 79
Intuitive definition of the Kleene function t_n 81
Eccentric notation for numerals 0–9 for coding Turing machines and computations 82
Examples of Turing machine and instantaneous description encodings 83
Relationships between intuitive "predicates" defined using logical operations and the primitive recursive functions really defined thereby 85

List of Displays

The concatenation predicate $w = xy$ 86
FORTRAN almost-ambiguous syntax constructions 87
The predicate $QUAD(x)$ asserting that x is a quadruple 88
The predicate $M(x)$ asserting that x has the partial appearance of a Turing program 88
The predicate $TM(x)$ which asserts that x is a syntactically correct Turing program 89
The predicate $TMQ(z,x_1,\ldots,x_4)$ which asserts that Turing program z contains a particular quadruple with elements x_1-x_4 89
The predicate $D(x,u,v)$ which asserts that x has the partial appearance of an instantaneous description in which the current state is u, and the scanned square contains v 90
The predicate $ID(x)$ which asserts that x is an instantaneous description 91
The predicate $YIELD(x,y,z)$ which asserts that x yields y on Turing machine z 91
The predicate $C(y,u)$ which asserts that y has the partial appearance of a numerical computation, in which the final code group represents the natural number u 92
The predicate $COMP_n(z,x_1,\ldots,x_n,y,u)$ which asserts that machine z on input $x_1,\ldots,x_n$ performs computation y with resulting value u 92
The Kleene T-predicate 93
The function U which recovers from a computation its computed value 93
Definition of $\varphi_z^{(n)}$ in the Kleene normal form 93
Cantor-like tableau for listing all partial recursive functions using the Turing machines which compute them 95
Form of the S-m-n theorem 98
Post canonical system production form 111
Post canonical system which generates non-multiply-declared identifiers 112
Proof of the declaration x;xxxx;xxx;xxxxxxx 113
Post canonical system productions to simulate a Turing computation 114, 115
The nonrecursive set K 115
Pairing function after Cantor's diagonal correspondence 124
General composition functions C_n^m 126
Operation codes of a register machine 131

List of Displays

Register program MUL2 for doubling (assembly language) 132
Yield operations of a register machine 132
MUL2 (formal description) 133
Computation by MUL2 of $2 \cdot 1 = 2$ 134
Register definitions for a Turing machine simulation 135
Definition of the macro D2R3 136
Initialization code for the Turing machine simulation 137
Simulating code for Turing machine quadruples 137, 138
Termination code 138
Simulation of SETZ, INC, JZDEC by Turing machine....................140
S-1-1 function obtained from pairing and composition 147
Format of RAM instructions 153
Yield operations of a RAM 154, 155
One-bit-word-length input routine (sample RAM) 156
Data structure for simulating a RAM with a register machine 157
Operation codes of a RASP 160
Transitions of the RASP 161
Yield operations of a RASP 162
Simulation of the RAM instruction INC 5(13) by a RASP 163
Instruction set of a RAM for complexity studies 171
ALGOL 60 programs which may and may not be patentable 175, 176

PREFACE

The word "theory" has two rather different general connotations. One has the character of speculation, an hypothesis or guess; this kind of theory is the opposite of "practice" and sometimes is criticized as being "idle." The other kind of "theory" is the scientific one, an explanation (as opposed to a catalog of facts) from general principles. In mathematics there is also a technical meaning, a body of definitions, axioms, and theorems which is a systematic presentation of a subject. The scientific and mathematical meanings become intertwined if the explanation of a phenomenon is mathematically expressed. From mathematics also comes the association of abstraction with theory, and (by way of those who have no interest in anything mathematical) a reputation as the more difficult part of any subject.

As a discipline, computer science occupies an interesting position with regard to theory and practice. On the one hand, the field has practical problems, important not only to the discipline, but of economic and social interest as well. So, as in a physical or social science, phenomena exist in computer science which require understanding and may even be controlled through that understanding. At the same time, the fundamental entities of the discipline, digital computers, are themselves entirely the product of human design, and in a sense represent an idealization of the way certain applied mathematicians performed calculations. In this aspect, the field is like mathematics in that the subject of study is under explicit control. The position is different in most other disciplines. For example, physics lacks the component of self-determination. How many physicists would have voted to scrap the kinetic-molecular theory in favor of Planck's work if the matter had been simply one of taste? Pure mathematics, on the other hand, need not really be concerned with the application of theory. There is no danger that someone will construct a rapidly converging Euler-Maclaurin series and threaten to destroy the world with it. Of course these positions are overdrawn, and the freedom of computer science to control its creations can also be illusional. Nevertheless, computer science theory is applied to practical computing as almost no other theory is applied.

xiv   Preface

One responsibility of theory in computer science is therefore to explain practical matters, and another to meet conventional mathematical criteria as systematic abstraction. These two goals are not incompatible, but neither are they close together. There is a considerable body of computer science which is really an enclave of pure mathematics in the discipline. The disappointing fact is that while computer science welcomes some mathematical experts, and recommends that students of the subject have a dose of theory as "preventative mathematics" (in case of a later attack of Fundamental Difficulties), not very many practical computer scientists attempt to understand and apply the deep results of theory.

This text attempts to draw upon mathematical work which applies to computer science, with two purposes. (1) By presenting the most elementary results in formal dress it can serve as an introduction to formal methods, and an entry to literature which might otherwise be difficult to read. (2) Even the beginnings of the mathematical theory have considerable explanatory power in the most concrete computing situations, and if the results are not new to practical people, perhaps the insights are. It might be taken as the goal of computer science theory to serve as a mental orientation in thinking about practical computing. This book tries to observe that goal.

As an advanced undergraduate or beginning graduate text, the presentation is self-contained. The reader should have a slight familiarity with the abstract idea of a function, and some exposure to prepositional calculus. He should be able to program in some high-level language, and should have seen an assembly language. All of these matters are covered in low-level undergraduate courses in computer science. Only a reader who is deficient in both mathematics and programming should have real trouble with the text; presumably such a person will not be at the advanced level.

An attempt is made to produce a readable presentation, despite the large number of displays and their abstract character. One technique used is the embedding of a display like

begin
comment *This ALGOL 60 program is included here to show that a good deal of complexity can be introduced in a sentence without losing track of where you were*;
procedure losetrack(position); **value** position;
losetrack(position);
string current;
current : = 'here';
if false then losetrack(current)
end

in sentences. The intent is for the reader to quickly scan the displayed object as if it were a parenthetical remark, then go back over it while reading the explanation given beneath it. Here, of course, the display is content free. Another technique is a certain affected hyperbole and innuendo within motivational sections. Nothing is stated which could not be defended, but at the same time the opposite position could often be defended with equal force. The slant of such remarks is obvious, and intended to have the same effect as waving a red cape at a bull with the difference that should the reader come charging into the material in response, it may not sidestep him. Within the text itself there is an occasional unexplained aside in parentheses (can you find an example of this?). These take the place of problems of the form "prove Theorem x" or "show that the statement near the bottom of page n is correct." Although usable as formal exercises, the intent of such remarks is to question the reader's understanding. It is presumed that he can do what is indicated relatively easily, and if not, something is wrong. The "official" problems both illustrate techniques and give results, and many are provided with solutions. Of course, the operations of working on a problem and looking at the solution do not commute when understanding is of interest.

The physical layout of the text is somewhat unorthodox. Equations, many displays, theorems, etc., are not numbered in any way, but a serious attempt has been made to force items into the index so that something vaguely remembered can be located quickly. This makes the book usable as a reference only if it has first been used as a text, and supports the narrative style which is intended to entice the reader to continue scanning even when the going gets rough. Where a reference to a previously appearing item is essential, that item will have been given a name, or will simply be repeated; cross references can then be by section only. Many displays are part equation, part figure, and woven into the surrounding text in a way that makes formal titles inappropriate. However, displays often stick in the mind, and indexing is not much help in locating what can only be recalled as a sort of blob at the bottom left of an unknown page. A descriptive List of Displays attempts to aid in finding such half-remembered figures.

Each chapter concludes with a brief list of references. The purpose of these sections is to credit the sources from which this text was drawn. In most cases the sources are accessible to students for a further treatment of material introduced in the chapter, but a few citations are historical or to more difficult current literature. No attempt has been made to locate the original source of most of the material, and the list of references collected at the end of the book is not a bibliography.

Let me acknowledge my own debts. R. W. Ritchie introduced me to the recursive-function-theory approach to computation theory, and consistently opposed a too-clever sweeping of difficult points under the rug of presentation. On the programming side, early use of Burroughs equipment was a continuing object lesson in doing things right even if no one can understand what has been done. In the preparation of the text, students in the Maryland core course in theory of computing provided initial motivation and a quantity of high-quality proofreading. H. P. Edmundson taught from the original notes, and devoted dozens of hours to discussing errors and confusions with me. A final debt is to technology, and unlike the people involved, technology could have done better. The IBM Selectric typewriter with various attachments is a boon to accurate representation of symbolic material. The pity is that when the whole thing has passed through fingers to paper, it must still pass through several other sets of fingers (and again be proofread) before printing. In a text on computing it is a duty to complain about the general unavailability of adequate document-preparation facilities.

1
INTRODUCTION

1.1 FORMAL THEORY AND INTUITION

The logical role of theory in computer science is somewhat like one role of symbolic logic in mathematics. In this application logic is used to systematize and explain informal mathematical thinking. In a sense the subject is a body of thought, which is studied by application of its own tools at a higher level. In computer science there is also a need for systematization and explanation, but the objects of this attention are not so much ways of thought as the realization of mental procedures in mechanical/electrical devices. In physical devices, the laws of physics apply, and as the devices are used by human beings the full range of social-science laws apply as well. But it remains true that the devices are man-made, and to understand them is not as difficult as understanding the hydrogen atom or the behavior of a crowd. Einstein said that God is only very subtle in making natural law—not damn mean. It may be that computer builders are mean enough, but they fortunately lack God's resources. Computer science is perhaps the only discipline in which instead of changing the theory to save the phenomenon, one can really change the phenomenon to save the theory, if that seems wise.

When we deal with fundamentals of computing it is therefore necessary to seek a clear picture of what is essential, and what is a matter of chance. If we cannot explain something properly, then we may not have to be concerned, for it may be only a random fact of life without implications. On the other hand, it may be intuitively the heart of the matter, and its explanation central to any theory. The ability to change the subject under discussion implies the responsibility of not abusing the privilege. The process of giving an explanation therefore proceeds something like this: First, an intuitive picture of the subject is sketched, as carefully as possible, but without details. Second, a mathematical description of the subject is attempted, guided by the intuitive outline, but seeking a "natural" expression rather than a perfect mimicry of intuition. The consequences of the mathematical definition may then be worked out, and their intuitive counterparts considered to check the "fit" with intuition. If there are obvious blunders, the mathematical definition is adjusted to eliminate them.

The formalization process has two difficulties: it is usually impossible to obtain all the consequences of a definition, and intuitive "fit" is a subjective matter. Thus we can never know that our work does not conceal a nasty surprise which will show it to be fundamentally incorrect, and even in the parts which have been explored, there may be no agreement about what the results mean. In compensation, formal notions are much easier to manipulate, and therefore results are obtained more rapidly within formalisms than in concrete settings; furthermore, results can be proved, and up to interpretation must stand unquestioned. Presentation of a formalism necessarily disguises all the trial and error that went into devising it, in order to avoid confusion. Also, it is usually assumed that the reader of a formal treatment will fight his intuitive battles elsewhere, and simply accept the mathematics as it is given. In an emerging discipline such as computer science these traditional attitudes may not be appropriate.

1.2 FINITE PROCEDURES

A "procedure" is intuitively something to follow, which implies that it is a given complete entity (otherwise we would say it was only part of a procedure), and that its author had in mind a follower and spoke to the latter's abilities. Associated with a procedure is a result which is to be obtained (although perhaps no guarantee that it will be attained). This implies that there is also associated an input, since if the following did not vary there would be no need for the procedure: the result could be obtained once and all else discarded.

The central theoretical issue in computation is certainly the nature of procedures which lend themselves to mechanical performance. At one time the specification of "mechanical" was more difficult than it is today, for we are now willing to attribute many marvels to cabinets with interiors of small electronic parts, and insist only on the existence of their definite boundaries through which no controlling intelligence can pass. Until recently, most people would not credit complex behavior in a device; today impossibly elaborate fakes are believed to be real. Because we build our machines to work perfectly, and do not often attempt to tolerate and circumvent failures by changing structure (as biological systems do), it is sensible to define mechanical performance as consisting of a fixed repertoire of precisely defined abilities, each of a circumscribed nature. Evidently then the mechanically manageable procedures are the ones which such devices can follow, consisting of component "steps" from the fixed repertoire.

It is important not to confuse a device (which has by definition a limited range of abilities) with a procedure which the device can follow. The difference is one of order: the procedure arranges a pattern of permitted steps in a sequence which is rather different from the simple unordered collection of abilities of the device.

1.2 Finite Procedures

Finally, there is the matter of arbitrary input and output which, intuitively, a procedure must be able to handle, or it will not be considered "general." It violates the idea of a well-circumscribed step performed by a mechanical device to in any sense "consider" an input all at once, when different inputs vary in complexity. A safer idea is to presume that a device may consider some limited portion of an input in a step, and produce output in the same way.

The flowchart is not the invention of the modern programmer, but high-speed machines have drastically increased its use. We use it to summarize the discussion of finite procedures. As all programmers know, the difficult thing about creating flowcharts is gaining precisely the correct level of expression in the component boxes. The flowchart of Fig. 1.1 always works, but its level is generally wrong for a mechanical computer (but not for the programmer, who has in effect been given such a chart, which is why he is trying to draw a more detailed chart). What is in the chart boxes corresponds to the permitted steps of the mechanical device, and the flowchart itself represents the procedure with which the device is to work. Existence of a step which examines a part of an input and use of that input to control the procedure are the permitted tests, and the only other kind of component dictated by our discussion is a way of producing a portion of an output. Other available operations depend on the details of the device.

As an example, consider a device which examines continuous metal chains of simple links, one link at a time. It has operations to advance to the next link and to detect the first and last. Let another operation test two links, the one currently under consideration and that considered just previously, to determine if one is the stronger. A final operation permits lighting a red light. Then the flowchart of Fig. 1.2 is a procedure for this device which tests the truth of the proposition that every chain has a weakest link (indicated by the

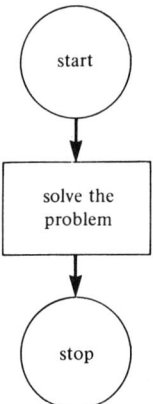

Figure 1.1

4   Introduction

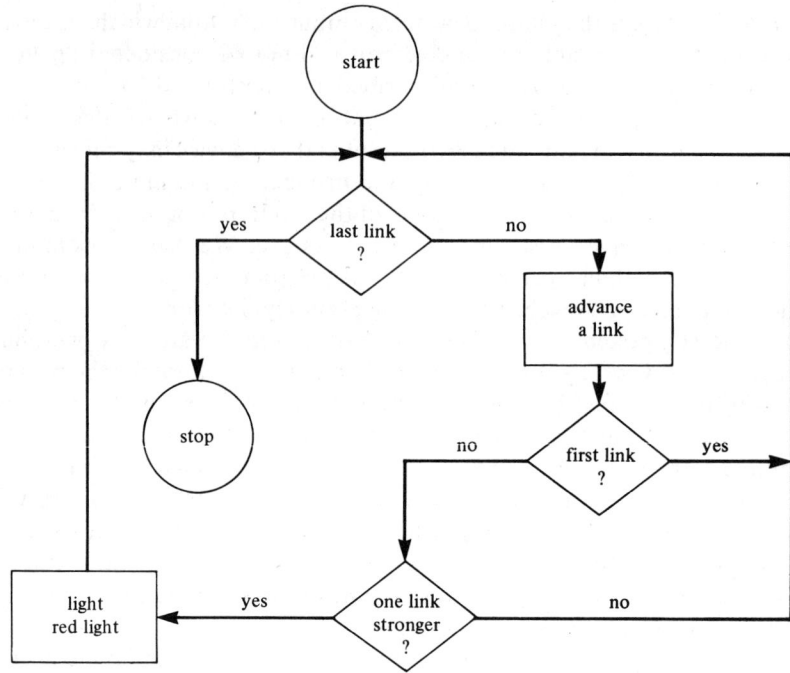

Figure 1.2

red light being lit when the last link of a chain is detected). Two interesting facts about this device and procedure are that to be intuitively mechanical, there must be some limit to the accuracy with which the determination of link strengths can be made, otherwise the device would have to be arbitrarily large or operate arbitrarily slowly; also, chains of fewer than two links are considered by the procedure to have no weakest link. (Those who object to this peculiarity should patch the flowchart. Can this be done if once on, the light cannot be turned off?)

1.3 EFFECTIVE PROCEDURES

Two important aspects of the finite procedures we have thus far considered are that there are very limited opportunities for them to malfunction, and that they can create no explicit intermediate results. (Of course, any procedure can malfunction in the sense that it does not realize a desired goal, but here we refer only to the prospect of never reaching any goal, which is an error we feel we could eliminate from any flowchart such as those presented in Section 1.2. As the example of that section indicates, there is a kind of intermediate result

1.3 Effective Procedures

recorded by steps along various paths taken or not taken, but the number of such paths is certainly limited in procedures which are themselves finite.)

Flowcharts more like those a programmer might actually write do make use of intermediate results; as we shall see, if there is no fixed bound on these, there is necessarily the possibility of a malfunction for which there is no general means of testing and repair. Consider the example of multiplying two numbers expressed in decimal numerals by the method of summing partial products. (An example with beads could be concocted—given a string of beads, the problem might be to detect patterns if the string were laid out beside itself repeatedly. But multiplication is the real example.) Certainly the description implied by the flowchart of Fig. 1.3 is one of those at the wrong level, and violates the requirement to examine the input in fixed-size pieces. A reasonable restriction on the device might be that one digit is the limit of input/output activity, and that its multiplication ability is confined to single-digit pairs, as is its ability to add. To use the grade-school procedure (which has just these limits) then requires some kind of "scratch paper" for putting down the partial products so that they may be added later. There are a number of problems of convention to be solved if we are actually to write the flowchart—the most difficult is how to imagine the input as consisting of two numbers in such a way that the device may obtain a digit from each as needed. Present purposes are served by avoiding the details, and considering only the number of digits which will be involved in the partial products before addition. There are cases in which for each partial product, $n \cdot m$ digits are required when a number of n digits is multiplied by one of m digits. There must be the smaller of n and m such products. To simplify matters to squaring, to square an n-digit number will require on the order of n^3 digits of partial product storage, plus a little extra for remembering carries and performing iterated addition later.

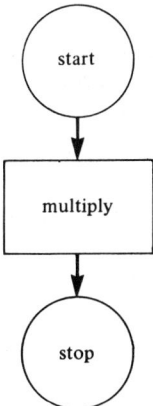

Figure 1.3

Perhaps there are clever ways to multiply that will require less scratch space, but it is difficult to imagine that it can be done without saving intermediate results whose size increases with the size of the input. It seemed intuitively correct to let mechanical devices examine arbitrary input and create arbitrary output so long as it was done a little at a time. Is it correct also to give them arbitrary scratch space if it is used in the same way? Probably most people who use computers would say so, because actual machines are not limited in this way. They use magnetic tape (among other things) for intermediate storage and, except for errors written into their operating systems, can use tape after tape, being limited only by the patience of the machine operator and the output of tape factories. But strictly speaking, once a device has indefinite scratch space, it is no longer finite, for it has no well-defined physical boundary, and in a sense grows as it works. Our intuition about its mechanical nature is saved by noting that on any one application only a finite amount of scratch work has been done before the result appears. Restricted to that much space, the device can solve only some problems of restricted size. The difficulty which has crept in is that should the device go on and on for some input, using more and more intermediate storage, it may be very difficult to tell if it is ever going to produce a result.

Before we investigate further the idea that the devices with unlimited scratch space are too powerful for us to really master, we should consider the other side of the coin: are such devices powerful enough to do whatever we ask of them? The only answer is that we have tried to allow anything which could be imagined as "mechanical," and hence might be constructed by men from parts whose workings are understood. There is considerable evidence that nothing further can be gained, in that the problem has been studied carefully at least since 1930, and the same result repeatedly obtained: all intuitively mechanical procedures have the same power, with remarkable indifference to their details. But of course no one can say what tomorrow will bring, even if he is willing to bet heavily on what it won't.

We return to the problem of examining the behavior of devices with unlimited scratch space. If there is no difference involving details, we may as well use a conventional programming language. Consider an implementation of a general-purpose language like ALGOL 60 or FORTRAN, and establish a convention for input and output from programs such that both are considered as strings of characters. A program of the language is such a string, but it may be considered also as a kind of transformation acting on input to produce output. Symbolize programs by upper-case letters when considering them as data strings, for example, P; use square brackets around the string name when considering it as a transformation, for example, $[P]$. It is not unreasonable to apply a program to itself as data, for example when listing a program which lists programs. If P were such a program, its output from itself as input would be written $[P](P)$ using the conventional functional notation. (It may or may not happen that such a lister treats details so that $[P](P) = P$.) Evidently any program could be applied to itself in this way, but for many there would be no output at all. (Let us agree to call a terminating diagnostic message "no output.") It is sensible to ask if one can decide whether or not a program will have any output when given its own character string as data. Certainly for some programs such an analysis can be carried out. But is there a general procedure which will work for any program? A precise form of this question is: does a program of the language exist with the property that its output is exactly *YES* if a program presented as data has output for itself as input, and exactly *NO* if it has none?

There is no such program for making the decision. If there were one, say T, it has by definition $[T](P) = YES$ if $[P](P)$ has a value, otherwise $[T](P) = NO$. It would be easy to modify such a T so that in place of the *YES* output for input P, the output would be the string $[P](P)$ concatenated with *YES*. To do so would require use of a built-in interpreter for the language, but writing this is at worst a practical problem. Suppose the modified program to be T' with $[T'](P) = [P](P)$ *YES* or $[T'](P) = NO$. Consider $[T'](T')$. This has some value, for T' has output for all inputs, by assumption of the existence of T. By the definition, the value must be $[T'](T')$ *YES*, which is impossible since this differs from $[T'](T')$ by three characters. There can thus be no such program T as was assumed.

The discussion appears to be some kind of trick, but this is not the case; rather, it expresses the central property of sufficiently powerful effective procedures. Many important details are suppressed in the informal discussion, and this kind of argument is certainly unreliable without details. In a careful discussion it also proves possible to characterize the programming languages which behave properly in their syntax-semantics division, in the sense that programs like T cannot be devised using some quirk of the syntax.

1.4 DIGITAL COMPUTERS

Electronic digital computers are the most complicated mechanical devices in existence today. The procedures (programs) executed on such machines are evidently archetype examples of the kind considered above, which in fact made it difficult to keep machines and programs out of the discussion.

A few cautionary remarks are in order, however. Access to the individual operations of computers has been restricted by the spread of high-level languages and assignment of basic operations as the unique prerogative of an operating system. There is nothing but good in this for most computer users, who may solve problems without knowledge of the arcane details. (The question of the priestly caste of systems programmers thus called into existence, and its social responsibilities, belongs elsewhere.) In considering fundamental questions, however, it is crucial not to confuse ideal features of programming

8 Introduction

languages with operations of the physical computing device. To give two important examples, the FORTRAN

   READ (9) ARRAY

in which a binary array is loaded is not one of the physical unit operations of any computer, since in principle the size of ARRAY's dimension is unlimited. In fact, a series of operations may be required to deal with such a statement. Similarly,

   integer i;
   for i := 0, i + 7 **while true do**
      begin x := cos(i) **end**

cannot be performed in any real machine without arranging arbitrary storage space to hold the successive values of the variable i; in fact, there is no limit to the amount of space so required. (There may be a way to accomplish the specified operation without arbitrary scratch space, but this depends on a peculiar property of the cosine function, and is appropriate only if i has no further useage; no existing compiler performs many optimizations of this kind.)

The point is not that one should distrust high-level languages (although that may occasionally be true) but that their operations hide use of arbitrary scratch space. Indeed, the fact that programming languages use unlimited intermediate storage implicitly is an argument for admitting it as intuitively available to procedures.

1.5 PLAN OF THE TEXT

Each chapter of this presentation is arranged as a relatively self-contained entity, ordered so that topics omitted from near the end will do the least damage to the understanding of succeeding chapters. The explicit dependencies are outlined below.

Three main topics are treated: (1) Finite automata, (2) computability, and (3) models of digital computers and programming languages. Topic 1 is self-contained, and other topics are related to it but without real dependence (but it is presented as a gradual exposure to formal methods which some students may welcome). Topic 2 is self-contained. Topic 3 draws heavily on (2) for its formal content, but parts can be read independently as exposition. The heart of the treatment is the presentation of Turing computability and the equivalence of the Turing-computable functions to the partial recursive functions.

Chapter 2 treats finite automata. An abbreviated treatment would omit Sections 2.7, 2.8, and 2.10 and thereby the deepest content of this section. Sections 2.11 and 2.12 are not explicitly used in other chapters.

Chapters 3–6 treat computability. The treatment of partial recursive functions in Chapter 3 is reduced to the minimum essential, but the details of

Sections 4.5–4.11 may be omitted in a survey. Section 4.15 and one of Sections 4.13, 4.14 may be omitted, but this will require some backfilling if Section 5.5 is included. The discussion of sets in Chapter 5 is important only because it contains the presentation of unsolvability; Sections 5.2, 5.3, 5.5, and 5.6 may be omitted if the subject is deemphasized. Similarly, Chapter 6 is quite technical and can be omitted entirely if the subjects are not of interest.

Chapters 7–9 consider application of formal methods to digital machines and programming languages. The treatment is concise only because it is similar in form to that of Chapter 4, but may be read independently as a survey by including only Sections 7.1, 7.3, and 9.1–9.3 for machines, or Sections 8.1–8.4 for languages.

Current application of the models presented in Chapters 8–9 is a discussion not so much of partial recursive functions as of their complexity. The topic is introduced in Chapter 10.

EXERCISES

1.1 Consider a device which has the ability to create its own procedure steps in the sense that one of its basic operations is to treat its own output as if it were part of a procedure being followed. Would such a device be effective in the sense of Section 1.3? Would it be finite in the sense of Section 1.2? Describe the action of such a device more carefully in terms of flowchart capabilities.

1.2 At the end of Section 1.3, a peculiar program T is discussed for a conventional high-level programming language, and the problems raised are claimed to be characteristic of devices with arbitrarily large intermediate storage. Explain where the unlimited storage arises in the argument. Consider applying the same argument to the finite procedures of Section 1.2. What is the result?

1.3 In a language with standardized input/output like FORTRAN or BASIC, write a program that lists programs, but whose listing of itself is not identical to itself.

1.4 Consider a programming language much like ALGOL 60, but with the following "test input" property of its syntax: each program is to specify, in a standard form, the output which it gives for the input *TEST*, or if there is no output, to specify this in a standard way. (For example, in ALGOL 60 the following would be an adequate form for each program to use: **if** instring = 'TEST' **then** outstring ('OK') **else begin** ⋯ **end**. The ellipsis would be replaced with the substance of the program, and 'OK' might be something more complex if 'TEST' were an input about which the programmer cared. On the other hand, if there were to be no output, the "outstring" could be replaced by "**for** i : = 0, i **while true do**" to force an unending loop at the test input.)

Show that the existence of such a piece of syntax implies the existence of a program T as in Section 1.3, and that no reasonable language therefore has the "test input" property.

1.5 For a particular digital computer with which you are familiar, carefully identify the operations and hardware devices which are clearly finite in the sense of Section 1.2, and those which might lead to potentially unlimited scratch space, as discussed in Section 1.3.

REFERENCES

The discussion of the intuitive significance of symbolic logic in mathematical reasoning is motivated by Rosser [1, Chapter I]. Rogers [2, Section 1.1] is the source of our Sections 1.2 and 1.3; Exercise 1.4 is a reworking of Rogers' Exercise 2-11. Many of the ideas about intuitive procedures were first caputred by Turing [3, 4].

2
FINITE AUTOMATA

2.1 "BLACK-BOX" INPUT/OUTPUT BEHAVIOR

Computing is an input-output process, not only at the level of conventional peripheral equipment, but in the component circuits of digital machines. From the study of such circuits, so-called *switching theory*, automata theory has grown. The basic device studied is a synchronous one presumed to be driven by an external clock pulse of some kind. At each tick of the driving clock, the device is presented with a digital input (that is, an electrical signal which takes one of a number of predefined values, small variations not considered), and responds with an output of the same kind. There are two ways to discuss the capabilities of such a device. First, its internal construction can be analyzed; this was the initial approach, which is useful only if there is some understanding of circuit elements and their connection. Second, the device can be viewed as a "black box" (so named because the standard color of experimental electronic enclosures was once black crinkle enamel) whose actions alone can be observed, in terms of inputs and outputs. The second approach certainly carries the practical restriction that there must be a finite number of cases to be studied or the device can never be mastered. The simplest experiment which can be performed is to provide just one input level from the finite number permitted (presumably these are printed on the box) and observe the output level which results. Repeating the test for each permitted input exhausts the capabilities of the simplest kind of box. A complication is that the box might contain something akin to a memory of previous inputs, in that the output might not always be the same for the same input. The essential restriction then becomes that some finite set of experiments must exhaust the tricks of any given device. The restriction is imprecise, and the characterization of finite machines demands precision.

A complication is caused by conducting experiments on a device which has an unknown history. This factor can be eliminated by imagining each device equipped with a "reset" button for standardization: pressing this button before an experiment guarantees that a repeatable result will be obtained. For the moment consider only such standardized experiments. A very general way to express the "finiteness" of the device is the following: all the infinity of possible sequences of input levels and the corresponding sequences of output response levels may be classified into a finite number of groups by the input. Each group may contain infinitely many input sequences, but the members are the same in the sense that if the device is reset, then presented with an input, there is no way to later distinguish which member of the group was in fact used. All later behavior of the device will be the same when preceded by any member of one group.

The "reset" button is an inessential convenience. For if all past behavior can at most represent one of a finite number of cases, then experiments conducted without the use of reset begin in one of those cases. Reset in effect selects one case as preferred; a device without a reset button might be thought of as comprising a finite collection of similar devices with reset, each standardized to a different starting point.

As an example, consider the input/output experiments shown in Table 2.1, conducted on a device with reset. (There are only two permitted input levels, represented by "0" and "1", and the same for output levels. The values represent input/output sequences, not positional numbers.) Now although we asserted that all experiments would divide inputs into a finite number of cases, there is no way to know when enough data have been collected to make the division properly. In this case we can distinguish two classes, but further experiments might distinguish more. Those that have appeared might be called the "ready to copy" class, and the "ready to reverse" class. In the former, a following input level will be simply reproduced as output; in the latter a following input symbol will be reversed. For example, experiments 3

Table 2.1

Experiment	Input	Output
1	0	1
2	1	0
3	00	10
4	10	01
5	01	11
6	11	00
7	000	101
8	010	110
9	100	010
10	110	001
11	001	100
12	011	111
13	101	011
14	111	000
15	0000	1010

and 4 show that "0" and "1" fall in different classes, since when these inputs are followed by "0" the result is different. Experiments 5, 6; 7, 9; 11, 13; 8, 10; and 12, 14 confirm this judgment. Other information consistently available is that the "ready to copy" class may contain "0", "01" (experiments 8, 12), "10" (experiments 9, 13), and "000" (experiment 15). The "ready to reverse" class may contain "1", "00", and "11". If indeed there are no more than two classes, by failing to use the reset, we should find that each experiment had only two possible outcomes, corresponding to accidentally being in the "ready to copy" or "ready to reverse" state at the outset.

2.2 FORMAL FINITE TRANSDUCERS

The difficulty apparent in describing the example makes an operational definition of a finite transducer very unattractive. We therefore present a formal mathematical definition, which will be argued to capture the essential features of the intuitive ideas. Although the traumatic introduction of mathematical ideas fits the purposes of this presentation, it is necessary to note that historically the formalism came about very gradually, and the elements of the definition are thought of as real entities by those whose training is more engineering than mathematical. As an example, one formal element of the definition is a finite alphabet of symbols which are used to construct input strings. These certainly correspond to the finite collection of permissible input levels in the intuitive device, but in the mathematics a set is a set, and its elements need not permit the unit "volts" to be appended as did the actual circuit levels. Similarly, another finite set in the mathematical definition is the states of the device. To the engineer, these are actual collections of switching elements. Again, a set is a set, and in the mathematics its elements need not be semiconductors.

Definition

A *finite transducer* is a 5-tuple $(\Sigma, Q, \Gamma, \delta, \omega)$ where Σ is a finite nonempty *input alphabet*, Q is a finite nonempty *state set*, Γ is a finite nonempty *output alphabet*, $\delta: Q \times \Sigma \to Q$ is the *state-transition function*, and $\omega: Q \times \Sigma \to \Gamma$ is the *output function*. ∎

The finite sets of the definition are clearly in accord with the intuitive model, if it is accepted that the states somehow correspond to the interior complication of the device. The behavior is entirely determined by the pair of mappings. Evidently, the device passes from state to state under the transition function, and as it does so the output function provides the responses. To go further with a verification that we have captured the essence of our intuitive transducers requires that we deal formally with sequences of input. The difficulties are almost entirely notational.

Definition

Let A be any finite nonempty set or *alphabet*, $A = \{a_1, \ldots a_n\}$. A *word* (*string*) over A is any finite sequence of elements from A, written carefully as $s_1, s_2, \ldots, s_k$ or $\{s_i\}_{i=1}^{k}$, the sequence being of *length* k, where each s_i, $1 \leq i \leq k$, is a_j for some $1 \leq j \leq n$. The less careful notation for such a string uses juxtaposition: $s_1 s_2 \ldots s_k$. The set of all words over A is

$$\bigcup_{k=0}^{\infty} \{s_i\}_{i=1}^{k}, \qquad s_i \in A, \quad 1 \leq i \leq k.$$

The peculiar sequence $\{s_i\}_{i=1}^{0}$ is called the *empty string* (*null string*), written Λ, while the set of all words over A is written A^*. ∎

The desired extension to the formal finite transducer is given precise form by extending the defining functions from the input alphabet Σ to Σ^*, by the following inductive definitions:

$$\hat{\delta}(q, \Lambda) = q, \qquad q \in Q,$$
$$\hat{\delta}(q, x\sigma) = \delta(\hat{\delta}(q, x), \sigma), \qquad q \in Q, \quad \sigma \in \Sigma, \quad x \in \Sigma^*;$$
$$\hat{\omega}(q, \Lambda) = \Lambda, \qquad q \in Q$$
$$\hat{\omega}(q, x\sigma) = \hat{\omega}(q, x)\omega(\hat{\delta}(q, x), \sigma), \qquad q \in Q, \quad \sigma \in \Sigma, \quad x \in \Sigma^*.$$

(The induction is on the length of the input string. Explicit use has been made of juxtaposition of strings instead of sequences.)

Since the definitions are framed so that $\hat{\delta}(q, \sigma) = \delta(q, \sigma)$ and $\hat{\omega}(q, \sigma) = \omega(q, \sigma)$ for all $q \in Q$, $\sigma \in \Sigma$, the hats over the functions will often be omitted; the context makes clear which is intended in all other cases.

The formal transducers may now be shown to have the property which was taken to be characteristic of intuitive transducers. The presence of a reset button is captured by adding a distinguished state to the

Definition

A *finite transducer with start state* is a 6-tuple $(\Sigma, Q, \Gamma, \delta, \omega, q_0)$ of which $(\Sigma, Q, \Gamma, \delta, \omega)$ form a finite transducer, q_0 being a distinguished member of Q, the *start state*. ∎

Theorem

Each finite transducer with start state $(\Sigma, \{q_0, \ldots, q_n\}, \Gamma, \delta, \omega, q_0)$ defines a partition of Σ^* into a finite number of classes $\Sigma_0, \ldots, \Sigma_n$ such that $\omega(\delta(q_0, x), z) = \omega(\delta(q_0, y), z)$ for each $0 \leq i \leq n$, for all $x, y \in \Sigma_i$, and for all $z \in \Sigma^*$.

2.2 Formal Finite Transducers 15

Proof

The classes are

$$\Sigma_i = \{x \in \Sigma^* | \hat{\delta}(q_0, x) = q_i\}, \quad 0 \le i \le n.$$

This finite set of sets must exhaust Σ^* since if any $x \in \Sigma^*$ were in no Σ_i, $0 \le i \le n$, then $\hat{\delta}(q_0, x) \notin Q$, contrary to the definition of $\hat{\delta}$. But then for each $0 \le i \le n$, for $x, y \in \Sigma_i$, we have

$$\hat{\delta}(q_0, x) = \hat{\delta}(q_0, y) = q_i,$$

so $\hat{\omega}(\hat{\delta}(q_0, x), z) = \hat{\omega}(\hat{\delta}(q_0, y), z)$ for all $z \in \Sigma^*$ since both are just $\hat{\omega}(q_i, z)$.

(The finite number of classes Σ_i of the theorem is not necessarily the smallest such collection since nothing prevents members of two such classes from being as indistinguishable (based on succeeding behavior) as are members of the same class. The point will arise again in Section 2.12.)

The finite transducer $(\Sigma, Q, \Gamma, \delta, \omega)$ may be described by conventional diagrams in an excellent way. Each state is represented by a circle containing its name, and the actions due to δ are shown by directed lines between the circles, labeled with values of input/output alphabet symbols: the input for the transition, and the output which accompanies it. For example, if $\delta(q_i, \sigma) = q_j$, where $q_i, q_j \in Q$, and $\sigma \in \Sigma$, this part of the transducer is represented by the part of the *state diagram* shown in Fig. 2.1.

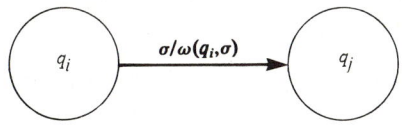

Figure 2.1

The transducer for which some experimental data were presented in Table 2.1 is described by $(\{0,1\}, \{q_0, q_1\}, \{0,1\}, \delta, \omega, q_0)$, where the functions are given by the table

$\delta(q,\sigma)/\omega(q,\sigma)$	σ	
	0	1
q_0	$q_1/1$	$q_0/0$
q_1	$q_0/0$	$q_1/1$

but this transducer is much more concisely described by the state diagram in Fig. 2.2 (at least this formal transducer agrees with the experimental data as far as it goes). (Which is the start state for the behavior with reset?)

16   Finite Automata

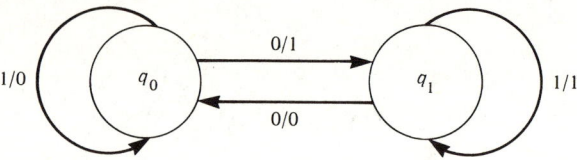

Figure 2.2

Two examples of finite transducers are of interest in connection with digital computer circuits. In both cases the formal model misses the mark, requiring some explanation to tie to the real world. The general copy machine ({a,b}, {q_0}, {u,v}, i,c), where i is the identity mapping $i(q_0,x) = q_0$ for $x =$ a or $x =$ b, and c is the copy mapping $c(q_0,$a$) =$ u, $c(q_0,$b$) =$ v, has the state diagram shown in Fig. 2.3 and evidently effects only a code change: a to u, b to v. Such devices are extremely common in computers, serving as interface modules between circuits whose codes (signal types and levels) are not the same.

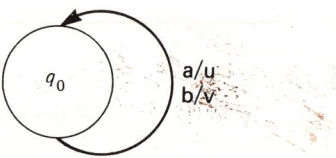

Figure 2.3

Perhaps the archetype finite transducer is the serial adder, designed to respond to two input sequences with a sum sequence. In practice the "inputs" are available as stored quantities, and the output is to be similarly stored, so the machine can operate backward from the right of the numbers to be added. Evidently this simplifies problems of alignment and carrying. However, our theory is not really up to a discussion of the problem, since it deals with only

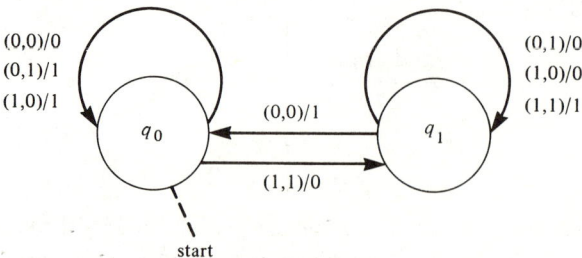

Figure 2.4

single-string inputs. The essence of a multi-input theory would clearly be a transition function defined on triples: a state and two input symbols. The state diagrams would have arrows labeled with input pairs. Then a binary adder might have the diagram shown in Fig. 2.4, from which the formal transducer (with start state) could be constructed if its definition were clear. There is a way to bring adding (and other multi-input ideas) under the theory we are using. Seeing two symbols at a time can be represented by seeing one symbol taken from a richer alphabet containing codes for all combinations of the two symbols. In the case of binary numbers, there are four such combinations, and with the correspondence indicated at the right, the adder might be drawn as shown in Fig. 2.5 with only a small loss in understanding. (Of course, this is not the only way to code a pair of input numbers. It might seem more reasonable to place them in the input sequence one after the other, using some special symbol to mark the transition. Apart from the fact that this is not very like what takes place in a computer, it certainly complicates the addition algorithm; indeed perhaps addition is impossible with this convention. The intuitive feeling is that it is unfair to present the device with a problem whose statement is so awkward. It is asking too much of a machine to do people work of that kind.)

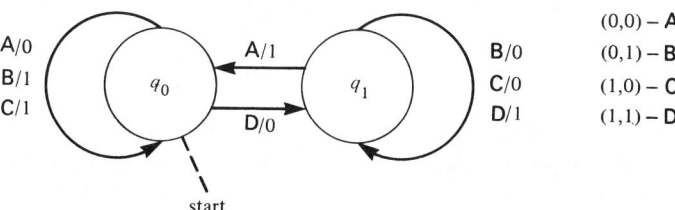

Figure 2.5

2.3 THE RELATION OF FORMAL TO REAL OBJECTS

The discussion of theory and intuition of Section 1.1 applies to formal transducers and the real objects which might be in black boxes. In what sense are we justified in substituting a treatment of the 6-tuple $(\Sigma, Q, \Gamma, \delta, \omega, q_0)$ as defined in Section 2.2 for a finite transducer which has been realized in hardware?

To a great extent, the choice of a formal object is a matter of taste, but there are some generally accepted rules. First of all, that some formal object must be studied is not seriously questioned. To conduct a discussion requires a common ground of abstraction, and lengthy laboratory experience cannot be conveyed on paper very well. (Indeed, what may be very clear in the laboratory loses clarity in the written report.) Second, there is no point in dwelling on the essential differences between abstractions and real objects, for example, that the former do not have physical properties such as price, size, color, etc. The difference is the very reason for the existence of formalisms, namely to strip away these details which are decided to be of no consequence. However, once that decision is made, it is not worth raising the issue at every turn. It is both a virtue and a failing of a formal transducer that you cannot burn it out by misusing it, but we don't talk about that aspect of the abstraction.

The matters of taste in formal theory come in judging how well the formal object "captures" the properties of the real one. This means that a point-by-point correspondence is established between the mathematical entities of the formal definition and the real entities, and a careful watch is maintained on how well the shadow of the formalism behaves in the real world. It is agreed that there shall be no obvious discrepancy in this behavior, but beyond that one can choose his own theory. For example, if the discussion of finite procedures in Section 1.2 is correct, and a finite transducer represents a (device and) procedure of this kind, then multiplication should be impossible for the formal transducers. There may be difficulty establishing a precise meaning for the statement "a finite transducer can multiply," but the arena in which to try is certainly the formal one, and the statement had better prove false, or those who feel that multiplication is not a finite procedure will never agree that the transducer theory is a good one. A more pedestrian illustration of this same principle was provided by the theorem that inputs to any (formal) finite transducer fall into a finite number of equivalent classes. If indeed this is the central property of a blackbox input/output device, then a formal object must have that property to be useful.

However, essential properties do not at all dictate the form of the complete formalism. An example is easy to give because it is an alternative in actual use. A transducer might as well have been defined as a triple (A,Q,m) in which A is an alphabet comprising all symbols for input and output, Q is a state set, and $M: A \times Q \to A \times Q$ is the combination transition-and-output function: in state q seeing (input) symbol a, $m(q,a) = (q',a')$ means that the device goes into state q' and gives output a'. There is simply no point in arguing details of comparison between this definition and the one given in Section 2.2; either would do, and the choice is a matter of taste. But of course it is essential not to change the rules in midgame, even if the new set of rules is just as fair, and the definitions of Section 2.2 must stand. Those who are offended are welcome to develop a parallel theory, and using the above definition should succeed, but there should be few takers. An alternative definition leads to a diluted understanding of the careful presentation because too much time is wasted in translating statements, and each gain in intuitive "feel" for the abstractions must be privately won.

However much we admit that it is silly to disagree about matters of taste, there is nothing easier to disagree about in fact. The borderline between important intuitive differences in definition and taste is not easy to draw. Again, there is a real example. The definition of a finite transducer given in Section 2.2

2.3 The Relation of Formal to Real Objects

follows intuitive ideas of G. H. Mealy, namely, that the way for a device to act is to use information about its current state and current input to determine both the next state to be entered and the output to give. This intuition appears in the formal definition in the domains of the transition and output mappings which operate on pairs. Another intuitive notion has an equally strong historical background. Following ideas of E. F. Moore, transitions of the transducer are still defined on state-symbol pairs. However, Moore imagined that the transducer's output was determined by state alone—as a matter of fact, the state to be entered, not by the previous state. This view is attractive from the standpoint of constructing actual devices, and is conceptually simpler. (A slot machine, for example, pays off not because of the state it was in when the handle was pulled, but because of the state it enters next.)

We will not use "Moore transducers" in this book except in discussion and exercises. When "finite transducer" is used, the Mealy version of Section 2.2 is always intended. Nevertheless, we outline the Moore definition as an alternative whose advocates might put up an argument about just what is taste and what is not.

The Moore transducer definition is not much different from that given in Section 2.2; only the domain of the output function must be changed. The real difference comes in the consideration of output strings—what the transducer does. To emphasize that the definitions are nonstandard, we will avoid the usual trappings of definitions. With input alphabet Σ, state set Q, output alphabet Γ, transition mapping δ, and output mapping ω, the Moore transducer has $\hat{\delta}: Q \times \Sigma^* \to Q$ just as in Section 2.2. However, the Moore output function $\omega: Q \to \Gamma$ cannot be extended to Σ^*, since it does not involve Σ. Thus a criticism of the Moore formalism is that its basic elements cannot be directly used to describe how the formal object is to act. A separate definition is required for the string which the machine gives as output for a given input string. To parallel the discussion of Section 2.2, call this output-string function ω', $\omega': Q \times \Sigma^* \to \Gamma^*$, with the inductive definition

$$\omega'(q,\Lambda) = \omega(q)$$
$$\omega'(q,x\sigma) = \omega'(q,x)\omega(\delta(\hat{\delta}(q,x),\sigma))$$

for each $q \in Q$, $\sigma \in \Sigma$, and $x \in \Sigma^*$.

According to this definition, there is an output associated with null input, and the output string is always one symbol longer than the input string. It is precisely such matters that some consider inconsequential, and others are prepared to defend at some length.

In the state diagram of a Moore transducer, only the input symbol labels the arrow passing to the next state. The symbols within the state circles represent the state name and the output which is delivered upon entering that state. For example, the Moore transducer of Fig. 2.6 does as

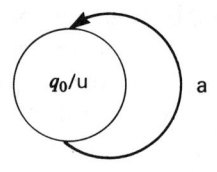

Figure 2.6

well as can be done with the code conversion from **a** to **u**. (Why is its best less than satisfactory?) (Can you draw a state diagram for a Moore transducer which simultaneously converts **b** to **v** in addition?)

2.4 RECOGNITION BEHAVIOR

In some applications the output of a mechanical device is less interesting than the input, in the sense that only two classes of input are of consequence: the acceptable and the nonacceptable. (In quality-control testing, for example, the items tested pass or are rejected.) Certainly such behavior can be described with finite transducers by establishing a criterion for pass/fail based on the output which arises from inputs. (If we actually wanted to carry out such a program, why would the Moore transducer be a better choice?)

A more compelling reason to consider only input behavior of finite-state devices is that this focuses attention on the transitions of the device, which seem to be the essential feature of its behavior. (Recall that we took as the characteristic property of the black box its ability to separate its inputs into a finite number of classes, and that the formal analog of this property was the finite number of states into which the machine could pass.) Device "memory" results from choice of transition paths, which is not output dependent. Intuitively, "recognition" is a process most often applied to single strings, not pairs of inputs as are some common function computations. All in all, the recognizer seems a more convenient object to study carefully than the transducer, yet it retains the most important intuitive ideas about finite procedures.

The choice of acceptance or nonacceptance can be signaled entirely without output by imagining that states come in two forms. The first, nonaccepting states, are voiceless, but the other, accepting states, give an indication when the device is in one. Perhaps a tone sounds or a light goes on. Thus as the intuitive device operates under the control of its synchronous clock, it emits a kind of binary code consisting of broken strings of tones or flashes. (For example, on an input which passed through no accepting state the device would appear quiescent; on the other hand, if it started out in an accepting state and made transitions only into such states, it would emit a steady tone or steady illumination.) A number of definitions might be adopted for such a device to approve of a complete input string, using everything from a complete prescribed pattern to just one state into which the input eventually drives it. The latter is a better choice, since it does not prejudge the length of the input.

Part of the historical basis for finite acceptors (to name the devices after their "success" results) is the judgment of inputs as part of languages. That is, a sensible question for consideration is whether or not such a device can decide questions of grammatical correctness. This study is outside the scope of the present treatment, but accounts for the terminology of input "sentences" and "languages" accepted by a device.

2.5 FORMAL FINITE ACCEPTORS

There is little disagreement about the definition of an acceptor model, probably because the theory is newer, and arises more from mathematics than engineering. The abstract viewpoint is also shown by the introduction of a nondeterministically operating device which would be difficult to construct.

Definition

A *finite acceptor* is a 5-tuple (Q,Σ,δ,q_0,A), where Q is a nonempty finite set of *internal states*, Σ is an alphabet, $q_0 \in Q$ is the *start state*, and $A \subseteq Q$ is the set of *accepting states*. The range of the *transition mapping* δ determines the type of acceptor; it is *deterministic* if $\delta: Q \times \Sigma \to Q$, or *nondeterministic* if $\delta: Q \times \Sigma \to 2^Q$. ($2^Q$ denotes the set of all subsets of Q.) ∎

By analogy to the finite transducer, the deterministic acceptor passes from state to state under the control of the transition function, and could be described by a state diagram stripped of its output symbols. (The purpose would be stripped along with the output; another definition is required to give acceptors a purpose.)

Nondeterminism has a motivation which is a little difficult to explain: it is introduced because it makes no difference in the power of the device. That is, it will be proved in Section 2.7 that whatever a finite nondeterministic acceptor can do, a finite deterministic one could do as well, and vice versa. What is different in the two ideas is the ease with which a nondeterministic acceptor can be "programmed" to accomplish some tasks. Nondeterminism incorporates patterns of trial and error procedures without requiring them to be explicit. A simple nondeterministic acceptor may therefore be equivalent to a complex deterministic one. Before it is possible to explain further, the defining purpose must be presented. In this the accepting states play the crucial role:

Definition

The deterministic finite acceptor (Q,Σ,δ,q_0,A) *accepts* a string $x \in \Sigma^*$ iff $\delta(q_0,x) \in A$. (For the deterministic case, the extension of δ to strings over the acceptor alphabet is accomplished exactly as for the finite transducer: $\delta(q,\Lambda) = q$ and $\delta(q,x\sigma) = \delta(\delta(q,x),\sigma)$ for all $q \in Q$, $\sigma \in \Sigma$, and $x \in \Sigma^*$.) ∎

The intuitive content of an acceptor is thus its behavior on various input strings—whether or not it accepts them. The adaptation of the state diagram to deterministic acceptors has two new elements: the starting state must be identified, and so must the accepting states. It is common to include an arrow from nowhere pinning the start state, and to use a double circle for accepting states. As illustration, one of the acceptors diagrammed in Fig. 2.7 accepts every string over its single-symbol alphabet; the other accepts only the null string. (It is no harder to draw one which accepts no strings, but the null-string case is the source of many "buggy" acceptors.)

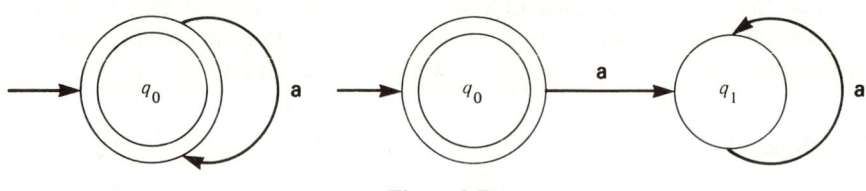

Figure 2.7

It is clear that the sense in which one acceptor is equivalent to another is that their accepting behavior is the same. But before we can discuss nondeterministic acceptance, we must find a way to extend the transition function to strings. Intuitively, at each step the nondeterministic acceptor makes a choice. It may have, for example, three states in the transition image for some particular symbol seen in some particular state. We want to capture the idea that it might choose to go into any one of these three states, and that acceptance is determined by any possible path which may result from such choices, the paths which end in nonaccepting states to be ignored as trials ending in error. Thus each of the steps resulting from succeeding applications of the transition function involves a selection of some state from the set of possibilities.

The extension of a transition mapping must agree with the unextended mapping on single symbols, so it must produce sets of states. We have tried to motivate the

Definition

The nondeterministic finite acceptor (Q,Σ,δ,q_0,A) *accepts* a string $x \in \Sigma^*$ iff $\hat{\delta}(q_0,x) \cap A \neq \emptyset$, where the extension $\hat{\delta}$ of δ is defined inductively by

$$\hat{\delta}(q,\Lambda) = \{q\}, \quad q \in Q,$$

$$\hat{\delta}(q,x\sigma) = \bigcup_{q' \in \hat{\delta}(q,x)} \delta(q',\sigma), \quad q \in Q, \ \sigma \in \Sigma, \ x \in \Sigma^*. \ ∎$$

(The idea of the definition is that at each step we collect all the transition-function images which could result from all the members of the set produced at the last step. Then acceptance means that in the set of all transition possibilities, at least one member is also an accepting state.)

The distinction between the hatted mapping and the one given with an acceptor need not be preserved in the nondeterministic case any more than it was for the deterministic, and furthermore there is no need to be careful about stating whether or not a given acceptor is deterministic or nondeterministic since the form of the mapping gives this away. In a state diagram, a nondeterministic acceptor might have several arrows leaving a state with the same symbol label on each and so indicate what sort of device it specifies. If this does not happen, it is easy to see that it does not matter: a nondeterministic acceptor with only singleton sets for transitions must do exactly what a deterministic version shorn of all the curly brackets would do. More care will be devoted to the relationship between the two kinds of acceptors in Section 2.7.

It is possible to illustrate "ease of programming" nondeterministic acceptors with a simple example. Consider designing an acceptor which will accept just inputs which start with **ba** and continue with an indefinite (possibly zero) number of **b**'s. A deterministic acceptor as in Fig. 2.8 is straightforward (ignore the dashed line at the top for the moment). However, suppose we seek to accept just indefinitely long (but at least one) repetitions of this pattern. No easy modification of the acceptor suggests itself, because there is no way to tell whether a particular **b** should be taken as the initial one of a new pattern or as just one more at the end of the old. By placing the label **b** on the dashed arrow

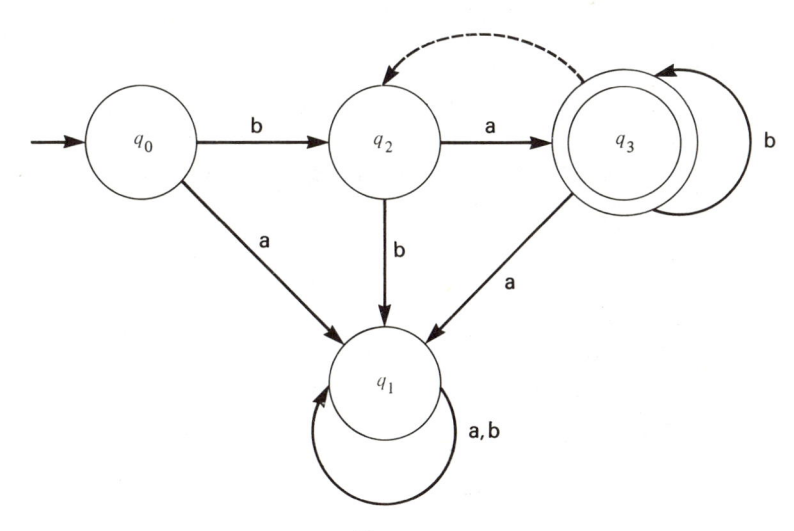

Figure 2.8

from q_3 to q_2 we create a nondeterministic acceptor which has the required properties. In q_3, on seeing a b it makes a choice about whether or not to begin a new pattern.

2.6 FINITE-STATE LANGUAGES

It is useful to have a name for the set of strings which an acceptor accepts:

Definition

A *finite-state language* is the set of strings accepted by some finite acceptor. ∎

(The adjective "regular" is much used with entities which have something to do with a finite procedure, and the sets accepted by finite acceptors are sometimes called "regular languages." In this presentation, such usage would be confusing, because we are going to establish its source in a proof that the finite-state languages can be defined in another way.) Note that we have not specified whether or not the acceptor involved in the definition is deterministic or nondeterministic, so for the moment either would accept (by different definitions) a finite-state language. The much heralded result of Section 2.7 will prove that there is no difference. A second note is in order about the exclusion part of the definition: the set of strings accepted does not, of course, include strings not accepted. This conflicts a bit with our usual linguistic habits in that we usually say "accept" in a sense which is not exclusive: if I accept all men as my brothers, then I certainly accept all black men as my brothers. But a finite acceptor could not do both of these things (if it cared about men as it does not): if it accepts all men, then it accepts all colors, and by failing to reject the non-black, it does not accept blacks; or, if it accepts blacks, it must necessarily reject all others.

Some examples will shed no light on race relations, but may help with finite-state languages. Given the singleton alphabet $\Sigma = \{a\}$, the following are all finite-state languages, because their acceptors have been discussed in

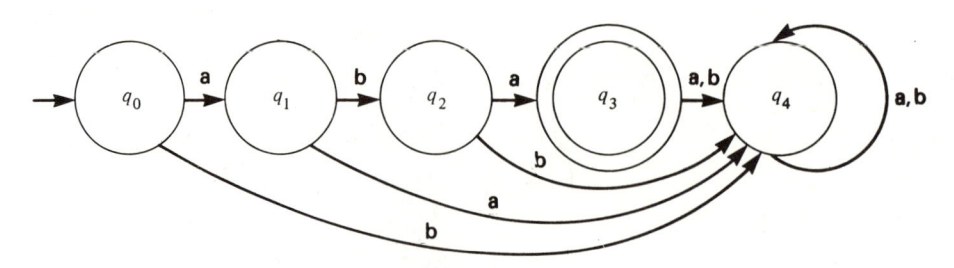

Figure 2.9

Section 2.5 (Fig. 2.7):

$$\Sigma, \quad \{\Lambda\}, \quad \emptyset.$$

If the alphabet has two symbols, $\Sigma = \{a, b\}$, then $\{a\,b\,a\}$ is a finite-state language, its acceptor being diagrammed in Fig. 2.9, and $\{a^k | k \geq 0\}$—in other words, all strings (including null) of only a symbols—is a finite-state language, accepted by the acceptor of Fig. 2.10.

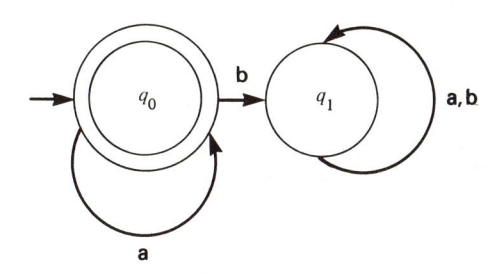

Figure 2.10

The entities something like identifiers in which a plays the role of any letter, and b of any digit, in phony Backus Normal Form

$$\langle id \rangle ::= a | \langle id \rangle a | \langle id \rangle b$$

is a finite-state language, its acceptor shown in Fig. 2.11.

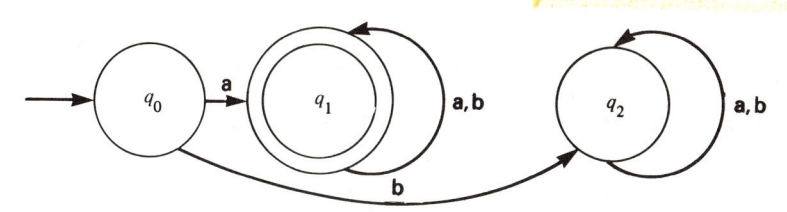

Figure 2.11

Finally, the strings which repeat patterns of b a followed by (perhaps) any other b at least once, comprise a finite-state language by display (Fig. 2.8 including the dashed line) of the nondeterministic acceptor at the end of Section 2.5.

2.7 EQUIVALENCE OF DETERMINISTIC AND NONDETERMINISTIC FINITE ACCEPTORS

It should be clear that the nondeterministic acceptor is potentially the more powerful device, since it may invoke choices which the deterministic acceptor cannot. This intuition is precisely captured by the

Theorem

The set of strings accepted by any deterministic acceptor is also accepted by a nondeterministic acceptor.   FA ⊂ NFA

Proof

Let the deterministic (Q,Σ,δ,q_0,A) be given. The appropriate nondeterministic acceptor is (Q,Σ,δ',q_0,A) in which $\delta'(q,\sigma) = \{r\}$ when $\delta(q,\sigma) = r$, for each $q \in Q$, $\sigma \in \Sigma$. Suppose either of these acceptors accepts a string. Then the other does so also, passing through exactly the same states. The nondeterministic acceptor has in fact no choices. ∎

The more interesting result is the converse: that the nondeterministic acceptor is not more powerful. At first it might seem difficult to "program" the choices of the nondeterministic operation explicitly. Further reflection indicates that only a sufficient quantity of states is needed. In a deterministic acceptor which possessed all the path choices of a nondeterministic one, the successful paths would lead to accepting states, and the trials ending in error to nonaccepting states. Thus the proper strings would be accepted.

Theorem

The set of strings accepted by any nondeterministic acceptor is also accepted by a deterministic acceptor.   NFA ⊂ FA

Proof

Let the set of strings accepted by the nondeterministic acceptor $M_n = (\{q_0,\ldots,q_n\}, \Sigma, \delta, q_0, A)$ be S. The deterministic acceptor $M_d = (Q', \Sigma, \delta^1, [q_0], A')$ is the one required. As indicated by the initial state, Q' contains elements symbolized strangely, which represent subsets of Q, but are notationally not sets. It is convenient to have an explicit notation for the state symbol which represents a subset of Q. We write

$$\{q_{i_1}, \ldots, q_{i_k}\}^\# = [q_{i_1} \ldots q_{i_k}]$$

the transformation eliminates the curly brackets in favor of square ones, discards commas, and places the elements in subscript order, that is, $i_1 < \cdots < i_k$, $1 \leq k \leq n+1$. Then we easily write the definition for the new components of the deterministic acceptor:

$$Q' = \{X^\# | X \subseteq Q \text{ and } X \neq \emptyset\},$$
$$\delta'(X^\#,\sigma) = (\bigcup_{q \in X} \delta(q,\sigma))^\#, \quad X^\# \in Q', \quad \sigma \in \Sigma,$$
$$A' = \{X^\# | X \cap A \neq \emptyset\}.$$

2.7 Equivalence of Deterministic and Nondeterministic Finite Acceptors

The proof that this acceptor is the correct one uses a lemma which displays a property of the extended δ':

Lemma

$$\delta'([q_0],x) = (\delta(q_0,x))^{\#}, \qquad x \in \Sigma^*.$$

Proof

Induction on the length of the string x.

Case 1. The length of x is zero. Then $x = \Lambda$, and by the two definitions for the extended transition functions for deterministic and nondeterministic acceptors, the left side in the lemma is $[q_0]$, the right is $(\{q_0\})^{\#}$, and these are indeed the same.

Case 2. The length of x is $n > 0$. The inductive hypothesis is that the lemma holds for all strings of length $n - 1$. Then let $x = y\sigma$, $y \in \Sigma^*$, $\sigma \in \Sigma$, and again consider the existing definitions for the extended transitions:

$$\text{deterministic: } \delta'([q_0],y\sigma) = \delta'(\delta'([q_0],y),\sigma);$$
$$\text{nondeterministic: } \delta(q_0,y\sigma) = \bigcup_{q \in \delta(q_0,y)} \delta(q,\sigma).$$

The former can be reduced to the latter by using the inductive hypothesis on the inner application of δ', since the string involved is of length $n - 1$. This gives $\delta'((\delta(q_0,y))^{\#},\sigma)$, a form to which the definition of δ' applies with the proper result. ∎

To complete the proof of the theorem, we show that a string is accepted by M_n if and only if it is accepted by M_d. The only difficult step in the following chain of equivalent statements is supported by the lemma.

Let $x \in S$, that is, M_n accepts x. This means that $\delta(q_0,x) \cap A \neq \emptyset$. By definition of A' this happens iff $(\delta(q_0,x))^{\#} \in A'$, which by the lemma may be written $\delta'([q_0],x) \in A'$, precisely the meaning of the statement that M_d accepts x. Thus M_d accepts S, as was to be proved. ∎

The finite-stage languages are thus shown to be those accepted by deterministic or nondeterministic finite acceptors alone, if such a restriction should be convenient.

We can illustrate the construction of the proof and the assertion that some nondeterministic acceptors are easier to understand than the equivalent deterministic acceptors, by constructing the deterministic equivalent of the nondeterministic device described at the end of Section 2.5 (Fig. 2.8). That device accepted repetitions of the pattern **ba** followed by an arbitrary number

28 Finite Automata

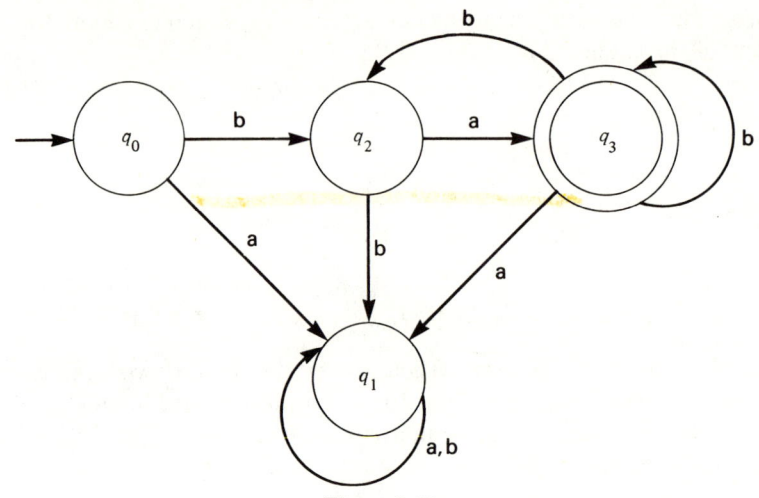

Figure 2.12

of b symbols. Its state diagram is repeated as Fig. 2.12. Part of the deterministic equivalent showing the composite state names and transitions is given in Fig. 2.13; its greater complexity is evident. (What part of the deterministic acceptor is omitted, and why?) (When performing the construction, is it apparent what parts to omit?)

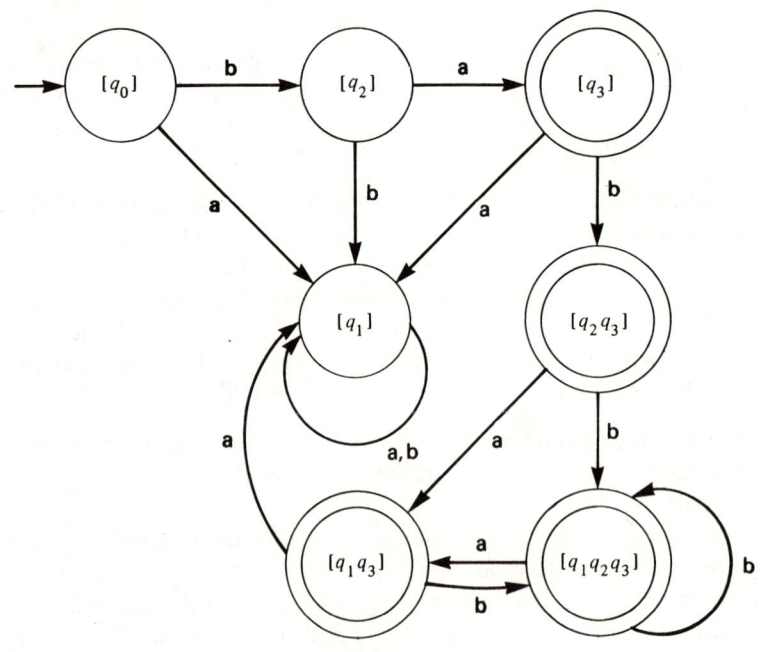

Figure 2.13

2.8 REGULAR SETS AND REGULAR EXPRESSIONS

We shall now describe two more classes of sets, associated with a kind of finite definitional procedure very different from the finite acceptor. The fact that these classes are only the finite-state languages in disguise will be the main result of this chapter. The first class arises from sets of finite strings by imagining any finite number of special operations to be performed on these basic sets. One operation is set union; the two others are:

Definition

The *set product* (ordinary, as opposed to Cartesian) of sets E and F (written: EF) is $EF = \{ef | e \in E \text{ and } f \in F\}$. Note the use of string concatenation; more care would require use of sequences again. The *Kleene closure* of set E (written: E^*) is

$$E^* = \bigcup_{n=0}^{\infty} \underbrace{E \ldots E}_{n}, \quad \text{where} \quad \underbrace{E \ldots E}_{0} = \{\Lambda\}.$$

$$(\underbrace{E \ldots E}_{n} \text{ means } \underbrace{E(E(\ldots (EE) \ldots))}_{n})$$

and is often written E^n.) ∎

Definition

The class of *regular sets* over an alphabet A is the smallest class containing the finite subsets of A^* and closed under the operations of union, set product, and Kleene closure. ∎

A second class of sets arises from a descriptive notation which strongly resembles a specification of a regular set. However, the notation is a strictly formal, symbolic matter, and must be related to sets with care.

Definition

The class of *regular expressions* over an alphabet A and the class of *sets described* by the regular expressions (for expression R, $S(R)$ denotes the set described by R) are inductively defined by:

Each $a \in A$ is a regular expression, describing the set $\{a\}$.
$\emptyset$ is a regular expression describing the empty set $\emptyset$.
If R is a regular expression, so is $(R)^*$, describing $S(R)^*$.
If R and T are regular expressions, so is $(R) \vee (T)$, describing $S(R) \cup S(T)$.
If R and T are regular expressions, so is $(R) \cdot (T)$, describing $S(R)S(T)$.
Nothing else is a regular expression. ∎

Theorem

The sets described by regular expressions are the regular sets over the same alphabet.

Proof

In one direction, by induction on the number of "connectives" ★, v, ·, in the regular expression; in the other, by induction on the number of closure operations which form the regular set. Since there is a clear correspondence between the inductive definitions, the proof is not interesting enough to write out in detail. ∎

Regular expressions are largely used to describe sets, and when ambiguities in the expression do not produce any doubt about which set is described, the expression is often written ambiguously. For example, since union and set product are associative, instead of the expression over {a,b}

$$(((a) \cdot (b)) \cdot (b)) \vee (((a) \cdot (a))\star)$$

one sees

$$(abb) \vee ((aa)\star) \text{ or even } abb \vee (aa)*$$

with decreasing precedence by analogy to arithmetic: ★, ·, v. Not only is the star often written in its easier-to-type form, but ∅ is often written for $\emptyset$. A multitude of notations exist, most containing some confusion between the expressions and the sets which are described. Here some pains have been taken to avoid such confusions. In describing sets, there are also many alternative forms for the same set. For example, although the regular expressions $E\star$ and $(E\star)\star$ are very different as strings of symbols, it is easy to see that $S(E\star) = S((E\star)\star) = S(E)*$. Many equivalences of this kind are not so easy to verify, since the only real method for establishing them in practice is detailed consideration of set memberships.

2.9 CLOSURE PROPERTIES OF FINITE-STATE LANGUAGES

Although the material of this section appears to be concerned with acceptors and their combination in various ways, the actual subject is regular sets. We investigate the results of applying the closure operations of regularity to sets which are accepted by finite acceptors, and note that the resulting sets are also accepted by finite acceptors. The existence of an acceptor for each finite set then shows that every regular set is a finite-state language. A reasonable framework for the discussion is a series of results within that statement.

2.9 Closure Properties of Finite-State Languages

Theorem

Each regular set is a finite-state language.

Proof

Although some details will be provided, most of the work is so straightforward that pictorial proofs appear adequate. The omitted argument is always an induction on the length of strings accepted. One such argument is given as convincing evidence that the others should not be given. For the closure results which make up the bulk of the proof, it is convenient to assume that all machines have the same alphabet. Versions in which different alphabets are used are easy to write and not much harder to prove, but the purpose is to consider regular sets, and the alphabet is eventually going to be fixed as that over which the set is formed. It is also convenient to assume that when two machines are combined, their state sets are disjoint, so that there can be no confusion caused by merging states.

Lemma 1

The class of finite-state languages is closed under union.

Proof

The lemma means that if $M_p = (P, \Sigma, \pi, p_0, A_p)$ accepts language L_p, and $M_r = (R, \Sigma, \rho, r_0, A_r)$ accepts language L_r, then $L_p \cup L_r$ is accepted by some finite acceptor. If M_p and M_r are chosen deterministic, then nondeterminism makes construction of the union acceptor very easy, for its mission is just to make a choice about whether to act like M_p or M_r. The acceptor is
$M = (P \cup R \cup \{q_0\}, \Sigma, \delta, q_0, A)$, where $q_0 \notin P \cup R$, $A = A_p \cup A_r \cup \{q_0\}$ if $\Lambda \in L_p$ or $\Lambda \in L_r$; otherwise $A = A_p \cup A_r$. The transitions are

$$\begin{aligned} \delta(q, \sigma) &= \{\pi(q, \sigma)\} \quad \text{if} \quad q \in P, \\ \delta(q, \sigma) &= \{\rho(q, \sigma)\} \quad \text{if} \quad q \in R, \\ \delta(q_0, \sigma) &= \{\pi(p_0, \sigma), \rho(r_0, \sigma)\}; \quad \sigma \in \Sigma. \end{aligned}$$

That is, the new acceptor has all the states of the two it combines, plus an additional start state, and makes its first move as a choice between the machines, thereafter acting like whichever machine was chosen. For $\Sigma = \{a, b\}$ and $\Lambda \in L_r$ the acceptors appear as shown in Fig. 2.14. About the only way to do the thing wrong would be to attempt to use q_0 to completely replace p_0 and r_0. This would fail since if either machine returns to its initial state, there could then be a crossover to the other machine, accepting some strings which are in neither language. As the construction is given, the abilities of the union

32 Finite Automata

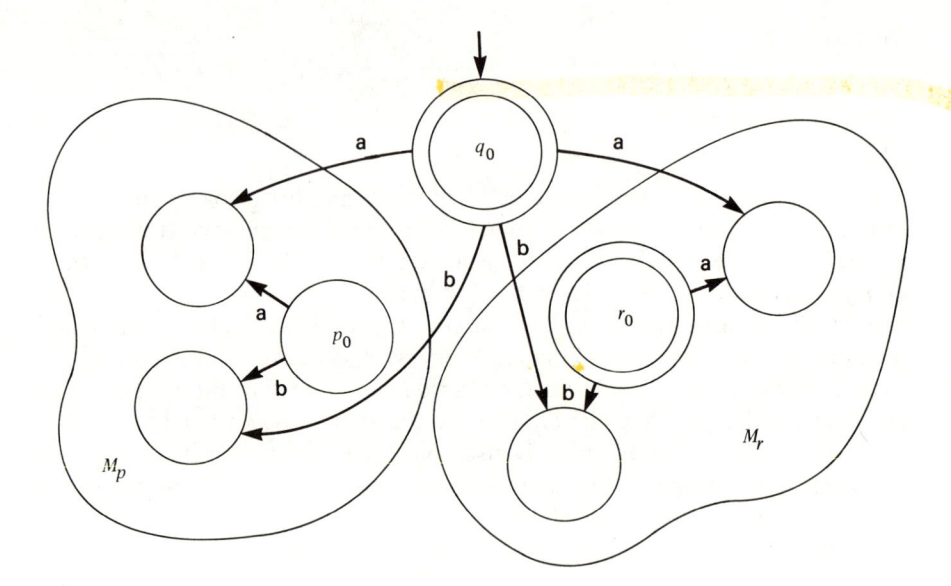

Figure 2.14

acceptor are exactly to mimic one or the other of the acceptors given for L_p' and L_r, with no additional paths to add extraneous members to $L_p \cup L_r$. ∎

Lemma 2

The class of finite-state languages is closed under set product.

Proof

Let deterministic M_p and M_r be given as in Lemma 1. The required nondeterministic acceptor for $L_p L_r$ is $(P \cup R, \Sigma, \delta, p_0, A)$, where $A = A_r$ if $\Lambda \notin L_r$, otherwise $A = A_p \cup A_r$. The transition function is given by

$$\delta(q,\sigma) = \{\pi(q,\sigma)\} \quad \text{if } q \in P - A_p,$$
$$\delta(q,\sigma) = \{\pi(q,\sigma), \rho(r_0,\sigma)\} \quad \text{if } q \in A_p,$$
$$\delta(q,\sigma) = \{\rho(q,\sigma)\} \quad \text{if } q \in R; \quad \sigma \in \Sigma.$$

That is, the nondeterministic acceptor acts as M_p until an accepting state is reached, then may choose to switch and behave as M_r does (skipping the state r_0 to keep pace with the input). Diagrammatically, when $\Sigma = \{a, b\}$ and $\Lambda \in L_r$, we obtain Fig. 2.15. ∎

Lemma 3

The class of finite-state languages is closed under Kleene closure.

2.9 Closure Properties of Finite-State Languages

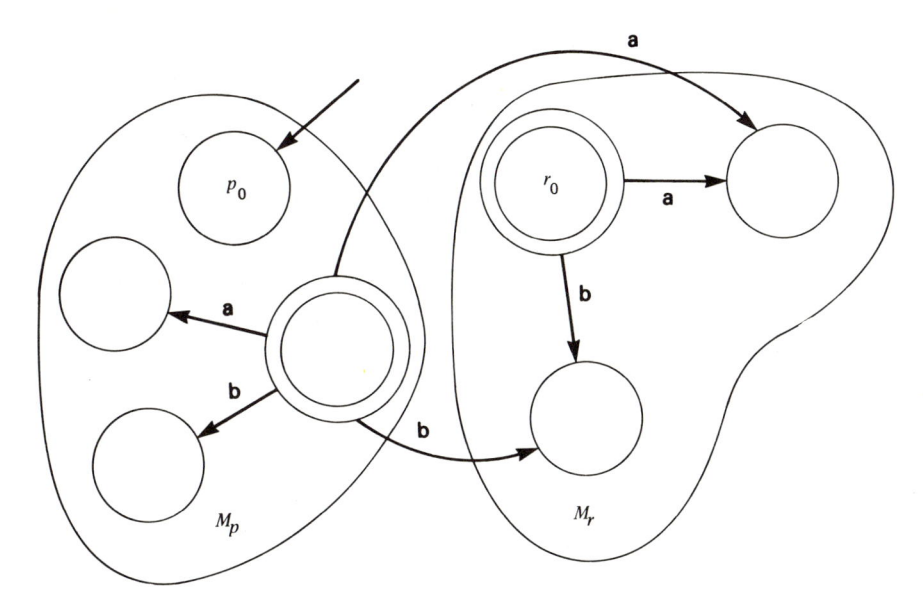

Figure 2.15

Proof

Let deterministic M_p be given as in Lemma 1. Then

$$M = (P \cup \{q_0\}, \Sigma, \delta, q_0, A_p \cup \{q_0\})$$

accepts L_p^*, where $q_0 \notin P$ and

$$\begin{aligned}
\delta(q,\sigma) &= \{\pi(q,\sigma)\} && \text{if } q \notin A_p, \\
\delta(q,\sigma) &= \{\pi(q,\sigma), \pi(p_0,\sigma)\} && \text{if } q \in A_p, \\
\delta(q_0,\sigma) &= \{\pi(p_0,\sigma)\}; && \sigma \in \Sigma.
\end{aligned}$$

The proof by picture can be constructed as a combination of those for Lemma 1 and Lemma 2: the new initial state avoids confusions which might be caused if p_0 is not itself accepting, and otherwise the new acceptor is a self-application of Lemma 2. However, since the Kleene closure is the most powerful regular operation, involving arbitrarily long strings of products, a formal proof is in order.

Suppose that $x \in L_p^*$. Then M accepts x by induction on the count k of the largest number of non-null strings of L_p of which x can be formed, $x = x_1 x_2 \ldots x_k$. ($x \in L_p^{k'}$ for some $k' \geq 0$, and thus either $x = \Lambda$, or some such $k' \geq 1$ exists. It happens that $k = k'$ only if $\Lambda \notin L_p$.)

Case $k = 0$. $x = \Lambda$. M accepts x since q_0 is an accepting state.

Case $k > 0$. The inductive hypothesis is that whenever $y = y_1 y_2 \ldots y_{k-1} \in L_p^*$ displays the greatest number of $y_i \neq \Lambda$ and $y_i \in L_p$, $1 \leq i \leq k-1$, then M accepts y. Then M accepts $x_1 x_2 \ldots x_{k-1}$, so there is a $q' \in A_p$ such that $q' \in \delta(q_0, x_1 \ldots x_{k-1})$. By definition of δ we then have that $\pi(p_0, \sigma) \in \delta(q', \sigma)$ for any $\sigma \in \Sigma$, so that it is as if M_p were presented with x_k alone. So M_p would accept x_k, and M can mimic the behavior of M_p. Thus M accepts x.

On the other hand, suppose that M accepts x. Then $x \in L_p^*$ by induction on the number of times r that M invokes the choice $\pi(p_0, \sigma)$ in accepting x.

Case $r = 0$. Except for its very first step and the choices which do not occur at all for count $r = 0$, M must mimic M_p, and thus $x = \Lambda$ or M_p accepts x, giving $x \in L_p^0$ or $x \in L_p^1$, and in either case $x \in L_p^*$.

Case $r > 0$. The inductive hypothesis is that for all y accepted by M invoking the choice $\pi(p_0, \sigma)$ $r-1$ times, $y \in L_p^*$. Let the given $x = yz$, where $q' \in \delta(q_0, y)$ is the state for which $\pi(p_0, \sigma) \in \delta(q', \sigma)$ for the rth time. Then $q' \in A_p$, and $y \in L_p^*$ by the inductive hypothesis. Since M accepts x, it is in an accepting state at the end of z, and thus its behavior on z is a copy of an acceptance by M_p, so $z \in L_p$, and $x \in L_p^* L_p \subseteq L_p^*$. ∎

With each of the regular closure operations proved to be of finite-state character in the sense of the lemmas, it remains only to start out properly.

Lemma 4

Each finite set of strings over alphabet Σ is a finite-state language.

Proof

Let any of the n strings of the set be $\sigma_1 \sigma_2 \ldots \sigma_m$, $\sigma_i \in \Sigma$, $1 \leq i \leq m$. Then

$(\{q_0, q_1, \ldots, q_m, q_z\}, \Sigma, \delta, q_0, \{q_m\})$ accepts this string if

$$\delta(q_{i-1}, \sigma_i) = q_i;$$
$$\delta(q_{i-1}, \sigma) = q_z \quad \text{if} \quad \sigma \neq \sigma_i, \quad 1 \leq i \leq m;$$
$$\delta(q_m, \sigma) = \delta(q_z, \sigma) = q_z; \quad \sigma \in \Sigma.$$

The example for $\Sigma = \{a, b\}$ and the string **a a b a b b** (Fig. 2.16) indicates how straightforward such an acceptor is. Having verified by similar means that each of the n strings of the given set has an acceptor, the Lemma follows by $n - 1$ applications of Lemma 1. ∎

The proof of the Theorem is now easy: given any regular set formed from some finite set of strings and any pattern of closure operations, we may con-

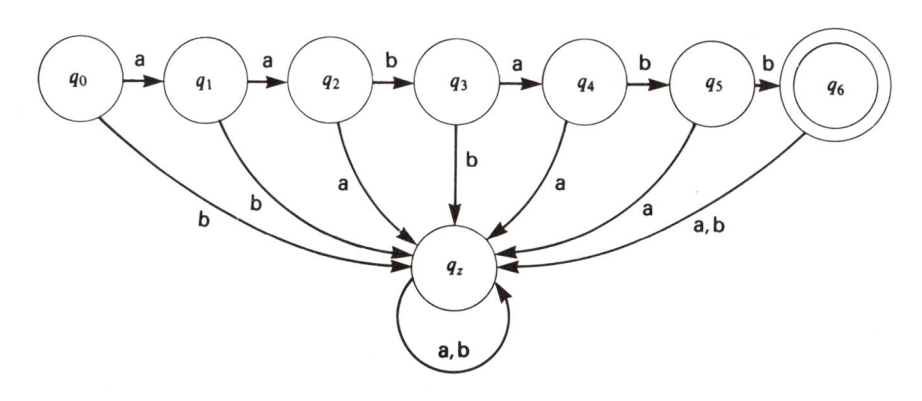

Figure 2.16

struct an acceptor for the set by the techniques of the lemmas, proving it to be a finite-state language. ∎

2.10 EQUIVALENCE OF FINITE-STATE LANGUAGES AND REGULAR SETS

The result of Section 2.9 is half of what we are seeking. In the other direction we must prove that given an arbitrary acceptor, the language it accepts is regular. Evidently this must be done by induction on the number of states in the given acceptor. The immediate difficulty is that there is very little connection between acceptors with n states and those with $n + 1$ states. All states of the larger acceptor may be linked by transitions in such a way that when a state is split off, the smaller acceptor is not related to the original in any comprehensible way, at least in accepting behavior. That is, the proof that if all n-state acceptors accept regular sets, then $(n + 1)$-state acceptors must also, does not go through easily. Indeed, both sizes of acceptors do accept exactly regular sets, as we shall prove, but the proof is not straightforward. Such situations are common in attempting induction, and the way out of the difficulty is always to generalize what is to be proved until induction does work. The generalization used here is roughly that a great deal more than the strings accepted by any acceptor are regular. The device defines many regular classes of input strings, and those accepted are an appropriate union of some such classes. Avoiding the union until after the induction is complete is a way to describe the technical trick by which the proof works.

Theorem

Each finite-state language is a regular set.

Proof

Let $M = (\{q_1,\ldots,q_n\},\Sigma,\delta,q_1,A)$ accept the language L. Consider the inductive definition of sets described by three indices

$$R_{ij}^0 = \{x \in \Sigma \cup \{\Lambda\} \mid \delta(q_i,x) = q_j\},$$
$$R_{ij}^k = R_{ij}^{k-1} \cup R_{ik}^{k-1}(R_{kk}^{k-1})^*R_{kj}^{k-1}$$

for each $i, j \leq n$. Since each R_{ij}^0 is finite (or $\{\Lambda\}$) it is a regular set, and because only union, product, and Kleene closure are used in the inductive step, so R_{ij}^k is a regular set for each k. These sets are designed to have the property that R_{ij}^k is the set of input strings which carry M from state q_i to q_j without entering any state whose subscript is strictly greater than k. Should that in fact prove to be the case,

$$L = \bigcup_{q_m \in A} R_{1m}^n$$

immediately gives the result: L is displayed as a finite union of regular sets, hence itself regular.

It therefore remains only to prove that for each $i, j \leq n$,

$$P_{ij}^k = \{x \in \Sigma^* \mid \delta(q_i,x) = q_j \text{ but for each } y, z \neq \Lambda, \, x = yz,$$
$$\delta(q_i,y) = q_m \Rightarrow m \leq k\}$$

are in fact R_{ij}^k in disguise, which we do by induction on k.

Case $k = 0$. The second condition in the definition of P_{ij}^0 can be satisfied only if x is a single symbol or Λ, so that there are no appropriate y, z to check, since there is no q_0. This reduces the definition of P_{ij}^0 to the definition of R_{ij}^0.

Case $k > 0$. The inductive hypothesis is that for all $i, j \leq n$, $P_{ij}^{k-1} = R_{ij}^{k-1}$. But P_{ij}^k is precisely all members of P_{ij}^{k-1} (because they continue to satisfy the higher-index definition), plus additional strings now qualifying under the second clause which failed to qualify at lower indices. The additional strings are obtained by the acceptor using state q_k. The most general way to do so is as follows: starting in q_i, the acceptor reaches q_k for the first time (that is, using only lower-numbered states), then returns to q_k an arbitrary number of times (using only lower-numbered states between returns), and finally leaves q_k for the last time, reaching q_j through lower-numbered states. Writing the three substrings of the string which forces such behavior as uvw, we have $\delta(q_i,u) = q_k$, but no initial segment of u reaches a state beyond q_{k-1}; the string v may be further divided into substrings $v = v_1 \ldots v_p$ such that for each substring v_r of v, $\delta(q_k,v_r) = q_k$, but no initial segment of v_r reaches beyond q_{k-1}, $1 \leq r \leq p$; and

$\delta(q_k, w) = q_j$, again invoking nothing past q_{k-1}. That is,

$$u \in P_{ik}^{k-1}, \qquad v \in (P_{kk}^{k-1})^p \subseteq (P_{kk}^{k-1})^*, \qquad \text{and} \qquad w \in P_{kj}^{k-1}.$$

The inductive hpothesis and closure under set product then provide the result. ∎

2.11 NONFINITE-STATE LANGUAGES. MULTIPLICATION

Experience with complicated regular expressions and finite automata with many states quickly conveys the idea that these devices are surprisingly powerful. It must be immediately noted that they have limitations which make the regular sets a strict subclass of the sets of strings over an alphabet which can be intuitively accepted by an effective procedure. The limitation is the central property of the finite machine—its fixed finite set of internal states, which limit its "memory". For example, the set of strings over a two-symbol alphabet which consists of a sequence of one symbol followed by a sequence of the other, the two being of equal length, has an obvious recognition algorithm. (Namely: look for the first occurrence of the second symbol, counting as you wait. When it is found, begin counting again, retaining the first count. Accept exactly when input terminates after the correct count of second symbols.) No finite acceptor can accept this set, for it necessarily exhausts its "memory" waiting for the switch in symbols. The result is worth a proof.

Theorem

$\{a^n b^n | n \geq 0\}$ is not regular.

Proof
Suppose it were, being accepted by the deterministic acceptor $M = (\{q_1, \ldots, q_k\}, \{a,b\}, \delta, q_1, A)$. The characterizing property for finite automata is that input strings are separated by the machine into at most k classes in that if x and y are in the same class $\delta(q_1, x) = \delta(q_1, y)$. (The proof in Section 2.2 was for transducers; it carries over without change for acceptors.) Thus the $k + 1$ strings $x_m = a^m$, $m = 0, 1, \ldots, k$ cannot fall into different classes. Two must fall together, say x_i and x_j, $i \neq j$. Then $\delta(q_1, x_i b^i) \in A$, the string being $a^i b^i$. But $\delta(q_1, x_j b^i) \notin A$, the string being $a^j b^i$, $j \neq i$. But these states are one and the same, since $\delta(q_1, x_i) = \delta(q_1, x_j)$ when x_i and x_j are in the same class. The contradiction means that there was in fact no such acceptor M, so the set is not a finite-state language, and hence is not regular. ∎

The technique of the proof requires a bit of practice to master. One must find a class of strings whose cardinality exceeds any given bound (a state count for a presumed finite acceptor), whose members have the property that some string affixed to any two members produces two strings respectively accepted and rejected by the acceptor. For example, the set of properly nested parentheses may be proved nonregular by this means; the strings to consider are exactly those of the Theorem, with a replaced by "(" and b replaced by ")".

Finite transducers suffer from the same limitations of "memory" as finite acceptors, and it is not difficult to discover transformations which they cannot perform. (Some arise from the nonfinite-state languages. For example, no transducer can output "1" when the input it has seen so far consists of balanced parentheses, and "0" when it does not; from such a transducer an impossible acceptor could be constructed.) One example parallels our discussion of addition in Section 2.2: no finite transducer can multiply. To prove this statement requires a careful definition of "multiply", and an agreement that the definition captures the essential features of the process. As we saw for addition, the problem may be complicated by an inappropriate way of encoding the operands. It seems best to follow digital computing (and the conventions that made addition easy) by requiring that a multiplication transducer be presented with its inputs in reverse binary, one bit at a time, with arbitrarily many leading zeros on both numbers. We can avoid the definitional problems of two inputs by restricting the problem to squaring the input, and in this form make precise some assertions made in Section 1.3 about multiplication requiring a nonfinite procedure.

With so many places for intuition to disagree, it seems best to state the formal result without mentioning multiplication:

Theorem

No finite transducer can respond to inputs of the form $0^n 10^n$ with outputs of the form $0^{2n}1$ for all $n \geq 0$.

Proof

Suppose $(\{0,1\},\{q_1, \ldots, q_k\},\{0,1\},\delta,\omega,q_1)$ were a transducer which violates the statement of the theorem. Consider the inputs $I_n = 0^n 1$, $1 \leq n \leq k+1$. As the transducer has only k states, by the fundamental theorem two of these inputs fall into the same input class, such that the transducer cannot distinguish them upon encountering subsequent input. Let these be I_r and I_s, $r < s$. The response required of the transducer on input $I_r 0^r = 0^r 10^r$ is $0^{2r}1$. Because the transducer cannot distinguish I_r and I_s, it must give as response to input $I_s 0^r = 0^s 10^r$ the output $x 0^{r-1} 1$ where the string x is of length $s + 1$. The number of bits before the "1" is therefore $s + r < 2s$, and the transducer fails to perform as specified. ∎

Of course, we interpret the insolvable problem as an inability to multiply 2^n times 2^n in binary, and thus conclude that finite transducers cannot multiply arbitrary numbers. It should be unnecessary to point out that digital computers do not multiply in this sense, and hence there is no inconsistency: the "multiplication" operator of a digital machine has a strictly limited range of inputs for which it works.

2.12 EQUIVALENCE PROBLEM FOR FINITE-STATE ACCEPTORS

No consideration has yet been given to the question of a "best" finite-state device for a specification. Historically, since finite machines were actually built from components purchased separately, the best machine was the one with the smallest number of states. The algorithm for reducing a given machine to its minimum state set while retaining exactly the same input/output behavior is no longer of the same importance in building computers, but serves to give a final characterization of finite devices: since they can be mechanically reduced to a minimum state set, an algorithm exists for deciding whether two arbitrary machines have the same behavior. The construction will be given for acceptors, but the transducer analog is similar. The essence of the construction is to lump all the states together, then "separate" them only when forced to do so by the behavior.

Suppose then that we are given an arbitrary (deterministic) finite-state acceptor, $M = (Q, \{\sigma_1, \sigma_2, \ldots, \sigma_k\}, \delta, q_0, A)$, which accepts the set L. We construct another deterministic finite-state acceptor as follows:

1. Eliminate from Q states which can never be used, by considering each in turn; a state must be in the range of δ to avoid elimination. Some state which is mapped to the one being considered must in turn appear in the range of δ, and so on in a reverse path back to q_0, otherwise the considered state cannot be entered.

2. Group together the remaining states of Q and successively refine the groupings, as follows: Initially, group all accepting states as Q_0^0, if $q_0 \in A$, or if $q_0 \notin A$, group all nonaccepting states. Then take $Q_1^0 = Q - Q_0^0$. Suppose that a series of such groupings has been successively carried out, resulting in the groups $Q_0^j, Q_1^j, Q_2^j, \ldots$ at the jth stage. Construct the groups at stage $j + 1$ by assigning to each $q \in Q$ a label of the form $r[i_1 i_2 \ldots i_k]$ where $q \in Q_r^j$, and $\delta(q, \sigma_1) \in Q_{i_1}^j, \delta(q, \sigma_2) \in Q_{i_2}^j, \ldots, \delta(q, \sigma_k) \in Q_{i_k}^j$. Finally, group together all the states for which the labels are the same, and assign these as the groupings $Q_0^{j+1}, Q_1^{j+1}, \ldots$ in any way, making sure that $q_0 \in Q_0^{j+1}$.

3. When stage m produces no further refinements, the new acceptor is $(\{Q_0^m, \ldots\}, \{\sigma_1, \ldots, \sigma_k\}, \delta_m, Q_0^m, A_m)$ where A_m is all groups containing any accepting state, and δ_m is defined by the group to which all members of any group pass under δ.

Finite Automata

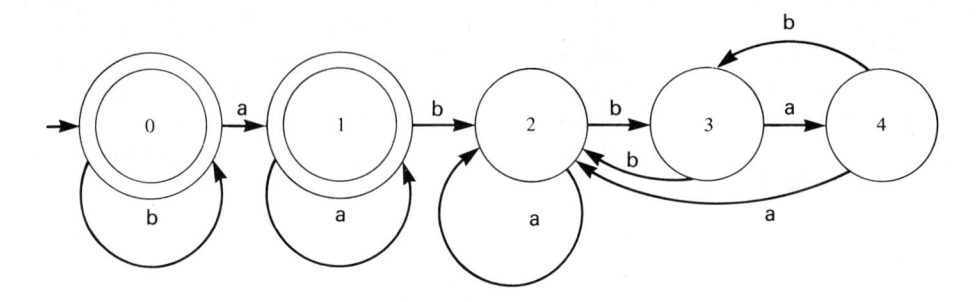

Figure 2.17

The state diagram of a machine to illustrate the construction is given in Fig. 2.17.

Table 2.2 gives the state-transition mapping in a form useful for the construction, and displays the first three stages of the splitting process, the last showing nothing new. The construction thus produces an acceptor in which all the nonaccepting states are represented by one group, shown in Fig. 2.18.

Table 2.2

σ	q	$\delta(q,\sigma)$	Q^0	Q^1	Q^2
a b	0	1 0	0	0[00]—0	0[10]—0
a b	1	1 2	0	0[01]—1	1[12]—1
a b	2	2 3	1	1[11]—2	2[22]—2
a b	3	4 2	1	1[11]—2	2[22]—2
a b	4	2 3	1	1[11]—2	2[22]—2

It is largely a matter of controlling the notation to prove that Step 3 of the construction may be carried out to produce a well-defined acceptor. Furthermore, the language accepted is unchanged by the construction, and in the new acceptor two states differ only if they must: only if some string will carry the acceptor from one into an accepting state, and from the other into a nonaccepting state.

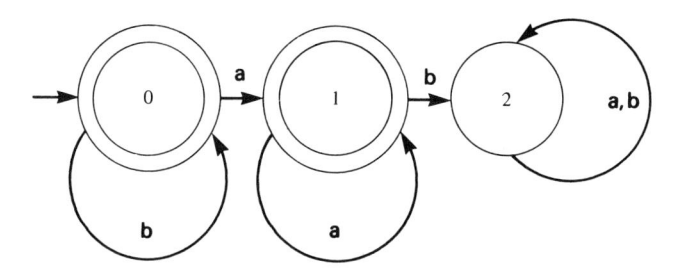

Figure 2.18

The problem of deciding whether or not two given acceptors accept the same language may then be solved by carrying out the construction on each, and noting whether or not the results are the same but for differences in the arbitrary assignments of the state names.

EXERCISES

2.1 In the "experimental data" presented for a particular transducer in Section 2.1 (Table 2.1), suppose that the results of the last experiment are:

Number	Input	Output
15	0000	1011

Give the state diagram of a formal transducer with this behavior. In what sense is it possible to specify "inconsistent" data on the performance of a finite transducer?

2.2 The Moore transducer defined at the end of Section 2.3 has output depending only on its internal state, not on the input symbol. Give a definition of a device which carries this idea over into the transition function as well. Why is such a device not a good model for the finite procedures described in Section 1.2?

2.3 Call two symbols of the input alphabet of a particular finite transducer "output equivalent" if there is no experiment of any kind which can be conducted on the transducer to distinguish one from the other by observing the output. Give a precise definition of this intuitive notion.

2.4 Give a complete formal specification for a finite transducer which "rounds off" binary fractions presented in reverse. Use {0,1,.} for the input and output alphabets. For example, the response to input "01010.00" should be "00000.00", but to "1100101.10" it should be "0000000.01".

2.5 Most programming languages which permit numerical applications have "constants" in the language. Consider such constants which may be arbitrarily long strings with or without initial sign, may have an embedded decimal point, but no exponential form. Give the state diagram of a finite acceptor for such constants, using the alphabet $\{+,-,\cdot,\beta\}$ where β represents a "generic digit" to save labeling transitions "0,1,2,3,4,5,6,7,8,9".

2.6 In FORTRAN IV, numbers such as those described in Exercise 2.5 may terminate in a bare decimal point, while in ALGOL 60 they may not. For example, one may write "1." in FORTRAN, but must write "1.0" in ALGOL. Give the state diagram for a finite acceptor which accepts exactly those constants of FORTRAN which are illegal in ALGOL.

2.7 Consider simpler "constants" than those of Exercise 2.5, which represent only integers without sign, but which are required to have no more than six digits. Can a finite acceptor accept such constants? Prove what you say.

2.8 Consider only languages which do not contain the null string. Give a precise definition of "acceptance" by a finite transducer with start state which agrees with the acceptor definition of Section 2.5 in the sense that for any given acceptor there is a corresponding transducer "accepting" the same set. By using Moore transducers, eliminate the restriction to languages not containing the null string.

2.9 Control-stream information on the UNIVAC 1108 under EXEC VIII follows rules something like the following:

> The initial character is "@". A sequence of optional blanks follows, then a string of alphabetic characters containing no blanks. This may optionally be followed by a comma and another alphabetic string without blanks. Next must come a blank (but there may be more than one), and finally a sequence of alphabetic strings, each containing no blanks, and set off from the others by a comma, which may be surrounded by an arbitrary number of blanks (or no blanks). The sequence of strings may be omitted entirely.

Specify a finite acceptor for 1108 control information, using a generic symbol for any alphabetic character.

2.10 Most processors used on the DEC System-10 timesharing system accept input of the form indicated by

DEV:FILE.EXT ← DEV:FILE.EXT, DEV:FILE.EXT, ...

to specify input files on the right and an output file on the left. Assuming that the letters used in the various DEV, FILE, and EXT are arbitrary alphabetic characters, and that these names are of any nonzero length, and that the punctuation characters may be surrounded by any number of blanks, and that the sequence at the right may be of any length, specify a finite acceptor for this kind of input, using a generic symbol for any alphabetic character.

2.11 At the end of Section 2.7 (Fig. 2.12) a deterministic acceptor is partly specified which is claimed to have the same behavior as another, nondeterministic acceptor. Give a complete formal specification of both acceptors.

2.12 Prove the following, where E is any regular expression:

$S((E\star)\star) = S(E\star)$
$S(\emptyset \cdot E) = S(E \cdot \emptyset) = S(\emptyset)$
$S(\emptyset \star) = \{\Lambda\}$

What is $S(\Lambda)$?

2.13 Write regular expressions which describe the sets

$\{a^k | k \geq 1\}$,
$\{a^i b^j | i, j \geq 0\}$ ($a^0 = b^0 = \Lambda$),
$\{a^{2k} | k \geq 0\}$,
$\{\Lambda\}$.

2.14 Given a regular expression R, give an algorithm for constructing another regular expression $R-$ such that

$S(R-) = S(R) - \{\Lambda\}$

that is, the null string is omitted from $S(R-)$.

2.15 Give a reasonable definition of the "complement" of a set of strings over a given alphabet, and prove that the finite-state languages are closed under complement. Use some set theory and closure under union to conclude that they are also closed under intersection, and therefore form a Boolean algebra.

2.16 Give examples to show why each of the closure operations for regular sets is necessary. That is, display sets which are regular only because of the existence of each operation, and would not be regular if that operation were omitted from the definition.

2.17 Given a finite acceptor for the set $L \subseteq \Sigma^*$, construct a nondeterministic finite acceptor for the set L^R of reversals of strings from L. ($\sigma_1 \sigma_2 \ldots \sigma_n \in L^R$ iff $\sigma_n \sigma_{n-1} \ldots \sigma_1 \in L$, $\sigma_i \in \Sigma$, $1 \leq i \leq n$.)

2.18 Let s^R be called the *reversal* of string s. Let E be a regular set. Define $P = \{ww^R | w \in E\}$. Prove that $P \neq EE^R$ (E^R as in the previous problem). Prove that P is not regular.

2.19 Give the state diagram of a finite transducer which multiplies by two according to the conventions of Section 2.11, and reconcile its existence with the statement that multiplication is beyond the abilities of finite procedures.

2.20 Consider the question raised in Section 2.2 about the ability of a finite transducer to add inputs presented to it serially with a separating mark between them. Suppose the coding of numbers is "offset unary," in which "1" represents zero, "11" represents one, "111" two, etc., and the separator is "0", so that the problem of adding one and one would appear as the input "110110". Answer this form of the question by displaying a finite transducer. What about the form of the question in which the coding of numbers is conventional binary?

2.21 Describe the intuitive notion of a "nondeterministic finite transducer," intended to make function computation easier. Give a formal definition of such a device, and of what it means for it to compute a function (of one input). Discuss whether or not your device is equivalent to a deterministic transducer, and whether or not it can compute the square function.

2.22 Define a *finite-state string machine* (fssm) to be a 6-tuple $(\Sigma, Q, \Gamma, \delta, \omega, q_0)$ where Σ is the input alphabet, Γ is the output alphabet, Q is the internal-state set, δ is the extended state transition function $\delta: Q \times \Sigma^* \to Q$, and $q_0 \in Q$ is the start state, just as for a finite-state transducer. However, the output function $\omega: Q \times \Sigma \to \Gamma^*$ produces strings of output symbols. The fssm $(\{b,1\}, Q, \{1\}, \delta, \omega, q_0)$ is said to *compute* the function f of two inputs iff

$$\omega(q_0, 1^{x_1} b 1^{x_2} b) = 1^{f(x_1, x_2)};$$

the output function is extended to $Q \times \Sigma^*$ by the recursive definition

$\omega(q, \Lambda) = \Lambda, \qquad q \in Q;$
$\omega(q, x\sigma) = \omega(q, x)\omega(\delta(q, x), \sigma), \qquad q \in Q, \qquad \sigma \in \Sigma, \qquad x \in \Sigma^*.$

Give a formal description of a fssm that computes the function of x and y, $3x + 2y + 5$. Prove that no fssm can compute the multiplication function.

REFERENCES

The sources of finite-state machine theory are in electrical engineering and the mathematics of formal languages. A presentation of the former viewpoint is the text by Booth [5], in which there is a sizable dose of "preventative mathematics." For formal languages a standard text is Hopcroft and Ullman [6]; the treatment of acceptors here is almost the same as theirs. However, regular languages are the least interesting of those treated by Hopcroft and Ullman, and we have entirely neglected the subject of grammars which concerns them. Salomaa [7] is a careful text concerned almost entirely with finite-state formalism, using regular expressions as the basis for a less orthodox treatment than given here.

3
NUMBER-THEORETIC FUNCTIONS

3.1 THE NATURAL NUMBERS IN. FUNCTIONS FROM $\mathbb{N}^n$ INTO $\mathbb{N}$

To continue the discussion of what can be accomplished by mechanical means requires passing to effective procedures which are nonfinite in some sense, as discussed in Section 1.3. It is equally necessary to make more precise just what accomplishments are desired. Two ideas which proved too much for finite-state automata suggest themselves in general form: finite transducers could not multiply, so computation of function values is the first idea; finite acceptors could not accept the set of strings of the form $a^n b^n$, so the general acceptance problem is the second idea. The Chomsky hierarchy of formal languages and the devices which accept progressively more difficult sets explore the second idea, but here we will compute functions.

The most fundamental class of functions is that called "number-theoretic;" these functions map n-tuples of nonnegative integers into nonnegative integers. To begin with these functions is certainly reasonable; Chapter 6 indicates why the discussion never passes beyond them. Digital computers deal in strings of symbols from a fixed character set, and all characters are converted to numerical codes internally. The special characters "−" and "." do not really introduce negative and fractional quantities if they are viewed as input/output characters.

The nonnegative integers are more often called the natural numbers. To write $\mathbb{N} = \{0, 1, 2, \ldots\}$ does little more than supply a symbol for this infinite set, and give a reminder that zero is a natural number. The three dots conceal a large "you know what I mean," and in this book the intuition that the counting numbers are God-given must suffice. Formal number theory would take us too far from the central topic of computing.

Number-theoretic functions may be classified in many ways, but three nested classes are of particular interest in the study of what can be computed. The smallest of these, the primitive recursive functions, is beyond the power of finite procedures, while the largest, the partial recursive functions, fails to exhaust the number-theoretic functions. The reason that these classes are interesting is that they correspond exactly to the use of three successively more powerful computing techniques, and specify functions in terms of the computing process. They therefore lend themselves to characteristic programming languages whose power allows just functions of the class to be computed. These languages are somewhat different than the usual high-level procedural ones, although they need not be. The differences are partly historical and partly simplifications which make proofs easier and correspond better with intuition about mechanical computation. In Chapter 4 we give full details of the most famous such language, devised by A. M. Turing, which is characteristic of the partial recursive functions.

Our treatment of functions is really only a prelude to the language characterization of Chapter 4. We need to establish the independent existence of the functions which will later be characterized, and do so as concisely as possible. Following the majority of the Turing presentation we return to functions in Sections 4.11 and 4.12. Church's lambda notation is used whenever functions are defined. Instead of writing something like $f(x,y,z) = x^2 + 2yz$, we write $f = \lambda x \lambda y \lambda z[x^2 + 2yz]$. This has the advantage of not confusing the function f notationally with one of its values such as $f(2,7,0)$, and the notation allows specification of functions without actually assigning them names, as in the constant function $\lambda x[3]$.

3.2 PRIMITIVE RECURSIVE FUNCTIONS

Each of the classes we will consider is defined by initial inclusion of a list of base functions, and by closure under operations which are intuitively effective.

Definition

Base functions:

$S = \lambda x[x'] = \lambda x[x + 1]$ the *successor function*;
$Z = \lambda x[0]$ the *zero function*;
$U_m^n = \lambda x_1 \ldots \lambda x_n[x_m]$ the *projection functions* (for each $n > 0$ and $1 \leq m \leq n$).

Closure operations:

$h = \lambda x_1 \ldots \lambda x_n[g(f_1(x_1,\ldots,x_n),\ldots,f_m(x_1,\ldots,x_n))]$ is said to be obtained from $g, f_1, \ldots, f_m$ by *composition*.

$$h = \lambda x_1 \ldots \lambda x_n \lambda y \begin{bmatrix} f(x_1,\ldots,x_n) & \text{if} & y = 0 \\ g(x_1,\ldots,x_n, y-1, h(x_1,\ldots,x_n, y-1)) & \text{if} & y > 0 \end{bmatrix}$$

is said to be obtained from f and g by *primitive recursion*. ∎

(It seems unnecessary to show that a function can be defined by primitive recursion to those acquainted with programs such as the ALGOL 60

integer procedure fact (n); **value** n; **integer** n;
fact := **if** n = 0 **then** 1 **else** n × fact (n − 1)

for the factorial.)

Definition

The class of *primitive recursive functions* is the smallest class of number-theoretic functions containing successor, zero, and projections, and closed under composition and primitive recursion. ∎

3.3 EXAMPLES. EXPLICIT TRANSFORMATION

Some examples will illustrate the way intuitive ideas about primitive recursion can be formally presented:

Addition $p = \lambda x \lambda y [x + y]$:

$$t = \lambda x \lambda y \lambda z [S(U_3^3(x,y,z))]$$

is primitive recursive by composition of the successor and projection base functions;

$$p = \lambda x \lambda y \begin{bmatrix} U_1^1(x) & \text{if} & y = 0 \\ t(x, y-1, p(x, y-1)) & \text{if} & y > 0 \end{bmatrix}$$

is primitive recursive by primitive recursion using the base function of projection and the primitive recursive t.

Multiplication $m = \lambda x \lambda y [x \cdot y]$:

$$u = \lambda x \lambda y \lambda z [p(U_1^3(x,y,z), U_3^3(x,y,z))];$$

$$m = \lambda x \lambda y \begin{bmatrix} Z(x) & \text{if} & y = 0. \\ u(x, y-1, m(x, y-1)) & \text{if} & y > 0 \end{bmatrix}.$$

Proper subtraction $d = \lambda x \lambda y [x \dotdiv y]$:

$$z_2 = \lambda x \lambda y [Z(U_1^2(x,y))];$$

$$b = \lambda x \lambda y \lambda z \begin{bmatrix} z_2(x,y) & \text{if} & z = 0 \\ U_3^4(x,y,z-1,b(x,y,z-1)) & \text{if if} & z > 0 \end{bmatrix};$$

$$d = \lambda x \lambda y \begin{bmatrix} U_1^1(x) & \text{if} & y = 0 \\ b(x, y-1, d(x, y-1)) & \text{if} & y > 0 \end{bmatrix}.$$

Constant $c_n = \lambda x[n]$:

$$s_0 = \lambda x[Z(x)],$$
$$s_1 = \lambda x[S(Z(x))],$$
$$s_2 = \lambda x[S(s_1(x))],$$
$$\vdots$$
$$s_{n-1} = \lambda x[S(s_{n-2}(x))],$$
$$c_n = \lambda x[S(s_{n-1}(x))].$$

Base-10 exponentiation $e = \lambda x[10x]$:

$$v = \lambda x \lambda y \lambda z \, [m(c_{10}(U_2^3(x,y,z)), U_3^3(x,y,z))];$$

$$f = \lambda x \lambda y \begin{bmatrix} U_1^1(x) & \text{if } y = 0 \\ v(x, y-1, f(x, y-1)) & \text{if } y > 0 \end{bmatrix};$$

$$e = \lambda x[f(c_1(x), U_1^1(x))].$$

When a definition involves several applications of primitive recursion, there is nothing to do but write them all out in this way; however, it is conventional to avoid listing a series of compositions by writing them all on a single line, so in the example concerning the constant function

$$c_n = \lambda x[\underbrace{S(\ldots(S(Z(x)))\ldots)}_{n \text{ times}}].$$

It is also common to technically violate the form of the inductive case of a primitive recursion; for example, one writes for addition

$$p(x,y) = S(p(x,y-1)).$$

When in doubt, however, exact details of the form may be required to justify a statement that a function is primitive recursive. Further liberties are taken in a slightly different direction. For example, the function $f = \lambda x[2x + 5]$ seems to be primitive recursive as a special case of addition, $f(x) = p(p(x,x),5)$. It is easy to justify all such usages.

Theorem (*Explicit transformations; constant substitution*)

Let $x_1, \ldots, x_n$ be distinct variables, and $z_1, \ldots, z_m$ chosen from among them or as constants, so that for each $1 \leq i \leq m$ there exists a $1 \leq j \leq n$ such that $z_i = x_j$ or constant k_i with $z_i = k_i$. Then if g is a primitive recursive function of m arguments, so is $f = \lambda x_1 \ldots \lambda x_n[g(z_1, \ldots, z_m)]$.

Proof

For each z_i, which is a variable, $1 \leq i \leq m$, there exists a $1 \leq j_i \leq n$ such that $z_i = x_{j_i}$. Or, if z_i is a constant, then $z_i = k_i$. Hence

3.4 Primitive Recursive Derivations. Totality of Primitive Recursive Functions

$$f = \lambda x_1 \ldots \lambda x_n [g(V_1(x_1, \ldots, x_n), \ldots, V_m(x_1, \ldots, x_n))],$$

where $V_i = U_{j_i}^n$ if z_i is a variable, or

$$V_i = \lambda x_1 \ldots \lambda x_n \left[c_{k_i}(U_1^n(x_1, \ldots, x_n)) \right]$$

if z_i is a constant, $1 \leq i \leq m$. ∎

3.4 PRIMITIVE RECURSIVE DERIVATIONS. TOTALITY OF PRIMITIVE RECURSIVE FUNCTIONS

In the careful examples displayed above there is a pattern of the following kind: the definition proceeds using a sequence of functions, each justified as primitive recursive in terms of previous ones, beginning with base functions and ending with the function being defined. It is precisely such a series of steps which characterize primitive recursiveness.

Definition

A *primitive recursive derivation* is a finite sequence of function definitions, each of which is

i) a base function, or
ii) obtained from previous definitions in the sequence by composition, or
iii) obtained from previous definitions in the sequence by primitive recursion;

the last element in the sequence is the function defined. ∎

It should be evident that a function is primitive recursive iff it has a primitive recursive derivation. (Actually, not all the previous examples meet the letter of the above definition since some include operations on base functions as well as functions earlier defined. For example, in the addition function, S and U_3^3 are composed in the very first line. To meet the above definition would require defining phony auxiliary functions first, say $S' = \lambda x [S(x)]$ and $U' = \lambda x \lambda y \lambda z [U_3^3(x,y,z)]$, then composing S' and U'. The sole reason for taking the somewhat too restrictive definition above is that it simplifies the initial step in the inductive proof that primitive recursive functions are defined for all argument values.)

Derivations provide the justification for considering the primitive recursive functions as "algorithmic", for they provide an intuitive computing procedure

50 Number-Theoretic Functions

for the function defined. The procedure is displayed in the proof of the following theorem:

Theorem

Each primitive recursive function is defined for all argument values.

Proof

(A function defined everywhere is called *total*.) Let f be primitive recursive, and let any argument values be given. We show that f is defined (and as a byproduct how to intuitively compute it) by induction on the length of any derivation for f.

Derivation length 1.   Then necessarily f is a base function, all of which are total (and intuitively computable).

Derivation length k.   Take as inductive hypothesis that all functions with any derivation shorter than k are total (and intuitively computable). Now consider the final line in the derivation, which defines f. It may be a base function, a case covered above. It may involve a composition, in which case the functions composed must have already appeared, with shorter derivations as a consequence. Furthermore, composition preserves totality (and is intuitively computable). The last case to consider is that in which the final line involves primitive recursion. The two functions employed are then total (and are intuitively computable) by the inductive hypothesis. The value of the first function may then be substituted in the second function as its final argument, then the resulting value substituted again. Continuing the process will yield a computed value corresponding to the given final argument, completing the proof. ∎

The derivation of the addition function given in Section 3.3 is repeated below, where care has been taken to follow the definition of a derivation strictly, and standardized names have been used for the functions defined:

$$f_1 = \lambda x[U_1^1(x)],$$
$$f_2 = \lambda x[S(x)],$$
$$f_3 = \lambda x \lambda y \lambda z[U_3^3(x,y,z)],$$
$$f_4 = \lambda x \lambda y \lambda z[f_2(f_3(x,y,z))],$$
$$f_5 = \lambda x \lambda y \begin{bmatrix} f_1(x) & \text{if } y = 0 \\ f_4(x, y-1, f_5(x, y-1)) & \text{if } y > 0 \end{bmatrix}.$$

The computing procedure specified in the proof of the theorem that each primitive recursive function is total can be illustrated by using this derivation to compute $f_5(3,2)$, assuming that computations of the base functions can be obtained. In order:

$f_1(3)$	is	3
$f_5(3,0)$	is	3
$f_3(3,0,3)$	is	3
$f_2(3)$	is	4
$f_4(3,0,3)$	is	4
$f_5(3,1)$	is	4
$f_3(3,1,4)$	is	4
$f_2(4)$	is	5
$f_4(3,1,4)$	is	5
$f_5(3,2)$	is	5

Note the iteration of f_3, f_2, f_4, and f_5 until the correct second argument is attained.

3.5 ENUMERATION OF DERIVATIONS, DIAGONALIZATION, NONPRIMITIVE RECURSIVE FUNCTIONS

A function may be primitive recursive without anyone necessarily being able to display a derivation for it. The essential point is only that a derivation be known to exist, even if no known procedure will find it. For example,

$$f = \lambda x \begin{bmatrix} 1 & \text{if Fermat's last theorem is true} \\ 0 & \text{otherwise} \end{bmatrix}$$

is primitive recursive, although it is not known (1973) which of the two indicated derivations

(1) $f = \lambda x [S(Z(x))]$ (2) $f = \lambda x [Z(x)]$

is correct.

However, not all intuitively computable functions are primitive recursive. In defining primitive recursive derivations, we might have insisted that the form of the derivation be precise—that only certain standard variable and function names be used, and a finite alphabet of symbols. Had we done this, it would have permitted us to carry out precisely a very interesting construction. Without the details, it goes like this:

> Consider only derivations of functions of one argument. Imagine listing all possible derivations in some standard order, say those of length 1, then 2, etc., ordered in any way you like within those of a given length. Since each derivation defines a primitive recursive function, we could then speak of the nth primitive recursive function, and symbolize it as p_n. (Unless we take

52 Number-Theoretic Functions

special care, the same function may appear more than once in the list, but this does not matter for present purposes.)

Intuitively, p_n is computable from a knowledge of n alone, since the derivations can be generated in order, and from the derivation the function can be calculated. We can then ask a very interesting question:

$$\text{Is } d = \lambda n [p_n(n) + 1] \text{ primitive recursive?}$$

The reason this question is interesting is that a negative answer would show that there are intuitively computable functions which are not primitive recursive. And a negative answer is correct. For suppose that d is primitive recursive. It is a function of one argument, and therefore would be p_i for some i. The function d must be defined at i, since primitive recursive functions are defined everywhere. But what is the value taken by d at i? By definition $d(i) = p_i(i) + 1$. But we assumed this to be $p_i(i)$ itself, which is impossible. Hence d, which is certainly intuitively computable, is not primitive recursive. (It is worth nothing that this result, obtained by *diagonalization* on the derivation listing, relies not at all on properties of primitive recursive functions except their totality and the effective nature of the listing itself. This means that any class of functions whose definitions can be listed in an intuitive sense is subject to the same difficulty and cannot encompass the intuitively computable functions. There are two ways out of the corner: a class of functions may be impossible to list, or may include members which are undefined at some points. The next classes we consider have exactly these characteristics, in that order.)

3.6 (TOTAL, GENERAL) RECURSIVE FUNCTIONS

Although historically primitive recursion was generalized by permitting multiple recursive definitions (the name *general recursive* was used), a more convenient definition gives the class as an explicit extension of the primitive recursive, by adding another closure operation. In composition and primitive recursion, the notation is standardized in other parts of mathematics (parenthesis ordering for composition and definition by cases for primitive recursion). The new operator is defined using the less standard "mu-notation," as in

$$\mu x[\ldots],$$

where the square brackets contain a logical predicate, usually written in terms of the variable which follows "μ", and the notation symbolizes the least x such that this predicate is true. If there is no such x, then $\mu x[\ldots]$ is undefined; however, no algorithm is implied for locating the value of x.

Definition

The function f is obtained from g by *restricted minimalization* iff for each $x_1, \ldots, x_n$ there is at least one y such that $g(x_1, \ldots, x_n, y) = 0$, and

$$f = \lambda x_1 \ldots \lambda x_n [\mu y [g(x_1,\ldots,x_n,y) = 0]]. \blacksquare$$

(We will insist that the item minimalized be a function having value zero; in fact, any relation may be used, but "closure" then is more difficult to define. See Exercise 3.7.)

Definition

The class of (total, general) *recursive functions* is the smallest class containing the successor, zero, and projection functions, and closed under composition, primitive recursion, and restricted minimalization. $\blacksquare$

It is not easy to construct an example of a function which is recursive yet not in fact primitive recursive. (The function d defined at the end of Section 3.5 is one, but its careful recursive derivation is very complex.) However, it is easy to construct a function whose primitive recursive derivation is more difficult to understand than its recursive derivation. This fact is the basis for statements that programming languages which permit minimalization (usually in the form of a controlled loop construction) are "more powerful" than those which do not. Exercises 3.11 and 3.12 explore these language-related ideas. A good case in point is the integer-division-by-two function $h = \lambda x [x \div 2]$, whose recursive definition in terms of multiplication and proper subtraction is

$$h = \lambda x [\mu y [(x \dot{-} 1) \dot{-} (y \cdot 2) = 0]].$$

The illustrated technique of successive trial is often useful for inverses.

In a rough intuitive way, the recursive functions supply the lack discovered in the primitive recursive functions, for minimalization seems to provide the mechanism for carrying out search operations such as locating something in a list, which is the heart of the diagonalization used to display a nonprimitive recursive function. The intuition is correct; in fact the recursive functions have not been effectively listed, and so diagonalization cannot be carried out. It will be some time (Section 4.11) before we are equipped to discuss this fact. What we can do immediately is show that each recursive function is total.

A recursive derivation may be defined by extending the definition of a primitive recursive derivation to permit restricted minimalization on previously occurring functions. Examining the proof of the totality of each primitive recursive function shows that it extends to the recursive functions if restricted minimalization preserves totality. The "restriction" does exactly that: since the function to be made zero *is* zero for some value of the argument which is to vary, that argument has a least value that forces zero. The intuitive computing procedure is of course to try the possible argument values starting at zero until the right one is found.

Since the totality proof carries over so well, what goes wrong with the procedure for turning derivations into a function listing that will support diagonalization? Intuitively, it is that same restriction. Suppose a listing of all possible recursive derivations were to be generated. In order to see if a given occurrence of an apparently valid restricted minimalization is in fact valid, it is necessary to check that the function minimalized does assume the zero value as required. Its appearance in the derivation in no way guarantees this, and it is not apparent how a test might be devised. (It is important to keep clear the difference between a plausibility argument such as this and a proof. Just because one cannot see how to do something is no particular evidence that it cannot be done. Neither is it convincing to display any number of ways that might be tried, and show that they all fail.)

Thus, although we can show that each recursive function is total, we have only a guess that this class exhausts the total functions which are intuitively algorithmic.

3.7 PARTIAL RECURSIVE FUNCTIONS

Paradoxically, by making a further extension to our functional class we regain the ability to make lists of derivations, but lose function totality. The final class is generally accepted as exhausting the intuitively algorithmic functions, a statement known as Church's thesis. The new operation is restricted minimalization with the restriction lifted.

Definition

The function ψ is obtained from g by (unrestricted) *minimalization* iff g is total and $\psi = \lambda x_1 \ldots \lambda x_n [\mu y [g(x_1, \ldots, x_n, y) = 0]]$. The class of *partial recursive functions* is the smallest class containing the successor, zero, and projection functions, and closed under composition and primitive recursion, and also under minimalization of total functions. ∎

It should be evident that use of unrestricted minimalization can lead to functions which are not everywhere defined, not total, hence "partial." For example,

$$\psi = \lambda x [\mu y [S(Z(U_1^2(x,y))) = 0]]$$

is partial recursive, and nowhere defined. (It is conventional to use Greek letters for partial functions; the strange symbol is a reminder that the function may also be strange, possibly undefined for some arguments.)

Consideration of partial functions raises some questions about our closure operations. In minimalization there is explicit provision for total functions only. In primitive recursion it seems evident that if the defining functions fail to be defined for some input values, then any use of these cases as the recursion unwinds in reverse creates points at which the new function is also undefined. For composition, consideration of functions such as $X = \lambda x [Z(\psi(x))]$ where ψ

is the function of the previous paragraph, indicates that two definitions are possible: we might ignore a lack of definition in an inner function if this is immaterial to the outer one, or insist that both functions be defined for the composition to be defined. The latter course is the one chosen, so in fact in the example, $X = \psi$. (This nowhere defined function appears often; it is called an *empty function*, since its graph is the empty set of ordered pairs. More computer programs are written for it than for all other functions combined. A common notation is $\psi = \emptyset$.)

It is easy to adapt the definition of recursive derivation to give a definition of partial recursive derivation—just change the restrictions on the functions which may appear in minimalizations. It remains unclear whether or not all such derivations can be effectively listed, since there is still a condition to be tested before a minimalization can be legally used. To illustrate the point about proof and plausibility, the result here is opposite to that for recursive functions. The partial recursive functions can be listed, and the listings can with justice be called programming languages. Until we make such a list (Section 4.11) these facts remain unproved, of course.

The inclusion of partial functions does eliminate diagonalization difficulties. Consider adapting the diagonal argument to a listing of the partial recursive functions of one argument, the xth function of the list written ψ_x. Define $\delta = \lambda x [\psi_x(x) + 1]$ as before, and suppose that this is a partial recursive function, occurring in the list, say at position i. Then is $\delta(i) = \psi_i(i) + 1 = \psi_i(i)$ the same contradiction? No. Our justification that δ appears in the list is that its computation could proceed by locating the proper list position, then following the partial recursive derivation which appears at that point, and when it produces a value, adding unity. But suppose when we do this that derivation produces no value, because the listed function happens to be undefined at the crucial argument. Then $\delta(i)$ is undefined, and there is no contradiction. What we have proved, then, on the assumption that partial recursive function lists can be made, and their searching is again partial recursive, as is simulation of an appearing derivation, is that the diagonal function is necessarily undefined at an argument that is its own position in the list.

It is clear that the three classes of functions we have defined are nested. However, we have proved nothing about this nesting except that the partial recursive functions strictly contain the others. It has been stated that the inclusion of the primitive recursive functions in the total recursive is strict. A final question concerns the total recursive function class and those partial recursive functions which happen to total. The definitions show that the former is included in the latter. It is true that the classes are the same, but again this is a result which must be deferred to Section 4.11.

We choose to now put aside the mathematical function classifications, and turn again to abstract machines, now with one component which is nonfinite. The machines are transducers, well adapted to computing functions, and to

EXERCISES

3.1 Give complete primitive recursive derivations for the zero function of n arguments, $Z^n = \lambda x_1 \ldots \lambda x_n [0]$; the factorial function $f = \lambda x [x!]$.

3.2 In the definition of primitive recursion the function defined must have at least two arguments. The form

$$f = \lambda x \begin{bmatrix} n & \text{if} & x = 0 \\ g(x, f(x-1)) & \text{if} & x > 0 \end{bmatrix}$$

is therefore not permitted (n is a natural number, and g is primitive recursive). Prove that functions defined in this way are primitive recursive. [*Hint:* Use an explicit transformation.]

3.3 Prove that

$$f = \lambda x \begin{bmatrix} g(x) & \text{if} & x = 0 \\ h(x) & \text{otherwise} \end{bmatrix}$$

is primitive recursive if g and h are.

3.4 Show that the functions

$$H_n = \lambda x \begin{bmatrix} 0 & \text{if} & x \leq n \\ 1 & \text{if} & x > n \end{bmatrix}$$

are primitive recursive for each natural number n. [*Hint:* Look for a relationship between H_n and H_{n-1}, and use induction.]

3.5 Write out a careful proof by induction that the function f defined in Exercise 3.2 is total if the function g is total.

3.6 Prove that the integer-divide-by-two function whose recursive derivation was indicated in Section 3.6 is primitive recursive.

3.7 For this problem only, call the class of functions defined with the restricted μ-operator, the "mu-recursive" functions. Show that the rather special form of the minimalization is not important, as follows: Consider a "restricted ν-operator"

$$f = \lambda x_1 \ldots \lambda x_n [\nu y [R(x_1, \ldots, x_n, y)]]$$

defining $f(x_1, \ldots, x_n)$ as the least y such that $(x_1, \ldots, x_n, y)$ is a member of the relation (set of $(n+1)$-tuples) R, this relation having the property that for each $x_1, \ldots, x_n$ there is at least one y such that the $(n+1)$-tuple is a member. Then define the "nu-recursive" functions as the smallest class containing the primitive recursive base functions and closed under composition, primitive recursion, and the restricted v-operator in the sense that

$$f = \lambda x_1 \ldots x_n [vy[R(x_1,\ldots,x_n,y)]]$$

is nu-recursive iff the characteristic function of the set R is itself nu-recursive. (The characteristic function is conventionally taken to have value 1 for $(n + 1)$-tuples in the set, value 0 for those not in the set.)

Show then that the mu-recursive functions and the nu-recursive functions are the same class, and hence that the more convenient mu-definition is not restrictive.

3.8 In the formula

$$\psi = \lambda \dot{x}[\mu z[p(x,\mu y[p(x,y) \dotdiv z = 0]) \dotdiv z = 0]]$$

the minimalization is to be interpreted as unrestricted. Suppose that the function p is known to be recursive, and to have the property that for all x and all z, there is a y such that $p(x,y) = z$; prove that ψ is primitive recursive. Discuss the situation if all that is known about p is that it is recursive.

3.9 Give in schematic form all the partial recursive derivations of length two lines. Avoid a possible difficulty by stating a convention for names of argument variables and functions to be used in derivations. What is the programming-language analogy to this difficulty about conventional names, and might programmers be willing to accept a similar convention?

3.10 Give a partial recursive derivation for the function

$$\psi = \lambda x \begin{bmatrix} 13 & \text{if } x = 1 \\ \text{undefined otherwise} \end{bmatrix}$$

3.11 Consider ALGOL 60 as a language of only typed procedures with arguments called by value. Each such procedure defines a function. Prove that every partial recursive function has an ALGOL 60 program of this kind. In what sense do actual implementations of ALGOL 60 fall short of allowing computation of any partial recursive function on a digital computer? In what sense is ALGOL 60 unsuited for specification of partial recursive functions because the language is too powerful?

3.12 Consider ALGOL 60 typed procedures as defining natural-number functions as in Exercise 3.11. How would you restrict the language further so that only the total recursive functions could possibly be computed? What restrictions would permit computing only the primitive recursive functions?

3.13 It can be shown (with some difficulty) that an equivalent definition of the partial recursive functions is as the smallest class containing all constant functions, projections, proper subtraction, addition and multiplication, and closed under composition and unrestricted minimalization. That is, enough arithmetic can replace primitive recursion (which is the difficult part of the proof). Under such a definition, prove that the functions defined in Exercises 3.3 (take g and h partial recursive) and 3.10 are partial recursive.

3.14 A function may be defined from each possible case involved in Fermat's last theorem:

$$f = \lambda x \begin{bmatrix} 1 & \text{if there are } a, b, c \neq 0, a^x + b^x = c^x \\ 0 & \text{otherwise} \end{bmatrix}.$$

This function is particularly simple if the theorem happens to be true. It could happen, however, that Fermat's last is not a theorem, and the behavior of f might then be complex. (For example, we know that $f(0) = 0, f(1) = 1$, and perhaps matters continue unsettled in this way.) Suppose that complete information were available about the behavior of f as a result of insight gained in trying to prove the theorem. Could it happen that f is not primitive recursive? Could f be partial recursive but not total recursive? Could f fail to be partial recursive?

REFERENCES

Landau's [8] axiomatic treatment of natural-number theory is intuitive, but careful, and directed toward fundamental ideas of what numbers are. The discussion of number-theoretic functions given here is very similar to Mendelson [9], although the definition of minimalization follows Davis [10]. The characterization of primitive recursive and recursive function classes by programming languages which is mentioned in Section 3.1 and the Exercises may be found in Meyer and Ritchie [11].

4
TURING COMPUTABILITY

4.1 PARTIAL-RECURSIVE-FUNCTION-DERIVATION "PROGRAMS"

Associated with each partial recursive derivation is an implied intuitive computing procedure, like that of a primitive recursive derivation with the addition of steps to take when a minimalization appears. Those steps are to start with zero for the argument to be minimalized, and see if indeed the appropriate function has zero value for this input. If so, zero is the least argument as required. If not, try one, and so forth. In this description lies the reason that we insist on total functions to be minimalized; otherwise, the least value might never be reached by the process which got stuck on an earlier computation at an undefined argument value. Although such a procedure associated with each derivation does not always produce a function value for a given set of arguments (if not, a minimalization will be at fault), it does yield the value when the function corresponding to the derivation has one. It would be sufficient for the purpose of continuing the discussion of function classes to use derivations as computing procedures. To anticipate Section 4.6, we would consider the form of the derivation to be the syntax of a programming language, with the semantics that the function computed by a program (derivation) is the partial recursive function derived.

There are two reasons why derivation programs are inadvisable. First, the syntax of such a language has a major flaw: one cannot in fact tell if a derivation is correct, precisely because there is no way to judge whether or not a function used in a minimalization is total, as required to meet the definition of partial recursive function. (As it happens, we could pass over this point by permitting minimalization to appear only once in a derivation, so that the function minimalized would necessarily be primitive recursive, hence total. This would seem to shrink the class of functions, but we could prove that it would not. See the Kleene normal-form theorem, Section 4.10.) The more important second reason not to use derivation programs is that another programming language is of greater historical importance, and today continues to be used in theoretical computer science. This language does not have the syntax problem of derivations, although it is not a language many programmers would choose over (say) ALGOL; the language was devised by A. M. Turing.

Programmers hardly have cause to feel smug that a language of any kind is used to discuss questions in recursive function theory. Turing, among others, could be said to have invented programming for the twin purposes of talking about functions (the program is a name for the function it computes), and capturing intuitive ideas of what can be accomplished by effective procedures (the partial recursive functions can be computed). Even the characterization of Turing's formal creations as programs is stretching a point. He thought of a person performing rote mathematical computations, working from a finite set of rules, employing unlimited scratch paper to transform an input into an output. The mechanical analog (eliminating the person) has the advantage that it may be expressed in a form itself suitable for input to a computation. Turing called his creations "machines," and they are now most commonly called "Turing machines."

4.2 TURING MACHINES

The primary purpose in presenting a complete theory of Turing computability is to have full details to fall back on when discussing difficult questions that appear to turn on tricks of expression. We encountered such a question at the end of Section 1.3, for example, and fundamental questions about programming are often of this kind. In fact, they do not turn on tricks, but this understanding has been gained only by considering a number of diverse languages in exactly the detail to be presented here, and noting the surprising similarity of results. (We consider another language in Chapter 7.) With the practice provided by study of finite transducers, the intuitive discussions need not be prolonged.

Definition

A *Turing machine* is a quintuple (Σ, Q, m, i, f) where Σ is a nonempty finite set (the *tape alphabet*) containing the very special character **b** (the *blank*), Q is a nonempty finite set of *internal states* of which i and f are members, the *initial* and *final* (*halt*) states, respectively, and $m: (Q - \{f\}) \times \Sigma \to Q \times (\Sigma \cup \{L, R\})$ is the *transition function*. ∎

In the remainder of this section we will make use of a particular example Turing machine which might be called the "Poor Richard" machine, or the "pennywise" machine. It will be called S, and its formal definition is

$$S = (\{\text{¢}, \text{b}, \$\}, \{i, q_0, f\}, m, i, f)$$

4.2 Turing Machines

where the transition function m is given by

$$q \begin{cases} \begin{array}{c|c|c|c} m(q,\sigma) & ¢ & b & \$ \\ \hline i & (i,R) & (q_0,R) & (i,¢) \\ \hline q_0 & (i,¢) & (f,L) & (i,\$) \end{array} \end{cases} \overbrace{}^{\sigma}$$

This is as far as we can now carry the example, since we do not yet have a definition of what a Turing machine does.

Intuitively, a machine is to pass from state to state directed by its input and present state, as a finite transducer does, but there may be an output which replaces the particular input, or a move to the immediately prior or succeeding tape symbol. All action should halt if the machine ever enters its final state; things should begin in the machine's initial state. Further definitions will be needed to actually force the machines to behave in this way, of course.

Before continuing, it is worth noting that for Turing machines, many definitions exist which differ in details. A common point of difference is whether or not the machine can move and output in one transition (our machines cannot, Turing's could). Such details are a matter of taste, and they complicate or simplify the proofs which form the theory of Turing computability. The point is that when one speaks of a Turing machine precisely, he must give some details of his definition or fail to be understood. It is a measure of how inessential the details are that such situations are uncommon.

Definition

An *instantaneous description* of a Turing machine (Σ, Q, m, i, f) is a triple (t, q, p) where nonnull $t \in \Sigma^*$ is the *tape*, $q \in Q$ is the *current state*, and the natural number p, $1 \leq p \leq \text{length}(t)$, is the *position of the scanned square*. ∎

Two instantaneous descriptions of the Poor Richard machine S are

$$(¢¢¢¢¢\$\$bb, i, 5) \quad \text{and} \quad (b\$b¢¢bbb\$¢, f, 9).$$

In the first, the machine is in state i scanning the last ¢ before the $; in the second, the machine is in state f scanning the rightmost $.

In almost every case an instantaneous description can be graphically represented by a diagram such as

$$t_1 t_2 \ldots t_p \ldots t_n$$
$$\underset{q}{\wedge}$$

showing a tape of length n with the position of the scanned square labeled with the current state. The only fault of the diagram is that when attention is con-

Definition

If X and Y are two instantaneous descriptions of Turing machine (Σ, Q, m, i, f), X yields Y iff one of the situations shown in Table 4.1 obtains (where $q, q' \in Q$, $t_1, \ldots, t_p, \ldots, t_n, \mathsf{a} \in \Sigma$). ∎

Table 4.1

	X	$m(q, t_p)$	Y
1)	$t_1 \ldots t_p \ldots t_n$, $\uparrow q$	(q', a)	$t_1 \ldots t_{p-1} \mathsf{a} t_{p+1} \ldots t_n$, $\uparrow q'$
2)	$t_1 \ldots t_p \ldots t_n$, $\uparrow q$	(q', R)	$t_1 \ldots t_p t_{p+1} \ldots t_n$, $\uparrow q'$
3)	$t_1 \ldots t_p \ldots t_n$, $\uparrow q$	(q', L)	$t_1 \ldots t_{p-1} t_p \ldots t_n$, $\uparrow q'$
4)	$t_1 \ldots t_p$, $\uparrow q$	(q', R)	$t_1 \ldots t_p \mathsf{b}$, $\uparrow q'$
5)	$t_p \ldots t_n$, $\uparrow q$	(q', L)	$\mathsf{b} t_p \ldots t_n$, $\uparrow q'$

The final two cases in the definition are a very nice way of making precise the "infinite" part of the Turing machine. Although any particular tape is finite, there is no limit to the size of tape which a given machine can write; as it moves off the existing tape, more is magically added. Such an operation is not foreign to those who write unlabeled multireel files on digital computers. (Note that there is no similar mechanism for stripping off extra end blanks, although there could be.)

Definition

A *computation* by Turing machine (Σ, Q, m, i, f) is a finite sequence of instantaneous descriptions $X_1, \ldots, X_k$ such that X_j yields X_{j+1} for each $1 \le j < k$, and the current state of X_1 is i, while the current state of X_k is f. We say that the computation *begins* with X_1 and *terminates* with X_k, and write $X_1 \to X_k$. ∎

The definition completes the formal machinery necessary to specify what a Turing machine does: it executes computations. For the Poor Richard machine S, the following is the kind of computation it is designed to execute: $(\mathsf{b}\$\mathsf{¢}, i, 1) \to$

4.2 Turing Machines

(b¢¢bb,f,4), in which the sequence of instantaneous descriptions is:

b\$¢ yields b\$¢ by case 2 since $m(i,\text{b}) = (q_0,R)$,
 $\underset{i}{\wedge}$ $\underset{q_0}{\wedge}$

yields b\$¢ by case 1 since $m(q_0,\$) = (i,\$)$,
 $\underset{i}{\wedge}$

yields b¢¢ by case 1 since $m(i,\$) = (i,¢)$,
 $\underset{i}{\wedge}$

yields b¢¢ by case 2 since $m(i,¢) = (i,R)$,
 $\underset{i}{\wedge}$

yields b¢¢b by case 4 since $m(i,¢) = (i,R)$,
 $\underset{i}{\wedge}$

yields b¢¢bb by case 4 since $m(i,\text{b}) = (q_0,R)$,
 $\underset{q_0}{\wedge}$

yields b¢¢bb by case 3 since $m(q_0,\text{b}) = (f,L)$.
 $\underset{f}{\wedge}$

When the computation begins as this one does, the machine justifies its name by saving pennies, but it is the dollar equivalent of "pound foolish."

These definitions are sufficient to specify the actions of our Turing machines, along the lines indicated following the first definition. The formal treatment is enough like that for finite-state machines that it is possible to draw a kind of transition diagram for the machines. Instead, we now introduce a notation which emphasizes the program nature of a Turing machine. It is the function m of (Σ,Q,m,i,f) which is the heart of the machine; from it the alphabet and states can be deduced, and by assuming that initial and final states will always be symbolized as i and f respectively, m specifies the machine. Thus a Turing program is a way of giving m as a collection of quadruples written without parentheses or commas:

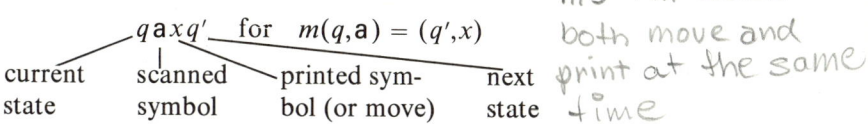

$q\,a\,x\,q'$ for $m(q,a) = (q',x)$

current state | scanned symbol | printed symbol (or move) | next state

[margin note: his Tm cannot both move and print at the same time]

is a quadruple, and writing a collection of them in any format is a program if the mapping m is thereby defined. The syntax of the language is thus specified (imprecisely), and the semantics is roughly that a program does what its transition function specifies. The language is very low level, which turns out to be useful in proving things about it, and nonprocedural, which could be blamed on

64 Turing Computability

Turing's intuition about the way people compute. (As we will see in Chapters 7 and 9, digital computer assembly languages are not much more procedural. One can still fault Turing's intuition, since all such languages are hard to use.)

The acceptance of sets such as $\{a^n b^n \mid n \geq 0\}$ is not the sort of work which will be assigned to Turing programs here, but we do not want to leave the impression that there is anything a Turing machine cannot do. Solving this acceptance problem which was beyond the ability of any finite acceptor also illustrates the conventions which could be used to define a "Turing acceptor" in general. The string to be tested is presumed to be encoded using the symbols 0 and 1 instead of a and b; this avoids confusion with the tape blank. The input is to be presented surrounded by blanks, with nothing to the left of the blank which the machine scans, nor anything to the right of the first blank encountered there. Acceptance is signaled by halt scanning a 1 and rejection by halt scanning a 0, the tape otherwise all blank. Since this is the first large Turing program to be displayed, comments will be provided to attempt a description of what is happening. The program of Table 4.2 is an order of magnitude larger than any to be presented in this form again, and so may be interpreted

Table 4.2

$ibRq_0$	$i0Li$	$i1Li$	At the left blank, go right. If scanning left (from q_4) ignore everything until the left blank.
$q_0 b 1 f$	$q_0 0 b q_1$	$q_0 1 b q_5$	Accept bb. Reject for too many ones (cleanup at q_5). Otherwise overprint leftmost zero.
$q_1 b R q_2$	—	—	Move right from blank produced at q_0. (For "—" see following.)
$q_2 b L q_3$	$q_2 0 R q_2$	$q_2 1 R q_2$	Skip over anything looking for the right blank, and when found, stop left of it.
$q_3 b b q_7$	$q_3 0 b q_7$	$q_3 1 b q_4$	Reject for too few ones at the right (cleanup at q_7). Otherwise overprint rightmost one.
$q_b b L i$	—	—	Move left from blank produced at q_3. Reuse the initial state.
$q_5 b R q_6$	—	—	Cleanup when error discovered at the left. Move right.
$q_6 b 0 f$	$q_6 0 b q_5$	$q_6 1 b q_6$	Overprint any nonblanks, and loop back to q_5. At right blank print reject and halt.
$q b L q$	—	—	Cleanup when error discovered at the right.
$q_8 b 0 f$	$q_8 0 b q_7$	$q_8 1 b q_7$	Overprint nonblanks and loop with q_7 till left blank, then reject.

(like any low-level program) as a sample of what not to do (write extensive low-level programs).

The algorithm is to be certain of a left zero, blank it out, seek the corresponding right one, blank it, and return. Success is then a blank tape at the time of checking for the left zero. In the specification of the program, "—" represents a quadruple of no consequence, since in some states some symbols can never be scanned. However, to specify a transition function, all the missing pairs of state and symbol must be filled in. A good plan would be to use the quadruple $q_x\, y\, y\, q_x$ for each missing state-symbol pair (q_x, y), causing a loop if the situation should arise. The example shows that the extra power of the Turing program results from its ability to move back and forth across the input, and to mark where it has been.

4.3 TURING COMPUTABILITY

To sharpen the semantics of the Turing language requires selecting part of the complete transition history as the meaning of a program. Since our interest is partly in partial recursive functions, we choose to single out the computed value—what is left on the tape at halt—and to restrict ourselves to numerical codes.

Definition

A *numerical computation on argument* $(x_1, \ldots, x_n)$ *with value* y by Turing machine $(\{b, 1\}, Q, m, i, f)$ is a computation that begins with an instantaneous description of the form

$$b1^{x_1}b1^{x_2}b \ldots b1^{x_n}b$$
$$\underset{i}{\wedge}$$

and terminates with one

$$b1^y b$$
$$\underset{f}{\wedge}$$

where $x_1, \ldots, x_n, y$ are natural numbers. The definition includes a convention, and is the one case in which our abbreviated notation for instantaneous descriptions is not precise enough. It is conventional to represent a tape which is blank but for one section as

$$b1 \ldots 1b$$

displaying only the nonblank section surrounded by a single pair of b symbols. But the convention then makes it impossible to tell what the numerical tape position of the scanned square actually is. In the definition, the tape of the beginning description has squares 1 through $(x_1 + \ldots + x_n + n + 1)$ exactly, with initial position 1. The final tape contains at least this many squares since there is no mechanism for deleting superfluous end blanks, but it may contain more, and the scanned square is not necessarily the first, although the tape is blank except for y ones. (Furthermore, it is as if blanks exist beyond the right end of tape so that $\underset{f}{\overset{\wedge}{\ldots\, b}}$ indicates a properly scanned zero.) ∎

Definition

A Turing machine *computes* the (partial) function ψ of n arguments iff whenever ψ is defined at argument $(x_1,\ldots,x_n)$ with value y, then there is a numerical computation on that argument with that value; and, whenever there is such a numerical computation, the function is so defined. A function which is computed by some Turing machine is called *Turing computable,* and the function of n arguments computed by machine $M = (\{b,1\}, Q, m, i, f)$ is denoted Ψ_M^n. ∎

For example, a Turing machine which computes the zero function Z has the program

$$\begin{aligned}
\text{N:}\quad & i\,1\,1\,i \\
& i\,b\,R\,q_0 \\
& q_0\,1\,b\,i \\
& q_0\,b\,b\,f
\end{aligned}$$

and is formally $(\{b,1\}, \{i, f, q_0\}, m, i, f)$, m given by the program. (We freely confuse names of machines and programs to write $\Psi_N^1 = Z$.) It is important to note that Turing programs do not in any way specify the number of arguments of functions computed. The example program does compute the zero function, but it also computes U_2^2 if considered as a two-argument machine, and a function of three or more arguments which is undefined if any argument past the first two is nonzero.

4.4 GRAPHICAL REPRESENTATION OF TURING PROGRAMS, EXAMPLES

As a programming language, like most low-level languages, the Turing one is hard to use. Fortunately, we only intend to write programs for all the possible partial recursive functions. It is not evident that this can be done, and it is less obvious that only partial recursive functions can be programmed. Establishing both results would prove the equivalence of the Turing comput-

4.4 Graphical Representation of Turing Programs, Examples   67

able functions and the partial recursive functions, which is what we now undertake. As a side effect of this work, all of the questions of Section 3.7 about relations between the recursive function classes will be answered, and we will see a prototype explication of the syntax and semantics of a programming language. The first half of the proof preceeds in the obvious way, and has in fact begun: all partial recursive functions will have Turing programs if the base functions have them, and the existence of a Turing program for any given functions implies the existence of one for a function defined with closure operations on these. We have a program for one base function, zero. Another for the successor is almost as easy to give: the method is to skip to the end of the input, then add a one, blank, and skip back.

To continue programming requires that we find a way to abbreviate the massive programs that result. Most of the difficulty arises from bookkeeping on the tape: to skip back and forth across argument values and mark positions requires too many quadruples, too many states, to keep track of easily. Furthermore, debugging even a small Turing program is not easy; here we must prove that indeed each of our programs computes the function we say it does. The solution to the difficulty is the same one which successful systems programmers employ when writing large machine-language systems for digital computers: we use subroutines. Digital computers have operators which make subroutines attractive for reasons of efficiency as well as understanding; however, in a large operating system, for example, the documentation is much the more important feature. Understanding is all we have to gain in Turing programming; indeed, it will often prove better to use an inefficient but proven routine than to devise an efficient one. Those who are offended by the inefficiency have no shortage of operating systems written according to their tastes, all badly in need of debugging for that very reason.

The kind of subroutines we shall define could be called "in-line" in the sense that from them we will construct larger programs by simple juxtaposition. But the concatenation also provides a measure of procedure-like isolation in the following sense: we will indicate how to compose machines so that any task which the "first" performs necessarily precedes tasks of the "second," and neither can possibly interfere with the other.

Given two Turing machines expressed as collections of quadruples, **A** and **B**, let **AB** denote the collection of quadruples obtained as follows:

> Systematically replace all the state names but f in **B** by new names which do not conflict with those of **A**. Suppose the replacement for i in **B** is i'; then replace f in **A** by i'.

Writing a string of machines such as **ABC** ... indicates that this process is carried out successively from the left, two machines at a time, **AB**, then the composite **(AB)C**, etc. Only the leftmost machine retains a state i; only the rightmost a state f. For example, we could use the new notation and the machine **N** for the zero function to define

$$\mathbf{N'}: \quad \mathbf{NN}$$

whose quadruples are obtained by making two copies of those for **N**, and modifying one copy according to the procedure defined above to obtain the composite machine

$i\,1\,1\,i$	$q_1\,1\,1\,q_1$	(The modified copy appears at the right; q_1 re-
$i\,b\,R\,q_0$	$q_1\,b\,R\,q_2$	places i, q_2 replaces q_0. What remains unchanged
$q_0\,1\,b\,i$	$q_2\,1\,b\,q_1$	in the copy, and what does change in the un-
$q_0\,b\,b\,q_1$	$q_2\,b\,b\,f$	modified copy?)

(Can a machine with fewer states behave just as **N'** does?) **N'** computes the zero function Z^2 of two arguments (and also U_3^3, etc.). Note that although often the machines combined compute interesting functions, the notation specifies successive use of any machines, even those whose functional behavior is not interesting.

A very useful combination of existing machines with tape alphabet {1,b} includes testing of the contents of the scanned square. We write

$$\ldots \mathbf{H} \begin{matrix} 1 \\ \nearrow \mathbf{J} \ldots \\ \searrow \mathbf{K} \ldots \\ b \end{matrix}$$

to indicate a construction from the quadruples of machines **H**, **J**, and **K** as follows:

> Presumably **H** has been adjusted to follow some string of machines, and **J** and **K** are to be similarly adjusted. But instead of merely equating final and initial states, add the quadruples $f'\,1\,1\,i'$ and $f'\,b\,b\,i''$ and replace f in **H** by f'. Then when **J** and **K** are adjusted, make sure that their initial states are replaced by i' and i'' respectively.

The effect is to choose to continue with machine **J** when the scanned square is a 1, or with **K** if a blank. The special case of the form

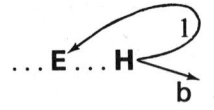

$$\ldots \mathbf{E} \ldots \mathbf{H} \begin{matrix} 1 \\ \curvearrowleft \\ \searrow \\ b \end{matrix}$$

illustrates two frequently used modifications of the added quadruples, in which i' is taken to be the initial state of the machine **E** (which state has perhaps been altered to something else as an earlier part of the renaming), and since the arrow labeled **b** leads to no machine, the i'' is taken to be f.

Of course, all these diagrams and conventions have no formal existence. They are merely convenient abbreviations which allow us to grasp the function of large Turing programs by viewing them as constructed from small components. From the abbreviations, the quadruples of the actual program which is abbreviated can be constructed according to the rules for renaming and adding "test" quadruples. When pressed about the details of some program, it may be necessary to unabbreviate.

As an example of building complex machines from simple ones, and the use of machines whose function-computing behavior is not the reason we consider them, consider the often occurring problem of moving across parts of a tape to the left and right. The basic components are evidently the machines

$$\mathbf{R}: \quad i \; 1 \; R \; f$$
$$\phantom{\mathbf{R}: \quad} i \; b \; R \; f$$

which just moves the scanned square to the right, and a similar machine **L** which goes to the left. (What functions do these machines compute?) In working with coded numeric arguments, it is common to be positioned on the b to the left or right of the code for a natural number, and to want to shift to the other side. The machines to shift right,

$$\mathbf{S}_R: \quad \mathbf{R} \begin{array}{c} 1 \\ b \end{array}$$

and an $\mathbf{S}_L$ similarly to shift left, do the job. As in any programming project, it is essential to have subroutines just powerful enough that their component parts are seldom needed, yet significant operations are performed. $\mathbf{S}_R$ and $\mathbf{S}_L$ are typical of appropriate machines for the partial recursive function programming now to be undertaken. (A summary of these component programs appears at the beginning of Section 4.5 as Table 4.2.)

In addition to shifting abilities, we will need component machines which print each possible symbol in the scanned square,

$$\mathbf{B}: \quad i \; 1 \; b \; f$$
$$\phantom{\mathbf{B}: \quad} i \; b \; b \; f$$

prints a blank, and a very similar machine **O** prints a one. With these tools, we can follow the suggested algorithm for a machine to compute the successor function, almost without pain. The program with $\Psi^1_\mathbf{P} = S$ is

$$\mathbf{P}: \quad \mathbf{S}_R \mathbf{O} \mathbf{R} \mathbf{S}_L.$$

(The third-applied machine **R** is essential not only to force the right-end blank from Case 4 of the yield definition, but also to arrange proper conditions for the application of $\mathbf{S}_L$, which must begin scanning a blank.)

Programs have been displayed for two of the partial recursive base functions as examples of function-computing Turing machines. But the real goal is to demonstrate half of the fundamental result that the Turing-computable functions and the partial recursive functions are the same. Since the theorem will be stated after we have constructed many machines, it is necessary now to indicate how one proves that a given machine does indeed compute a given function. Perhaps there should be a "royal road" for people with substantial programming experience: anyone used to considering programs working on data and examining the cases which may occur should believe that the machine **N** computes Z and the machine **P** computes S. If pressed for a proof, details of the particular program must be taken into account. For example, **N** can be analyzed directly: it halts on the first blank to the right of the one it initially scanned, and never prints a one, sufficient to certify it for the input zero. As it moves right it further eliminates any intervening one, enough for correct results on any nonzero input. For the program **P** it would be unwise to write out all the quadruples as a first step in the proof. Rather the analysis should make use of the subroutines to show that the result is always one longer than the initial configuration. These two programs are typical of those we will produce: analysis of the functions they compute is direct, and really no more informative than the remarks used to motivate the programs themselves. A formal proof by induction on the length of the input string could be given, but the inductive hypothesis would often go unused. To avoid such embarrassing demonstrations the emphasis will be on explaining each program thoroughly, as a sort of proof preventative.

The remaining base functions are the projections, and by introducing one further convention they can all be shown as one diagram. When it is necessary to apply some component machine several times, its name will be shown with a superscript in parentheses for the number of applications. Should the superscript be zero or negative, the machine does not in fact appear at all. Sometimes the repetition required is on several machines; in that case they will be grouped with parentheses and the group superscripted. As an example that we do not actually need, the zero function of n arguments is computed by the machine

$$\mathbf{N}_n: \quad \mathbf{N}^{(n)},$$

and the machine

$$\mathbf{K}_3: \quad \mathbf{NP}^{(3)}$$

computes the constant function $\lambda x\,[3]$ of one argument.

The machines for the projection functions $U_k^n = \Psi_k^n = \mathbf{I}_k^n$ are given in Fig. 4.1,

$$\mathbf{I}_k^{n\cdot}: \quad \mathbf{N}^{(k-1)}\mathbf{R} \begin{array}{c} \overset{b}{\longrightarrow} \mathbf{N}^{(n-k)} \\ \underset{1}{\longrightarrow} \mathbf{LS}_R \mathbf{N}^{(n-k)} \mathbf{L} \end{array} \begin{array}{c} b \\ 1 \end{array} \mathbf{RS}_L$$

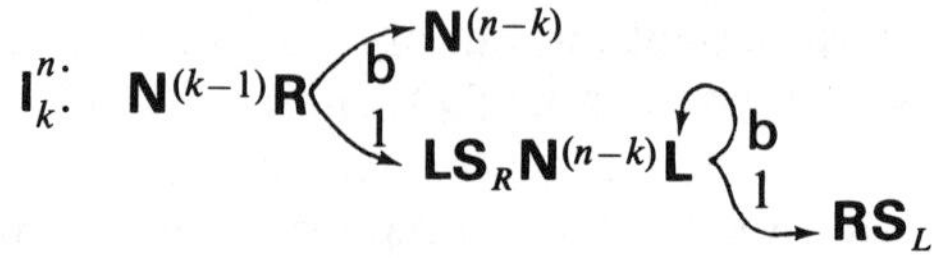

Figure 4.1

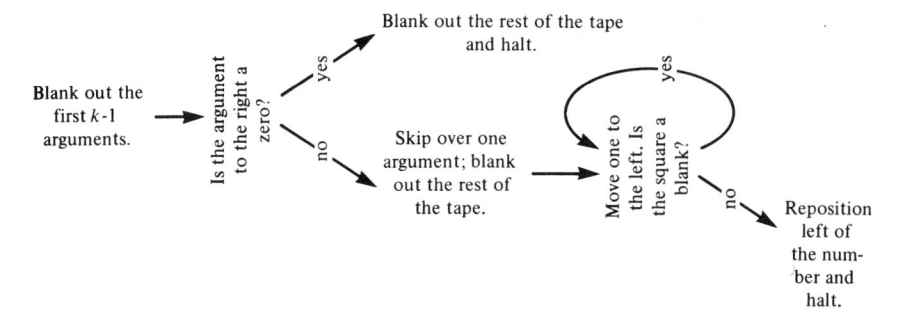

4.4 Graphical Representation of Turing Programs, Examples 71

```
                          Blank out the rest of the tape
                                  and halt.
                              ↗
                          yes
Blank out the      ┐ ┌                         ┌── yes ──┐
  first k-1    →   │ │                         ↓         │
  arguments.       │ │ ──no──→  Skip over one  Move one to
               Is the argument  argument; blank  the left. Is
               to the right a   out the rest of  the square a
               zero?            the tape.        blank?
                                                         │
                                                         no
                                                         ↘
                                                      Reposition
                                                       left of
                                                       the num-
                                                       ber and
                                                        halt.
```

Figure 4.2

which is complicated enough to require an explanation. Fig. 4.2 shows a very convenient kind of commentary which can be written to follow the two-dimensional form of the program. The algorithm is evident from this comment diagram. A feature of the projection machines (which will occur again) is the treatment of a zero argument as a special case. This is the payment for simplicity in coding a zero as simply a pair of consecutive blanks: one can never depend on the presence of any ones to serve as a marker which can again be located. After skipping argument number k the projection machines must eventually find it again, and that will be impossible should it be a zero. Of course, finding it in that special case is unnecessary, and the given machines take advantage of this fact.

All of the machines we have produced never move left of the initially scanned square although all but the successor machine do not necessarily scan the same square at the end of a computation as at the beginning. A simpler successor machine would be

OL

if there were no reason not to move left of the starting point. But there is reason to keep to the right; the reason lies in the computations which must yet be performed with Turing machines to show that all partial recursive functions are Turing-computable. We must show that when a closure operation invokes an already defined function, then a machine can be found for the newly defined function, in terms of the machine for the one already defined. Our conventions for writing composite machines lend themselves well to such constructions, but for one difficulty: if the details of the machines used are not available, we cannot be sure that the interface between them will operate smoothly. For example, we might wish to compute a function which is obtained from several others by composition. A reasonable way to do so is to perform conputations of the inner functions so as to leave a tape which appears to be a coded tuple of their values, to which the machine for the outer function may be directly applied. The scheme of performing the inner computations successively to the right would founder if any machine such as the **OL** successor one were used, for it destroys information to the left. Even the machines that do not go left are not immediately suitable for such schemes, unless they can be made to return to the initial square at the end of their computations. If that can be arranged, the position of argument codes can be guaranteed. The obvious way to repair the machines **N** and **I**$_k^n$ is the same, and can be made available for general use by adding two component machines to our list: the first, **X**$_n$, shifts a tape containing an n-tuple to the right by one square, inserting a one as a mark to the left; the second, **F**, presumes that a computation has been performed starting with such a marked tape, resulting in a computed value which lies to the right of the mark, with an indefinite number of intervening blanks. It moves the result to the left and deletes the mark, so that answers are in the position where the first argument once began. With these machines, **X**$_1$**NF** is a machine for the zero function, and **X**$_n$**I**$_k^n$**F** for the projections, which never move left of the original scanned square, and always terminate scanning it.

$$\mathbf{X}_n: \quad \mathbf{S}_R^{(n)}(\mathbf{L} \xrightarrow[1]{b} \mathbf{RORS}_L \mathbf{RBL})^{(n)} \mathbf{OR}$$

(Recall the convention about repeating groups of component machines. The arrow terminating at the end of the repeating group of course means that in the test quadruples the state chosen on scanning a blank is the newly named initial state of the lead-off machine in the next repeat of the group, save in the final occurrence, when it is the initial state of the penultimate **O** machine.) The algorithm for **X**$_n$ works from the right of the initial n-tuple. Positioned at the right of one of the code groups which is to be moved to the right, and with an extra blank already available from previous moves, no action need be taken if the code group to the left is for a zero. If not, a one is appended to its right end, and removed from its left end. In any case, things are now set up to do the same to the code next to the left. When the whole string has been moved the leading one can be inserted, and the scanned square placed to its right. (Incidentally, in the **X**$_n$ and **F** machines the payment is greatest for the coding choice which makes it impossible to distinguish a zero code from the end of the tape. Were it not for this choice, we could make a single machine which would serve instead of **X**$_n$ for all n, by coding zero as something nonblank, and seeking the tape end by looking for a double blank. The inconvenience soon disappears, and one of the advantages purchased is not technical: we have chosen the "natural" coding, and made it work. This argues that there has been no cheating in the argument that Turing machines can perform all partial recursive function computations.)

The **F** algorithm (Fig. 4.3) is to "roll" the value to the left one bit at a time, appending a bit to its left and removing it from the right, until it bumps up against the marker bit presumed to exist at the left end of tape. That mark is

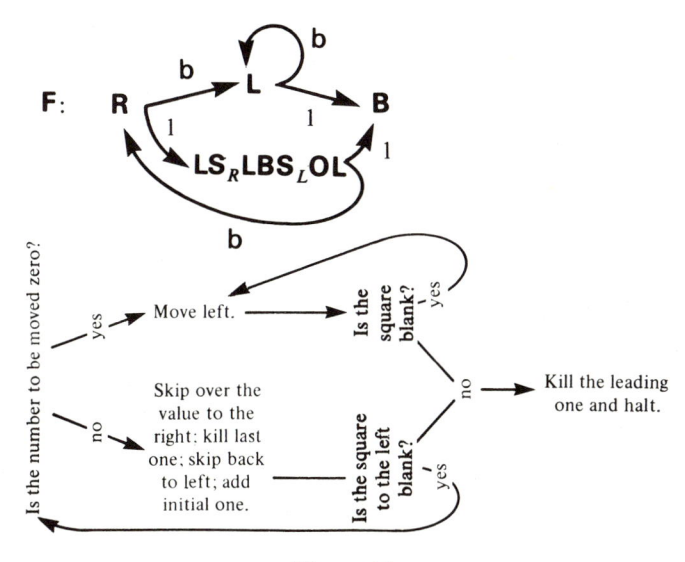

4.4 Graphical Representation of Turing Programs, Examples

Figure 4.3

then finally removed. A zero value presents the special case of nothing to roll, so the mark is simply sought and deleted.

We now have the means to constrain computation which never moved left to further return to the same initial square, and it is time to state the requirements formally:

Definition

The Turing machine Z *positively computes* a function ψ of n arguments iff

1. $\psi = \Psi_Z^n$ (that is, Z computes ψ);
2. Case 5 in the definition of yield (Section 4.2) is never invoked in a numerical computation on n arguments by Z (that is, no blanks are added at the left end of the tape).
3. The scanned square in the instantaneous description which begins any numerical computation on n arguments by Z is the same as the scanned square in the instantaneous description which terminates it.
4. If $(x_1,\ldots,x_n)$ is an n-tuple for which ψ is not defined, then there is no computation by Z which begins with

$$\underset{i}{b}1^{x_1}b\ldots b1^{x_n}b.$$

A function is *Turing positively computable* iff some Turing machine positively computes it. ∎

74   Turing Computability

Our machines **P** and **N** and I_k^n were designed to meet conditions 1 and 2 of the definition; **P** met condition 3, and the others were forced to meet it by prefixing and suffixing X_n and **F**; since all these functions are total, condition 4 is satisfied because its hypothesis is never true.

Condition 4 is necessary to verify composition and primitive recursion closure, because we permit a Turing machine to enter its final state, yet perform no numerical computation (because it scans the result incorrectly). If a machine which halts in this way were followed by another machine, the second could conceivably ignore the improper stop, and continue in such a way that the composite machine performs a numerical computation. This would cause the function computed by the composite machine to be defined where the composition function is undefined, and destroy a proof that the composition operation could be effected directly with composite machines. For positive computation the situation is legislated out of existence. (Actually, what we will need is the somewhat stronger guarantee that the situation of condition 4 cannot arise even if there is an arbitrary string on the tape to the left of the scanned square in the initial instantaneous description. Condition 2 implies that condition 4 is enough.)

4.5 TURING COMPUTABILITY OF EACH PARTIAL RECURSIVE FUNCTION

It is past time to announce what we are doing:

Theorem

Each partial recursive function is Turing computable.

Proof

The method is display of the Turing programs which compute any given function, in the sense that from a partial recursive derivation an appropriate Turing machine can be constructed. In fact, we will prove something stronger (because it is easier than the weaker case): every partial recursive function is positively computable by a Turing machine. We summarize what has already been obtained in a

Lemma 1

The base functions are Turing positively computable.

Proof

Consideration of the programs $X_1 N F$, **P**, and $X_n I_k^n F$ given in Section 4.4. ∎

In arguing for closure, most of the computation is devoted to a kind of bookkeeping which orders and controls component computations so that they

4.5 Turing Computability of Each Partial Recursive Function

do not destroy arguments, but do place results in the correct order. Positive computation is essential here, but one more building-block machine is also invaluable for positioning arguments out of harm's way. The additional machine is C_k, which presumes that it is viewing a k-tuple of code groups in the usual numerical code. It copies the first code group across all the intervening ones, so that at termination the tape contains the code for a $(k + 1)$-tuple of which the first and last code groups are the same, the scanned square immediately following the first one.

$$C_k: \quad R \overset{b}{\underset{1}{\leftarrow}} BS_R^{(k+1)} O RS_L^{(k+1)} O$$

The algorithm is straightforward: the first bit of the number at the beginning of the tape is examined, and if a nonzero code group is first, its initial bit is deleted, then replicated $(k + 1)$ code groups to the right. (The first time, the last code group is a zero, to which the bit originally at the left end of the tape is appended.) After the bit has been placed at the right, the machine skips back and reinserts it in its original position, but then scans one more bit into the first code group. As soon as the blank at the right end of the first code group is encountered, the work is done, even to the correct scanned square.

Table 4.3

Machine	Summary of Action
N	$\underset{i}{b 1^x b} \rightarrow \underset{f}{b b^x b}$
R [L]	Shift the scanned square one to the right [left].
O [B]	Prints a one [blank] on the scanned square.
S_R	$\underset{i}{b 1^x b} \rightarrow \underset{f}{b 1^x b}$
S_L	$\underset{i}{b 1^x b} \rightarrow \underset{f}{b 1^x b}$
X_k	$\underset{i}{b 1^{x_1} b 1^{x_2} b \ldots b 1^{x_k} b} \rightarrow \underset{f}{1 b 1^{x_1} b 1^{x_2} b \ldots b 1^{x_k} b}$
F	$\underset{i}{1 b^x b 1^y b} \rightarrow \underset{f}{b 1^y b b^x b}$
C_k	$\underset{i}{b 1^{x_1} b 1^{x_2} \ldots b 1^{x_k} b} \rightarrow \underset{f}{b 1^{x_1} b 1^{x_2} \ldots b 1^{x_k} b 1^{x_1} b}$

76   Turing Computability

Table 4.3 summarizes the component machines for reference. Only **L**, $\mathbf{S}_L$, and **F** move to the left, while $\mathbf{X}_k$ and $\mathbf{C}_k$ make use of blank tape beyond the right blank shown.

Lemma 2

The class of Turing positively computable functions is closed under composition.

Proof

Suppose that functions $\phi_1,\ldots,\phi_m$ are computed by Turing machines $\mathbf{Z}_1,\ldots,\mathbf{Z}_m$ respectively, and that **Y** computes χ, all positively. Then the composition function

$$\lambda x_1 \ldots \lambda x_n [\chi(\phi_1(x_1,\ldots,x_n),\ldots,\phi_m(x_1,\ldots,x_n))]$$

is positively computed by the program using

$$\mathbf{A}: \quad \mathbf{C}^{(n)}_n\,\underset{1}{\mathbf{Z}}\,\underset{L}{\mathbf{S}}^{(n)}\,\mathbf{C}^{(n)}_{n+1}\,\underset{R}{\mathbf{S}}\,\underset{2}{\mathbf{Z}}\,\underset{L}{\mathbf{S}}^{(n+1)}\ldots \mathbf{C}^{(n)}_{n+m-1}\,\underset{R}{\mathbf{S}}^{(m-1)}\,\underset{m}{\mathbf{Z}}\,\underset{L}{\mathbf{S}}^{(n+m-1)}$$

to obtain the proper string of arguments; then

$$\mathbf{X}_n \mathbf{A} \mathbf{N}^{(n)} \mathbf{Y} \mathbf{F}$$

for the composition itself. In **A**, there are m machines which operate one after the other, the jth being of the form

$$\mathbf{C}^{(n)}_{n+j-1}\,\mathbf{S}^{(j-1)}_R\,\mathbf{Z}_j\,\mathbf{S}^{(n+j-1)}_L$$

and acting to first copy the original n-tuple across the $n + j - 1$ code groups then on the tape, reposition viewing the copy, compute the jth inner function (positively, of course), thus leaving its value in place of the n-tuple, and finally reposition back at the left end of the tape, which grows eventually to the form of the input n-tuple followed by an m-tuple of the inner function values. It is necessary to mark this tape at the outset, since after the **A** machine is done, the argument n-tuple is erased, the outer function computed (positively, although it need only stop properly and keep right—the return to initial square is unnecessary), and the final value shifted back to standard position.

Lemma 3

The class of Turing positively computable functions is closed under primitive recursion.

4.5 Turing Computability of Each Partial Recursive Function

Proof

Suppose that Z_0 positively computes ϕ, and Z_1 positively computes χ. Then the function

$$\phi = \lambda x_1 \ldots \lambda x_n \lambda y \begin{bmatrix} \psi(x_1,\ldots,x_n) \text{ if } y = 0 \\ \chi(x_1,\ldots,x_n, y-1, \phi(x_1,\ldots,x_n, y-1)) \text{ if } y > 0 \end{bmatrix}$$

is positively computed by the program of Fig. 4.4. Appropriately, this is an example of "recursive programming." That is, the machine starts the computation at the given argument, and part way through determines that the result for the previous argument is needed, so starts computing that, and so on until finally for a zero argument a computation can be completed, and the process can unwind back out to the completion of the desired result. The more pedestrian approach would start computing from the zero argument until the desired one was reached. (This is "iterative programming", and although such a program is a little more difficult to understand because of bookkeeping problems, it does use less tape, since each computation can take place over the previous one.) The given "recursive" algorithm first checks for an input argument involving no recursion, and in that case applies Z_0. Otherwise it marks the tape, and inserts a leading zero after the mark, which will be used to flag the top level of the recursion. The $(n + 1)$-tuple to the right of this inserted zero now has its final value decremented, and is copied across itself. The decremented final value must be zero before Z_0 applies, so the decrementing and copying continues until this is the case. The analog to this process in an ALGOL 60 recursion would be the successive stacking of call parameters as the routine encounters itself at execution time. When finally the copied $(n + 1)$-tuple ends in zero, Z_0 is applied to the first n of the copied values. It leaves an $(n + 2)$-tuple $(x_1,\ldots,x_n, 0, \phi(x_1,\ldots,x_n))$, the first $n + 1$ values remaining from the copy sequence. But this is precisely the proper argument for the program Z_1, and

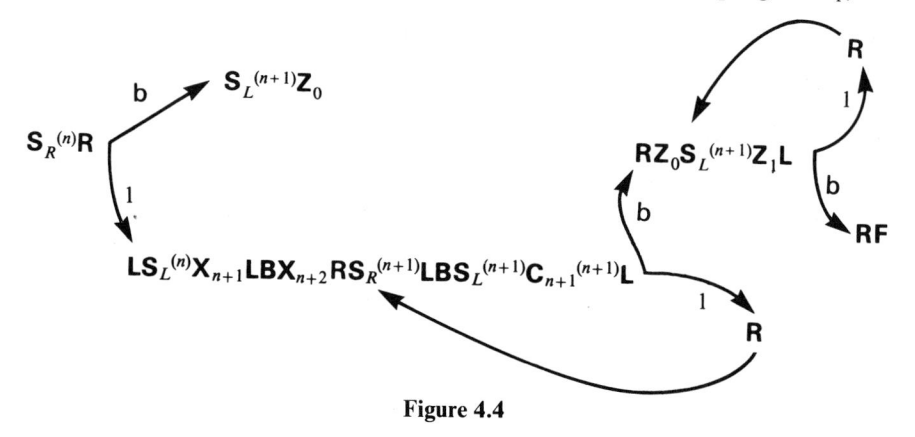

Figure 4.4

78   Turing Computability

when it has finished the $(n+2)$-tuple $(x_1,\ldots,x_n,1,X(x_1,\ldots,x_n,0,\psi(x_1,\ldots,x_n)))$ is at the end of the tape. Further applications of $\mathbf{Z}_1$ complete the calculation, which is done at detection of the initially created zero marker just to the left after $\mathbf{Z}_1$ is used. No zero could appear there as part of an argument string. This repeated use of $\mathbf{Z}_1$ has the ALGOL 60 analog of execution and exit from a procedure which designated itself, cutting back the argument stack in the process. When the marking zero is detected, the final result is all that remains on the tape, and it need only be shifted into place. Fig. 4.5 gives the pictorial flowchart. ∎

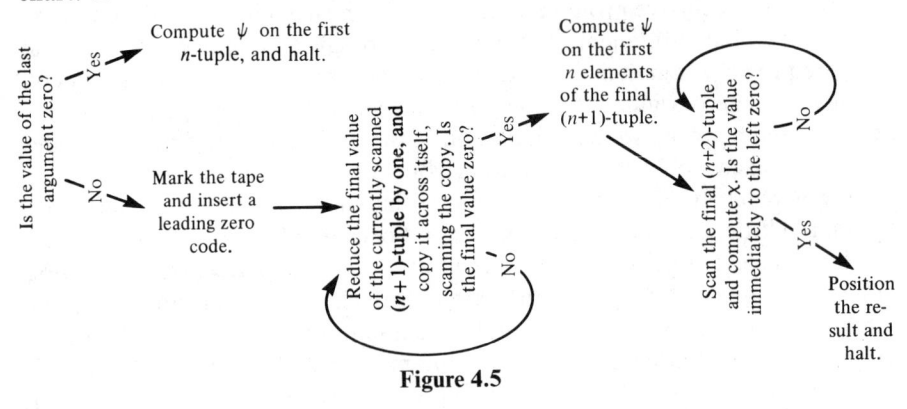

Figure 4.5

Those who prefer interative programming get their chance next.

Lemma 4

The class of Turing positively computable functions is closed under minimalization.

Proof

Suppose that $\mathbf{Z}$ positively computes f. Then the function

$$\lambda x_1 \ldots \lambda x_n [\mu y [f(x_1,\ldots,x_n,y) = 0]]$$

is positively computed by the machine of Fig. 4.6; its comment diagram is Fig. 4.7.

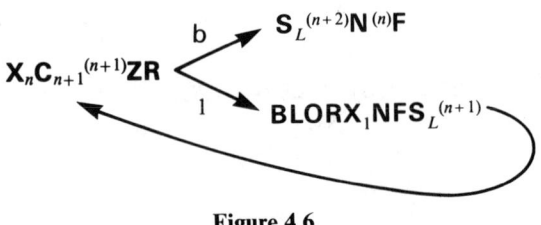

$$X_n C_{n+1}{}^{(n+1)}ZR \quad \xrightarrow{b} \quad S_L{}^{(n+2)} N{}^{(n)} F$$
$$\xrightarrow{1} \quad BLORX_1 NFS_L{}^{(n+1)}$$

Figure 4.6

4.6 Arithmetization. Gödel Numbering. Syntax and Semantics of Languages

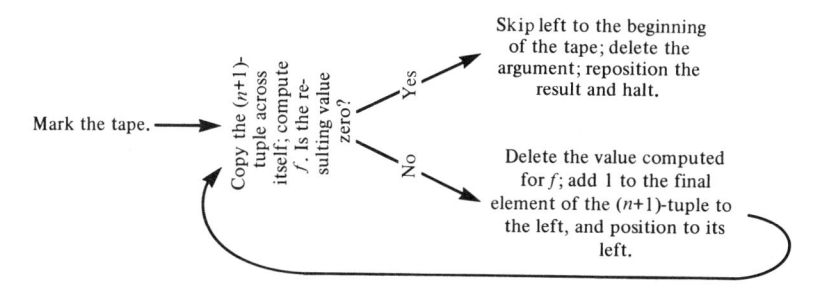

Mark the tape. → Copy the $(n+1)$-tuple across itself; compute f. Is the resulting value zero?
- Yes → Skip left to the beginning of the tape; delete the argument; reposition the result and halt.
- No → Delete the value computed for f; add 1 to the final element of the $(n+1)$-tuple to the left, and position to its left. (loop back)

Figure 4.7

(Although the tape is presented with an n-tuple, the initial copy reproduces as $(n + 1)$st element the zero which is at the end of any proper input tape. In the deleting- and adding-one code which is used when the minimalized function fails to be zero, the actual order tries to take advantage of position for a little efficiency.) Note that the machine takes advantage of the totality of f in simply trying all values for the final argument. ∎

Given any partial recursive function, there is a corresponding partial recursive derivation, specifying a series of functional definitions from the base functions and closure under three operations. By creating Turing programs according to the lemmas in parallel with the derivation, at the final line we will have a program which positively computes the function derived. ∎

Since we have spent so much time computing positively, it should be noted that we will not need this notion again, and that in particular there is no excuse to confuse it with Turing computability itself. The latter notion is the one we continue to explore.

4.6 ARITHMETIZATION. GÖDEL NUMBERING. SYNTAX AND SEMANTICS OF LANGUAGES

There are two levels to the work we do with Turing machines. On the surface, proofs are in progress showing that the functions which are Turing computable are exactly the partial recursive functions (the theorem of Section 4.5 is half of this result). At the same time, however, we presist in viewing the sets of quadrupless of a Turing machine as a program from a programming language encompassing all such sets of quadruples meeting our definition, and studying these programs to better understand programming languages. In the work above, this second level consists of conveying a feeling for the language through a number of examples (which happened to be just those needed for the surface-level proof). To stretch a point, perhaps one could even learn something about programming in general from the work of Section 4.5: to accomplish any large task in a low-level language it is essential to invent a way to avoid checking the large final program all at once. Use of prechecked components combined in such a way that there are no hidden connections is one such way. Obviously this corresponds to the usual digital machine-language use of subroutines; there are those who believe that there is no other reasonable way to write (for example) an operating system in such a language.

Indeed, the usual promotional introduction to a programming language displays sample programs which graphically convey the "power" of the language. "Power" often has more to do with economy of programming than with function-computing ability, so Section 4.5 was somewhat more focused than a typical language introduction. The second half of the result we are seeking—that each Turing-computable function is partial recursive—serves two purposes on the surface level. In addition to support for the proposition that "intuitively computable" and "partial recursive" describe the same class of functions, it happens that the form of the proof will also answer all the questions concerning the nesting of the function classes left open at the end of Section 3.7. At first sight, there might seem no parallel to more usual programming languages at the second level: no one goes about proving that his pet language is limited in what it can do. However, most of the insight into properties of programming languages in general is gained from the proof; it is not the result, but the method which provides information at the second level. For the method of proving that each Turing-computable function is partial recursive is to precisely describe the syntax and semantics of the language, the latter in such a way that the meaning assigned to a program is the function it computes (in a form which makes it easy to identify that function as partial recursive).

In one way it would be appropriate to define our Turing machine syntax and semantics as nearly as possible in the way programming languages are usually defined. A grammar would generate the syntax, and semantics would be defined using that grammar, perhaps with English as the metalanguage of the semantics. This approach would be familiar, and would certainly justify the orientation that the Turing language is like any other, for all its low-level nonprocedural nature. One difficulty which would certainly arise would be that of gaining enough precision in the semantics to carry out the surface-level proof, and in relating the semantics to partial recursive functions.

Perhaps there is better reason to follow the historical development, as this chapter does, even though it is rather unlike conventional syntax and semantics. The precision is no problem, and that is the most important reason for adopting historical methods. The interesting side effect of this decision is that the illumination of fundamental properties of syntax and semantics may actually be better than if the ground were more familiar. Those who define and describe programming languages do not always agree about just what constitutes syntax and what semantics, and too often the semantic metalanguages are imprecise.

4.6 Arithmetization. Gödel Numbering. Syntax and Semantics of Languages

It therefore clears the air to approach language definition using the tools of the recursive function characterizations.

The goal is specifying Turing machine syntax and semantics is to mimic the computations of an arbitrary machine with a recursive function, in the sense that the function judges whether or not a given machine, with given input, produces a given computation. The function computed by the machine is then somehow related to the least computation which is correct for each input. More precisely, we will show that there is a primitive recursive function t_n such that

$$t_n(z, x_1, \ldots, x_n, y) = \begin{cases} 0 & \text{if } z \text{ is the number of a Turing machine which on} \\ & \text{argument } x_1, \ldots, x_n \text{ performs the numerical} \\ & \text{computation whose number is } y \\ \text{nonzero otherwise} \end{cases}$$

and that another primitive recursive function U obtains the value computed from a computation, so that

$$U(\mu y [t_n(z, x_1, \ldots, x_n, y) = 0])$$

as a function of $x_1, \ldots, x_n$ is what machine numbered z computes—evidently partial recursive.

There is no hope of devising the function t_n without introducing some conventions concerning machines and computations, because the first and last arguments of this function as previously defined are not numbers. Turing machines are 5-tuples with rather complicated components; computations are sequences of instantaneous descriptions, also complicated. In a sense we have been working with a reference language up to now, but presently need an implementation language. This requires a defined character set and rules to code the "reference" entities into it. The coding requires more than usual care because of its purpose. Language implementors always use such care, but here we make its necessity explicit: the game must not be lost in the coding. To give a crucial example, suppose that the character set we adopt contained "!" (it doesn't). We might then arrange that when writing strings of characters, only those starting with "!" were to be Turing machines. We could then recognize that such a string is in fact a machine by looking at its first character. It is evident that such a procedure is cheating in a fundamental way: "Turing-machine-ness" is not to be decided during the process of coding, but after coding. Intuitively the code should accomplish nothing more than bringing the entities we want to consider into considerable form. That means coding things like machines and computations into numbers, in as mechanical a fashion as possible. No one can prove that nothing is hiding in the coding, but general agreement may be attainable.

The idea of assigning numerical values as codes for entities which are not numerical perhaps seems obvious to programmers who use machines to do just that. It is necessary to look at history to see what a brilliant suggestion this is. The inventor is K. Gödel, who called the process "arithmetization"; it is now called "Gödel numbering" as well. These names are usually reserved for more than just a numerical coding of nonnumeric entities, however, Gödel insisted that the encoding be intuitively effective in the sense that given an entity to be coded, the number can be obtained by rote; furthermore, decoding is also effective: given a number, the entity it codes may be regained undamaged in a mechanical way. These requirements are not met by many of the "internal codes" of digital computers. In a typical machine a memory word has at least four possible decodings: as an integer, a floating-point value, a string of characters, or an instruction; the word in no way flags which code was in effect at its creation. It might be said that the conflict between J. von Neumann's idea of ignoring the meaning of stored data and Gödel's concept that data have such a meaning is what makes an occupation of programming. The programmer and his brainchild, the program, keep track of the von Neumann transgressions against the Gödel coding.

In any case, we now proceed to create a Gödel numbering for Turing programs and computations, and to construct the function t_n. The presentation employs a kind of "keypunch code" which uses decimal digits as characters. The advantage of such a code is that it is easy to read, and familiar to digital machine programmers (although their memory dumps may come in another base). The disadvantage is that pains must be taken to avoid ambiguity in decoding. If it is easy and natural to think of 7 as the code for "L", 2 as the code for "b", and 5 for "f", so that 77 is the code for "LL", it is not so natural to prevent 77 being decoded as "Lbf" (that is, 72 + 5). The gain in readability seems worth the loss to decoding complication. Instead of writing digits, most often we will write what they code, using a special typeface to keep things straight. This may be thought of as merely the eccentric notation for the numerals shown in Table 4.4.

Table 4.4

Usual digit	New Notation	Comments
0	(none)	Not used.
1	⊔	Separator symbol.
2	b	Tape blank symbol.
3	1	Tape one symbol.
4	i	Initial state symbol.
5	f	Final state symbol.
6	q	Symbol used to construct state names.
7	L	Left move symbol.
8	R	Right move symbol.
9	/	Symbol used to implant a state within a tape.

4.6 Arithmetization. Gödel Numbering. Syntax and Semantics of Languages 83

Many details of the coding are apparent from the informal discussion (what tape has the number 232?). One confusion can arise, since 1 in the new notation is coded 3, while 1 codes a ⊔, but the symbols are really distinct. There will be considerable use of 0, 1, and 10 as numbers of the sort that can be counted on the usual complement of fingers. There will be some symbols with multiple use, but this situation is familiar in most high-level languages, and we will make no errors as bad as using "( )" for both subscripts and function calls, to cite a horror all FORTRAN compilers tolerate.

The tape coding is the obvious one. For a Turing machine, we choose to make some simplifications. The machine is of course a 5-tuple, but throughout our "programming" we used only the collections of quadruples which define the transition mapping, having noted that the other 5-tuple elements can be deduced therefrom. We then choose to implement only collections of quadruples. Furthermore, arbitrary state sets cannot be captured within any finite collection of symbols, so we standardize state names. Those which are not i or f are required to be finite strings of q symbols, but not all possibilities need arise in a machine—that is, qq and qqqq could appear without q or qqq. (There is nothing difficult about allowing arbitrary identifiers in the ALGOL 60 sense, but the extra symbols are a bother.) Quadruples of a machine will then be coded just as they would appear with a single blank separating the parts. This happens to be as in the few examples of Section 4.3. If one prefers state names like "q_{87}" he can imagine that 88 q symbols in a row is an abbreviation. Thus 413181666 is an example of a quadruple which we have previously written as $i\ 1\ Rq_2$. To combine quadruples into a machine we use a double blank to separate them. Thus our blank convention is not at all like that of many programming languages, since leading and trailing blanks are not used, and within a machine blank counts are important. As an illustration, the machine **N** for the zero function has a number

$$41313141141218161161312141116121215$$

which we previously wrote

$$i1\,1\,i\quad ibRq_0\quad q_0 1bi\quad q_0 bbf.$$

Instantaneous descriptions are the elements of the sequence which is a computation, and are in turn made from tapes, states, and scanned squares. We mimic our pictorial notation without going off a line by writing the tape, with the current state enclosed between solidi, just to the left of the scanned square. For example, (b1b,i,1) is a common beginning instantaneous description, which we encode /i/b 1 b or 949232. For the sequences of instantaneous descriptions of a computation, a single blank separates the components. We would thus code the computation of our machine **N** (Section 4.3) on input 1 as

$$9492321296932129492212296921229592.$$

A footnote may justify the coding for machines and computations as intuitively mechanical and concealing nothing. The machine coding happens to be the input format for a Turing machine simulator implemented on a PDP-10 system, and the simulator prints instantaneous descriptions in their coding. Of course, the author of the simulator was trying for clarity rather than concealment.

4.7 "PREDICATES" AND FUNCTIONS

Historically, instead of the function t_n a primitive recursive "predicate" was developed—a propositional function of $n + 2$ places taking the value *true* when the arguments represented a Turing machine, its n-tuple input, and the resulting computation, otherwise *false*. The predicate has a famous name: the Kleene T-predicate T_n. Such a presentation goes together with a minimalization operation which operates on arbitrary predicates or relations instead of zero values of functions. The difficulty with the presentation is that of defining closure when what is minimalized is not a function; we have chosen to avoid the complications by avoiding predicates. (The essential idea appears in Exercise 3.7.) However, in the long chain of definitions which leads to t_n, the intuitive content is better expressed by intuitive "predicates" than by functions. We hack our way out of this dilemma by writing predicates but meaning functions. A series of primitive recursive functions will indeed be given, but associated with each one is a condition which obtains if and only if the function takes a zero value. This condition is the intuitive predicate, and it will be given a name as well as the function. Successive functions are then defined if new predicates are defined from the old, providing we can associate functional operations with the logical ones which apply to predicates. Intuitively then the full machinery of the propositional calculus is available in function building.

For example, consider the function of two arguments (we abandon the lambda notation for discussing predicates) defined by

$$eq(x,y) = (y \dotminus x) + (x \dotminus y),$$

which is primitive recursive (composition; addition; proper subtraction). It happens that $eq(x,y) = 0$ iff $x = y$. Hence the intuitive predicate associated with eq is equality. How might we then construct a second function neq which would correspond to inequality? The logical situation is that $x \neq y$ holds iff $\sim(x = y)$ holds. We arrange this for the functions by

$$neq(x,y) = 1 \dotminus eq(x,y).$$

That is, to gain the logical negation, use proper subtraction from 1.

We write predicates with capital letters corresponding to the small letters of the functions unless there is some more standard notation (*e.g.*, *EQ* is not used for equality). The general situation is then that primitive recursive functions f and g will have been defined taking a zero value if and only if predicates

4.7 "Predicates" and Functions

F and G hold. To define a new predicate H is then to define a new primitive recursive function h according to the following rules:

predicate	defines the primitive recursive function
H iff $F \vee G$	$h = f \cdot g$
H iff $F \wedge G$	$h = f + g$
H iff $\sim F$	$h = 1 \dotdiv f$
H iff $F \supset G$	$h = 1 \dotdiv (f + (1 \dotdiv g))$

The interconnections between the connectives are preserved; in the case of $F \supset G$ the definition as $\sim(F \wedge \sim G)$ is used (why is the simpler $g \dotdiv f$ incorrect?).

The major intuitive power of the predicate notation arises from the use of the logical operations of quantification. To stay within the primitive recursive functions requires a restriction, however, so only "bounded quantification" will be incorporated:

predicate	function
$\exists y \leq x_i [F(x_1,\ldots,x_n,y)]$ $(1 \leq i \leq n)$	$f(x_1,\ldots,x_n,0) \cdot f(x_1,\ldots,x_n,1) \cdot \ldots \cdot f(x_1,\ldots,x_n,x_i)$
$\forall y \leq x_i [F(x_1,\ldots,x_n,y)]$ $(1 \leq i \leq n)$	$f(x_1,\ldots,x_n,0) + f(x_1,\ldots,x_n,1) + \ldots + f(x_1,\ldots,x_n,x_i)$

(For the first of these read "there exists a y less than or equal to x_i such that $F(x_1, \ldots, x_n, y)$ holds." If no y makes $F(x_1, \ldots, x_n, y)$ hold, or one no larger than x_i makes it hold, the predicate intuitively agrees with the usual $(\exists y)[F(x_1, \ldots, x_n, y)]$ of the first-order predicate calculus. The difference is that if given $x_1, \ldots, x_n$ there is a y such that $F(x_1, \ldots, x_n, y)$ holds but every such last argument is larger than the given x_i, then $(\exists y)[F(x_1,\ldots,x_n,y)]$ holds, but $\exists y \leq x_i [F(x_1, \ldots, x_n, y)]$ does not.) By multiplying all possible values of f with the first n-tuple of arguments fixed and the final argument varying over the allowed range, a zero value results only if one or more of the multiplicands is itself zero. The resulting function is primitive recursive because it can be defined with a primitive recursion:

$$g = \lambda x_1 \ldots \lambda x_n \lambda z \begin{bmatrix} f(x_1, \ldots, x_n, 0) & \text{if } z = 0 \\ g(x_1, \ldots, x_n, z-1) \cdot f(x_1, \ldots, x_n, z) & \text{if } z > 0 \end{bmatrix}$$

and an explicit transformation:

$$\lambda x_1 \ldots \lambda x_n [g(x_1, \ldots, x_n, x_i)],$$

taking the definitions freely in the usual way which might be converted to a precise definition. (The discussion of "for all y less than or equal to x_i, $F(x_1, \ldots, x_n, y)$ holds"—the second predicate above—exactly parallels this discussion of the bounded existential quantifier.)

To illustrate this machinery we define the two kinds of nonsymmetric inequalities. The traditional logical definition of $x \leq y$ is $(\exists u)[y = u + x]$, so letting y be the bound we have defined $leq(x,y)$ which is 0 iff $x \leq y$ as

$$leq(x,y) = eq(y,0 + x) \cdot eq(y,1 + x) \cdot \ldots \cdot eq(y,y + x).$$

We have $x < y$ iff $x \leq y \wedge x \neq y$, so

$$ls(x,y) = leq(x,y) + neq(x,y)$$

has been defined.

Henceforth we will dispense with the function names (one exception appears below in the function c), since they will not be used to write new names; the discussion will deal only with predicates.

The heart of our coding schemes is concatenation, and this 3-ary predicate $w = xy$ (w is x concatenated with y) can be constructed from the primitive recursive exponentiation function. Care is required to avoid a uniqueness problem, but the way is partly prepared by avoiding the use of the zero digit in the coding above. Define the concatenation predicate by

$$w = xy \quad \text{iff} \quad (y = 0 \wedge w = x) \vee \exists u \leq w[u \neq 0 \wedge w = 10^u \cdot x + y \wedge 10^{u-1} \leq y \wedge y < 10^u].$$

The basis of the definition is the usual one of the positional system: x is scaled u places to the left of y ($w = 10^u \cdot x + y$). In discussing the esoteric points of the definition, it is convenient to write concatenation as "&"—unnecessary in nonpathological cases. It is arranged that:

Anything is itself concatenated with zero, such as $1 = 1$ & 0.	$(y = 0 \wedge w = x)$
The concatenates do not overlap in the sense that $23 \neq 1$ & 13.	$(u \neq 0, y \wedge 10^u)$
No zeros appear at the junction between x and y as a part of y, so $102 = 10$ & 2, but $102 \neq 1$ & 2.	$(10^{u-1} \leq y)$

The concatenation predicate is elaborate because it must guarantee that decoding using implicit concatenation is unique. For example, if the predicate $w = xy$ holds when $w = 74$ and $x = 7$, we want to be assured that $y = 4$ is the only possibility, and similarly the other way around: $y = 4$ would force $x = 7$. We have avoided using the zero digit to code any basic symbol, so no zeros need appear in our code numbers. This convention permits concatenation to forbid an internal zero to cause ambiguity. A simpler predicate might allow a situation like $w = xy$, $w = 704$, $y = 4$, and both $x = 7$ or $x = 70$. The given predicate declares that 704 is 70 & 4, but is not 7 concatenated with anything. Thus we are unable to talk about zeros properly, and so must not use them. (This situation occurs in programming languages without reserved words, such as

FORTRAN, where the problem character is the blank (space). The usual treatment is to ignore occurrences of blank, but it is only good fortune that avoided ambiguities in FORTRAN, for example in

$$DO5I = 1,5$$
$$DO\ 5\ I = (1.,5.)$$

and

$$2\quad FORMAT(I5,X5H) = (I2)$$
$$FORMAT(I5,X5H) = (I2)$$

and in a formal treatment it seems better to avoid dependence on luck.)

Multiple concatenation is defined by pairs,

$$w = x_1 x_2 \ldots x_n \quad \text{iff} \quad \exists u_2 \leq w[w = x_1 u_2 \wedge \exists u_3 \leq w[u_2 = x_2 u_3$$
$$\wedge \cdots \wedge \exists u_n \leq w[u_{n-1} = x_{n-1} x_n] \ldots]],$$

and concatenation frequently occurs implicitly in that a string is an initial segment of, is a final segment of, or is embedded in another:

$$x\ BEG\ y \quad \text{iff} \quad \exists w \leq y[y = xw]$$
$$z\ END\ y \quad \text{iff} \quad \exists w \leq y[y = wz]$$
$$x\ ELT\ y \quad \text{iff} \quad \exists u,v \leq y[y = uxv].$$

Evidently the last three predicates will be useful in describing our codes. A convenience tailored to discussion of repeating digits such as appear on tapes and in the machine states is

$$x\ ALL\ y \quad \text{iff} \quad \forall z \leq x[(z\ ELT\ x \wedge z \wedge 10 \wedge z \neq 0) \supset z = y].$$

A peculiarity of the *ALL* predicate, essential in coding tapes and annoying at other times, is that while as expected iii *ALL* i (that is, 444 *ALL* 4), it is unexpected that when the first argument is zero, the second is immaterial and the predicate holds. That is, zero is *ALL* anything you like.

4.8 THE SYNTAX PREDICATE $TM(z)$

Most of the predicates above have general application; now some are presented which apply particularly to Turing machines as sets of quadruples. The names chosen sometimes correspond to entities which we have defined for machines, but more often the material included in a given predicate is more a matter of convenience than of adherence to what its name promises.

$$ALPH(x) \quad \text{iff} \quad x = b \vee x = 1$$
$$STATE(x) \quad \text{iff} \quad x = i \vee x = f \vee \exists y \leq x[x = qy \wedge y\ ALL\ q]$$

express the properties of being the Gödel number of a legal tape symbol and state name, respectively. In the latter, the last disjunction cannot be simply

'x *ALL* q' because then we would have $STATE(0)$. The syntax of four particular entities joined by blanks is of some importance:

$$QUAD(x) \quad \text{iff} \quad \exists x_1, x_2, x_3, x_4 \leq x [x = x_1 \sqcup x_2 \sqcup x_3 \sqcup x_4$$
$$\wedge STATE(x_1) \wedge x_1 \neq \mathsf{f} \wedge ALPH(x_2)$$
$$\wedge (ALPH(x_3) \vee x_3 = \mathsf{L} \vee x_3 = \mathsf{R}) \wedge STATE(x_4)],$$

and illustrates implicit decoding using concatenation. The $QUAD$ predicate is a gentle introduction to an important way in which our syntax differs from that of some practical languages (but not from their implementations). It is certainly essential that we have $STATE(\mathsf{f})$, yet a part of our machine definition forbids the occurrence of this one state as the first element of a quadruple (because it is omitted from the domain of the transition mapping). There is no question but that transitions are part of semantics, yet we have incorporated a transition restriction into the syntax by checking for that f. This point is one about which there is disagreement, but the position taken here is not intended to be in doubt: We put into syntax each and every idea that we can force in, on the grounds that semantics is hard enough when it is certain what was parsed; by leaving too many openings for programs to be nonsensical, semantics becomes an impenetrable thicket. It cannot help but be easier to specify what programs do if we have a good idea what they look like, and are sure they follow some rules which we arbitrarily impose. There is no purpose to syntax but as the ground on which to define semantics. We will see this attitude appearing again in the next two predicates, particularly in the "final pass" of the parse, which is *TM*. (Incidentally, another analogy to the f-restriction in $QUAD$ is that we are simply forbidding the appearance of a reserved word in a context where other words of its syntactic class are permitted.)

The primary feature of the following predicate is the device it uses to indicate a sequence of elements and their spacer, when the length of the string is unknown. Except for the additional conditions on i and f there are those who would consider that this predicate covers all of Turning-program syntax. No such person accepts the remarks about syntax and semantics above.

$$M(x) \quad \text{iff} \quad \exists t \leq x [QUAD(t) \wedge t \, BEG \, x] \wedge \exists v \leq x [QUAD(v) \wedge v \, END \, x]$$
$$\wedge \forall t, u, v \leq x [(tuv \, ELT \, x \wedge QUAD(t) \wedge QUAD(v)$$
$$\wedge \forall u_1 \leq x [u_1 \, ELT \, u \supset \sim QUAD(u_1)]) \supset u = \sqcup \sqcup]$$
$$\wedge \mathsf{i} \, ELT \, x \wedge \mathsf{f} \, ELT \, x$$

asserts that something begins to look like a Gödel number of a machine if it is a sequence of quadruples with double-blank spacers.

The analog of what is not included in *M* but is a part of Turing-program syntax is symbol-table information in a conventional compiler or interpreter. In some languages one must declare identifiers before use, and in most languages consistency of identifier use is required; the same identifier cannot at once be an array and a procedure name in FORTRAN, for example. Such conditions are often omitted from the formal "syntax" of languages, and their misuse referred to as "semantic errors." From our point of view this is nonsense. Turing machines have constraints which are not unlike those of identifier-laden languages, concerning the state-name occurrences in a machine: once a name appears anywhere in any quadruple, it is required to appear properly in others so that the transition function is completely defined. Furthermore, the first two elements of a quadruple must not appear duplicated in several quadruples without the rest of those quadruples also being duplicates. These properties are evidently analogous to requiring proper identifier use following implicit declaration, and consistency of identifier usage. Those who believe that such matters cannot be put into formal syntax are simply wrong (even for typical block-structured languages); those who believe that symbol tables should not be syntax are in the wrong implementation group at this time. Thus

$TM(x)$ iff $M(x) \wedge \forall\, u_1, u_2, u_3, u_4, u, v_1, v_2, v_3, v_4, v \leq x [(u\ ELT\ x$
$\wedge QUAD(u) \wedge u = u_1 \sqcup u_2 \sqcup u_3 \sqcup u_4$
$\wedge v\ ELT\ x \wedge QUAD(v) \wedge v = v_1 \sqcup v_2 \sqcup v_3 \sqcup v_4)$
$\supset ((u_1 = v_1 \wedge u_2 = v_2 \supset u = v) \wedge (u_4 \neq \mathbf{f} \supset \exists\, w, w_1 \leq x [w\ ELT\ x$
$\wedge QUAD(w) \wedge w = u_4 \sqcup w_1])$
$\wedge\, \exists w, w_2 \leq x[w\ ELT\ x \wedge QUAD(w) \wedge w \neq u \wedge w = u_1 \sqcup w_2])].$

The paraphrase of this predicate is that something is a Gödel number of a Turing program iff it has the correct symbols and spacers, and any two of its component quadruples are identical if their first two elements agree (this guarantees a single-valued transition function), and if a state name appears anywhere, then both scanned-symbol options **b** and **1** appear with that name as first element (**f** is an exception). Although we will make no use of it formally, we have with the definition of *TM* also defined a primitive recursive function *tm* which takes the value zero iff its argument is the number for a Turing machine. It is unfortunate that we lack the alphabet convention to allow the nonzero value taken by *tm* when the argument is not such a number to be **SYNTAX ERROR**.

Although *TM* is certainly of the correct form to define a language syntax, in the semantics to follow we will almost always need a form which isolates the basic element of the machine we are considering: the quadruple and its four components. (Statements, or "constructs," would be the analogous notion for more conventional languages.) The predicate we need is

$TMQ(z, x_1, x_2, x_3, x_4)$ iff $TM(z) \wedge \exists x \leq z [x\ ELT\ z \wedge QUAD(x)$
$\wedge\, x = x_1 \sqcup x_2 \sqcup x_3 \sqcup x_4].$

which breaks out full details of the quadruple, but also insists that it be part of a syntactically correct Turing program. It is at this point that the Turing language has it all over any more usual high-level language, since its "constructs" always have the same four crucial elements, and are easily isolated within a program for the specification of semantics.

4.9 THE SEMANTIC PREDICATES $T_n(z,x_1,\ldots,x_n,y)$

Before continuing to obtain the Kleene T-predicates for Turing machine semantics, a warning is in order about the form of the remaining work: it appears no different from what has gone before. We continue to devise predicates, and use no operations we have not already used. Why then has the syntax stopped and the semantics begun? Of two answers, only the less interesting can be explained immediately. Intuitively, *TM* is all there is to syntax because the things it approves are exactly codes for the Turing programs written as quadruples according to our earlier definition. Thus the first reason for calling *TM* the syntax predicate is that it does what syntax checking for any language implementation does: judges the programs presented. The semantics to follow applies the judgment of other predicates not to programs, but to their purported computations. It might not be wrong to call this syntax—it is certainly judging strings of symbols mechanically—but syntax of Turing computation rather than programs. The notion may seem strange because we are accustomed to leave such matters to hardware engineers. Computations take place inside digital computers at a speed which forbids examination, and with a lack of error which is remarkable. Only when programs malfunction is the computation laboriously traced as a last resort in debugging. In the proof we are anticipating by building the T-predicates, the question is whether or not the computation process is partial recursive in character, so we must capture recognition explicitly to prove that it is.

The deeper reason for making the syntax-semantics division at this point is also the answer to the question: why not include the syntax of computations in the programs, as part of official syntax? This would be desirable from many standpoints, not the least of which is that since computations include information about whether or not programs perform properly, the question of program correctness could then be treated. Sadly, the reason that we do not include computations in syntax is that to do so would compromise the most important property of syntax—effective recognition of programs. This assertion will be proved when we consider unsolvable problems, of which the Turing "halting problem" in Section 5.4 is one. (We therefore take another unambiguous position on a point of programming-language theory: along with believing that symbol tables are syntax, we assert that the "meaningfulness" of programs is not syntax if meaningfulness incorporates the notion of computation.)

We begin the semantic considerations with a parallel to the *M*-predicate which judges the symbol juxtapositions for instantaneous descriptions:

$D(x,u,v)$ iff $\exists w \leq x[w = /u/v \wedge w\ ELT\ x \wedge ALPH(v)$
$\wedge\ \forall t \leq x[t\ ELT\ x \wedge \sim(t\ ELT\ w) \wedge t < 10 \supset ALPH(t)]]$.

4.9 The Semantic Predicates $T_n(z, x_1, \ldots, x_n, y)$

The first argument is the description being judged, the second stands for the current state, and the third is the contents of the scanned square. Most of the predicate is devoted to assuring that the tape has nothing but b and 1 outside the local disturbance caused by incorporating something between solidi left of the scanned square.

Each of the possible positions of the scanned square (left end of tape, right end, or strictly in the middle) has its own form:

$ID_L(x,u,v,z)$ iff $D(x,u,v) \wedge x = /u/vz$
$ID_R(x,y,u,v)$ iff $D(x,u,v) \wedge x = y/u/v$
$ID_N(x,y,u,v,z)$ iff $D(x,u,v) \wedge x = y/u/vz$.

The variable names x, u, and v in these definitions are respectively the description, the current state, and the contents of the scanned square. Other variables represent the remainder of the tape contents left and right as appropriate. Occasionally we do not care about details so long as one of these holds:

$ID(x)$ iff $\exists y,u,v,z \leq x [ID_L(x,u,v,z) \vee ID_N(x,y,u,v,z) \vee ID_R(x,y,u,v)]$.

The ID predicates and TMQ are enough to write the heart of the semantics, the way in which one instantaneous description leads to another in accordance with the program quadruples. The predicate $YIELD(x,y,z)$ asserts that the last argument is the code number of a Turing program, and that this program authorizes the transition from one instantaneous-description code to another, as given by the first two arguments. In a bastard symbolism, "$x \to y$ on z."

$YIELD(x,y,z)$ iff $\exists x_1, x_2, x_3, x_4 \leq x \exists y_1, y_2, y_3, y_4 \leq y$
$[(ID_N(x,x_1,x_2,x_3,x_4) \wedge ID_N(y,y_1,y_2,y_3,y_4)$
$\wedge ((TMQ(z,x_2,x_3,y_3,y_2) \wedge x_1 = y_1 \wedge x_4 = y_4)$
$\vee (TMQ(z,x_2,x_3,\mathsf{R},y_2) \wedge y_1 = x_1 x_3 \wedge x_4 = y_3 y_4)$
$\vee (TMQ(z,x_2,x_3,\mathsf{L},y_2) \wedge x_1 = y_1 y_3 \wedge y_4 = x_3 x_4)))$
$\vee (ID_R(x,x_1,x_2,x_3) \wedge ID_R(y,x_1 x_3, y_2, \mathsf{b})$
$\wedge TMQ(z,x_2,x_3,\mathsf{R},y_2))$
$\vee (ID_L(x,x_1,x_2,x_3) \wedge ID_L(y,y_2,\mathsf{b},x_2 x_3)$
$\wedge TMQ(z,x_1,x_2,\mathsf{L},y_2))]$

The predicate considers each case in the definition, and ties the action to the enabling quadruple in the syntax. (The order in which cases are listed is: printing, moving right, left, off tape right, left.)

Although we are now in a position to assert that in a sequence of instantaneous descriptions, one yields the next properly, a momentary digression will complete the stock of predicates needed to assert that a machine performs a numerical computation. This predicate is a reversal of the sort of thing we have been doing up to this point. Heretofore an intuitive notion was essentially nonnumeric, we coded it, then asserted that the code was in the

92   Turing Computability

correct form. In the case of numerical values on a tape, we already have a code, forced on us at an early stage by the Turing machine's inability to handle anything but a symbol at a time. The contiguous string of 1 symbols is intended to represent a number, and we want to assert that a number for the string (in our code, for example 33333 or 11111) is to be taken as a natural number argument on a tape (in the example a count of the fingers on most left hands). The apparent difficulty with the predicate is that the line between what is code and what is number is crisscrossed too often. As a helpful example, 33333 CODES 5:

$$x\ CODES\ y \quad \text{iff} \quad (x = 0 \wedge y = 0) \vee \exists u \leq x[x\ ALL\ 1 \wedge 10^{u \dotdiv 1} \leq x$$
$$\wedge\ x < 10^u \wedge y = u].$$

It is convenient to specify a Gödel number of a numerical computation in two stages, the first serving to force proper elements in proper order (with a useful side effect):

$$C(y,u) \quad \text{iff} \quad \exists t, t_1, y_1 \leq y[t\ END\ y \wedge ID_N(t,y_1,\mathsf{f},\mathsf{b},t_1 t_2) \wedge y_1\ ALL\ \mathsf{b}$$
$$\wedge\ t_1\ CODES\ u \wedge t_2\ ALL\ \mathsf{b}]$$
$$\wedge\ \forall t,w,v \leq y[(twv\ ELT\ y \wedge ID(t) \wedge ID(v)$$
$$\wedge\ \forall u_1 \leq y[u_1\ ELT\ w \supset\ \sim ID(u_1)]) \supset w = \sqcup].$$

The final condition requires that all interior elements (separated by the single-space spacers) are instantaneous descriptions; part of the first condition makes the final element an instantaneous description; nothing is said of the initial element. The side effect is that the second argument of the predicate is the Gödel number of the value computed by the machine which has properly halted in order to satisfy C. This is apparently premature, since nothing is present to force a proper initial configuration of the tape, and YIELD has not been incorporated between the instantaneous descriptions. But C does force the proper appearance on a computation, however inconsistent the details may be, and hence the corresponding primitive recursive function c will later be useful in recovering the result of a computation through the second argument. Other constraints will have to deal with the remainder of the computation itself.

$$COMP_n(z,x_1,\ldots,x_n,y,u)$$
$$\text{iff} \quad C(y,u) \wedge \exists t,t_1 \leq y[t\ BEG\ y \wedge ID_L(t,\mathsf{i},\mathsf{b},t_1)$$
$$\wedge\ \exists w_1,\ldots,w_n,t_2 \leq y[t_1 = w_1 \mathsf{b} w_2 \mathsf{b} \ldots \mathsf{b} w_n \mathsf{b} t_2 \wedge t_2\ ALL\ \mathsf{b}$$
$$\wedge\ w_1\ CODES\ x_1 \wedge \ldots \wedge w_n\ CODES\ x_n]]$$
$$\wedge\ \forall d_1, d_2 \leq y[ID(d_1) \wedge ID(d_2)$$
$$\wedge\ \exists d \leq y[d = d_1 \sqcup d_2 \wedge d\ ELT\ y]$$
$$\supset YIELD(d_1,d_2,z)]$$

is the entire specification of the numerical computation with Gödel number y on argument $(x_1,\ldots,x_n)$ with value u on Turing machine with Gödel number

z. The predicate supplies all the deficiencies of C: the initial instantaneous description is specified, including the code groups for the input, and each instantaneous description of the computation is required to yield the following one on the machine. We have then actually overshot the Kleene T-predicates, which assert that a computation takes place without naming its computed value (although of course there is one):

$$T_n(z,x_1,\ldots,x_n,y) \quad \text{iff} \quad \exists u \leq y[COMP_n(z,x_1,\ldots,x_n,y,u)].$$

It remains only to display the means of recovering the computed value from a computation, which as promised is accomplished by a kind of "bounded minimalization" of the function c defined from the predicate C above. The function is therefore primitive recursive by much the same arguments supporting bounded quantification in Section 4.7. The recoverer of a final tape value is

$$U = \lambda y[(1 \dotdiv c(y,0))\cdot 0 + (1 \dotdiv c(y,1))\cdot 1 + \ldots + (1 \dotdiv c(y,y))\cdot y].$$

Each of the $1 \dotdiv c$ terms reverses the value of the c-function, and so all will be zero save the one for which c is zero; that term will be 1. Multiplication by the second argument which made the appearance of a proper computation thus selects that second argument as the value of U. U is a total function, being primitive recursive, but it is of no interest what happens when the input argument does not happen to be a proper computation.

4.10 PARTIAL RECURSIVENESS OF EACH TURING-COMPUTABLE FUNCTION

In Sections 4.7 through 4.9 the function t_n described in Section 4.6 was defined. That function is constructed in such a way that there should be no doubt that it is primitive recursive. That in addition it captures the essence of Turing-machine computations is partly a matter of correctly defining t_n, and partly a matter of agreeing that nothing is hidden in our codings. It remains only to formally state the result, and establish an important notation:

Theorem

Each Turing-computable function is partial recursive.

Proof

Given any Turing machine Z and any argument count n, let z be a Gödel number for Z as described in Section 4.6. Define

$$\varphi_z^{(n)} = \lambda x_1 \ldots \lambda x_n [U(\mu y[t_n(z,x_1,\ldots,x_n,y) = 0])].$$

By the construction of Sections 4.8 and 4.9 we have $\varphi_z^{(n)} = \Psi_z^n$ and the theorem. ∎

The formula for $\varphi_z^{(n)}$ was expensive to obtain, but well worth the price. Many of its implications are associated with the name of S. C. Kleene.

Theorem (*Kleene Normal-Form*)

Each partial recursive function may be written as the composition of a primitive recursive function with a minimalization of another primitive recursive function.

Proof

As defined, $\varphi_z^{(n)}$ has exactly this form. The function minimalized is t_n, and the outer function is U, both primitive recursive. Since any partial recursive function is $\varphi_z^{(n)}$ for some z, we have the normal form. ∎

In defining $\varphi_z^{(n)}$ the first argument z to t_n is a fixed parameter. (Thus there is an implicit composition with a constant function inside t_n.) If the Turing-machine number is accorded full argument status the result has two often used names:

Theorem (*Enumeration; Universal Turing machine*)

There is a partial recursive function E_n such that

$$E_n = \lambda z \lambda x_1 \ldots \lambda x_n [\varphi_z^{(n)}(x_1, \ldots, x_n)]$$

and hence a *universal Turing machine* with Gödel number e_n such that $\varphi_{e_n}^{(n+1)} = E_n$.

Proof

$E_n = \lambda z \lambda x_1 \ldots \lambda x_n [U(\mu y [t_n(z, x_1, \ldots, x_n, y) = 0])]$. This is partial recursive by considerable design, and a Turing machine exists for any partial recursive function, from Section 4.5. ∎

For a more conventional programming language than the Turing language, the function E_n (or the program e_n) would be called an interpreter. It takes as data not only the arguments but also a program, then arranges to treat the arguments as that program would. It is the primary content of the theorem that the interpreter exists for the entire language, and not just for single programs. The existence of a language interpreter is strong support for the contention which has been in the background from the outset that the functions we are considering are those which are "effectively calculable," or "computable by algorithm." It supports the part of this statement which asserts that what we have defined are functions so computable.

4.11 TOTAL PARTIAL RECURSIVE FUNCTIONS. EFFECTIVE ENUMERATIONS

Advance billing of Section 3.7 claimed that the work of Sections 4.6 through 4.10 would answer some questions about number-theoretic function classes. We first deal with the identify of the class of total recursive functions and the class of partial recursive functions that are total.

Theorem

The class of total Turing computable functions (and hence total partial recursive functions) is exactly the class of recursive functions.

Proof

Evidently each recursive function is (positively) Turing computable, by a subset of the proof (Section 4.5) that each partial recursive function is. When the machine searching for a least number is guaranteed to find one, that total function results. Consider then any total Turing-computable function

$$f = \lambda x_1 \ldots \lambda x_n [U(\mu y [t_n(z, x_1, \ldots, x_n, y) = 0])]$$

computed by a machine numbered z. Its totality can arise only from the existence of the essential y for each argument tuple, and hence in this case the partial recursive derivation of the Kleene normal form is in fact a recursive derivation. ∎

Next consider the possible listing of partial and total recursive functions. The very notation "$\varphi_z^{(n)}$" implies that the partial recursive functions can be listed for each fixed number of arguments by listing the Turing programs. Each such program is the subscript of a function, and all partial recursive functions appear (with duplications). The effective procedure for listing Turing programs uses trial and error with the predicate *TM* determining whether or not the trial is an error. To produce a list of all partial recursive functions the Cantor correspondence between the integers and pairs of integers is easily adapted. Imagine a listing tableau:

$$\begin{array}{ccc} \varphi_{z_0}^{(1)} & \varphi_{z_0}^{(2)} & \cdots \\ \varphi_{z_1}^{(1)} & \varphi_{z_1}^{(2)} & \cdots \\ \vdots & \vdots & \end{array}$$

and a sequence obtained by following the arrow:

$$\varphi_{z_0}^{(1)},\ \varphi_{z_1}^{(1)},\ \varphi_{z_0}^{(2)},\ \varphi_{z_2}^{(1)},\ \ldots$$

Listing only the recursive functions (or in light of the theorem above picking the total functions from a partial recursive list) is not an effective process if we take on faith enough of the equivalence of effectiveness and partial recursiveness to make the diagonal argument work. For if $r_0, r_1, r_2, \ldots$ were a list of the 1-ary recursive functions, and there were no other effectively computable total functions, then $\lambda x[r_x(x) + 1]$, if considered effectively computable by virtue of the list, should be found therein, yet if it appears at position u, we have the contradiction $r_u(u) = r_u(u) + 1$. We can remove the vagueness in this argument about whether or not the presumed $\lambda x[r_x(x) + 1]$ is total recursive (Section 5.5), but proof of the impossibility of doing something effectively must necessarily retain an intuitive component.

The original difficulties in answering the listing questions involved the decision as to whether or not minimalization of functions should be permitted since there was no way to determine if the function minimalized met a nonmechanical criterion (was total, for example). How then is it possible that the criterion is undecidable for listing recursive functions, yet somehow the partial recursive functions can be listed? The Kleene normal-form theorem is the answer: for any partial recursive function, there is a derivation which includes exactly one minimalization. This implies that the function minimalized (it is always t_n) is primitive recursive, hence total, and the criterion is met. Given an arbitrary purported partial recursive derivation, we still have no way of deciding whether or not its (more than one) minimalizations are permissible, but we have a sufficient list of preferred derivations for which the problem does not arise.

4.12 CHURCH'S THESIS

To what extent have we captured the functions which are intuitively computable by algorithm with our Turing programs? The Turing machine was designed to argue that its operations are mechanical, by limiting them severely, and so it is plausible that each Turing program is an algorithmic procedure. In the other direction we have less evidence. The question is whether or not all algorithmically computable functions have Turing programs, and evidence supporting an affirmative answer would be a display of Turing programs for apparently hard-to-compute functions. But we have done better than that. We really have been considering two intuitive computing processes, those of Turing machines, and those implied by partial recursive derivations. The two have different origins and no apparent connection, yet the functions computed proved to be the same class. Such a result is a surprise, and usually indicates some kind of mathematical invariance. To this rather skimpy evidence has been added a great deal more of the same kind: an intuitively satisfying computing device or procedure has been devised for the purpose of capturing the intuitive idea of "effective computation," and has then been found to be capable of computing exactly the partial recursive functions. Each investigator might be said to have been considering a conjecture that the intuitively computable functions and his precise class of functions arising from carefully describing "computing" are the same. It would be Turing's thesis that the Turing-computable functions (a precise class) are just those which can be intuitively computed (not so precise). One name is commonly used for a summary conjecture in light of the equivalence of all such precise characterizations to the partial recursive functions. *Church's thesis* asserts that the intuitively computable functions are the partial recursive functions. It will remain unproved so long as our collective intuitions resist being brought into lockstep by a definition.

In our argument that the recursive functions could not be effectively listed, we really made two uses of Church's thesis of a fundamentally different character. The "essential" use occurs when we asserted that because no partial recursive function exists for doing something, that thing cannot be done at all by any conceivable effective procedure. There can be no objection to such usage; in making such an assertion one is simply affirming that he agrees with Church about the equivalence of the intuitively computable functions and the partial recursive functions, good company to keep. But we also made an "inessential" use of Church's thesis, by not providing details about a particular recursive function, one which was to assume the same values as other functions in a list. We gave an intuitive procedure for looking through the list, and thus for computing the function. To then conclude that the function is partial recursive—by inessential use of Church's thesis—can be criticized as sloppy mathematics, and one hardly commits blunders to place himself in Church's company.

Inessential use of Church's thesis is controversial in recursive function theory. Those who work with programs and the functions they compute quickly develop an excellent intuition about when an intuitive procedure can in fact be turned into a careful function definition. At the same time, those who must write extensive programs also develop a reluctance to begin such projects, particularly if it is necessary in the end to prove that the program does what it is supposed to do. The power of methods making inessential use of Church's thesis—and their freedom from error in good hands—is perhaps tipping the balance in favor of informality. In this text, we use Church's thesis when it is convenient. The next section contains a typical example.

4.13 PARAMETRIZATION (*S-m-n*) THEOREM

A loose paraphrase of the enumeration theorem of Section 4.10 is that the syntax of the Turing language is adequate to support its semantics: the interpreter program is able to work out correct function values from a program and its data. (Note that there is no guarantee that the interpreter can mimic the details of computation for the programs it interprets.) The symbolism for single-argument function with interpreter E_1 (for which e_1 numbers a Turing program) is that $E_1(x,y) = \varphi_{e_1}^{(2)}(x,y) = \varphi_x^{(1)}(y)$ for all Turing programs x and all arguments y. The interpreter deals with an argument as if it were a program, and does so for all programs uniformly.

It would be very convenient to be able to reverse this process: given a program for a multi-argument function and some fixed argument values, to be able to find a program which acts on any remaining arguments as the original program did on the full set. For example, in two-argument functions we would like to create from program (number) x and argument y a new program (number) z such that $\varphi_x^{(2)}(y,t) = \varphi_z^{(1)}(t)$ for all t. (Applied to the interpreter itself this would amount to finding a way to specialize it to interpret just one program.) It would be particularly nice if the calculation of the new program z were in some way the same no matter what x and y might be. Such an ability would also be a complement to the enumeration theorem in the sense that it would indicate that the syntax of Turing programs is rich enough to express internally one important semantic element: reading of input. For the program z would compute the same function as x without in any sense "reading" y as x does; y is somehow incorporated into z. In conventional programming languages this idea is exactly expressed in the existence of constructions for setting the values of data structures internally (with assignment statements, for example) as an alternative to setting them with input statements.

If the motivation provided above is weaker than that for the enumeration theorem, the theorem it attempts to describe is just as powerful. It will be at the heart of the proofs in Sections 5.4 through 5.6, and 8.4 and 8.5. Some further discussion appears in Section 6.3.

Theorem (*S-m-n*; *Parametrization*)

For every $m, n \geq 1$ there is a total recursive function S_n^m such that for each program z,

$$\varphi_{S_n^m(z,x_1,\ldots,x_m)}^{(n)} = \lambda y_1 \ldots \lambda y_n [\varphi_z^{(m+n)}(x_1,\ldots,x_m,y_1,\ldots,y_n)]$$

for each $(x_1, \ldots, x_m)$.

Proof

By Church's thesis. Given the Turing program z and $x_1,\ldots,x_m$, proceed as follows to calculate $S_n^m(z,x_1,\ldots,x_m)$: Create some quadruples for a new Turing machine whose sole action is to transform a given tape containing the codes for an n-tuple into a tape which has that n-tuple displaced to the right, and the codes for $x_1,\ldots,x_m$ placed before it. Certainly such a machine exists for any fixed $x_1,\ldots,x_m$. However, we are required to go further and find a way of creating the machine from these m values no matter what they may be. In the notation of Section 4.4 we indicate how this can be done for displacing one argument and inserting one before it (which applies to the S-1-1 theorem, then). The machine needed is

$$\mathbf{X}_1^{(x_1+1)} \mathbf{L}^{(x_1+1)} \mathbf{B}$$

which uses the tape-marking machine to insert one more than the proper number of ones before the given argument, then change the first of these to a blank. The idea is that creating this machine given x_1 is a mechanical process, since it is only necessary to utilize two machines ($\mathbf{X}_1$ and $\mathbf{L}$) $x_1 + 1$ times. Now obtain the quadruples from the given program z and preface them with the displacing machine. Obtain a number for the resulting program, which evidently acts to create an $(m + n)$-tuple tape from an n-tuple one, and then compute

$$\varphi_z^{(m+n)}(x_1,\ldots,x_m,y_1,\ldots,y_n);$$

that is, we have constructed a program which acts as S_n^m is supposed to act on $(z,x_1,\ldots,x_m)$. ∎

The inessential use of Church's thesis in the above proof saves us the tedious programming task of coding and decoding the Turing programs involved. We believe it can be done; indeed, all the constructions in Sections 4.4 and 4.5 rely on this belief. But we would rather not give the quadruples of the program that does it. The theorem is of sufficient generality to confine the Church's thesis argument. In succeeding work we will cite the parametrization theorem rather than invoke similar arguments by Church's thesis. Then if pressed to supply full details, they will be lacking in just one place.

4.14 SYNTACTIC COMBINATION OF PROGRAMS FOR COMPOSITION

To illustrate application of the S-m-n (well, S-2-1) theorem we obtain a result with a more convenient interpretation in terms of programming language syntax and semantics. Its paraphrase is that there is a mechanical means of combining two arbitrary Turing programs into a program which computes the composition of the functions the two compute. This indicates that the Turing syntax is adequate to express subroutine-like behavior in which one program acts "inside" another. (But note that our juxtaposition of machines cannot in general be used to obtain the result since we do not know that the programs involved do not interact in the unpleasant way which necessitated the definition of positive computation at the end of Section 4.5.)

The theorem is also a convenient place to introduce a convention in wide use: Whenever argument counts are omitted, the implied count is 1. Thus φ_x means $\varphi_x^{(1)}$, the enumeration function E is really E_1, etc.

Theorem (*Syntactic Composition*)

There is a total recursive function C such that for any two Turing programs z_1 and z_2,

$$\varphi_{C(z_1,z_2)} = \lambda x[\varphi_{z_1}(\varphi_{z_2}(x))].$$

Proof

We first require that $\lambda z_1 \lambda z_2 \lambda x[\varphi_{z_1}(\varphi_{z_2}(x))]$ be a partial recursive function of three arguments, say $\varphi_g^{(3)}$. The enumeration function E proves it so, for

$$\lambda z_1 \lambda z_2 \lambda x [E(U_1^3(z_1,z_2,x), E(U_2^3(z_1,z_2,x), U_3^3(z_1,z_2,x)))] = \varphi_g^{(3)}$$

defines φ_g in an acceptable form. The S-2-1 theorem then gives

$$\varphi_{S_1^2(g,z_1,z_2)} = \lambda x[\varphi_g(z_1,z_2,x)]$$

for all z_1 and z_2, and an implicit use of the constant function with value g gives

$$C = \lambda z_1 \lambda z_2 [S_1^2(g,z_1,z_2)]. \blacksquare$$

(Note that the enumeration theorem enters to eliminate an inessential use of Church's thesis in saying that the composition function can be computed by the obvious procedure of computing the functions successively, and the S-m-n theorem eliminates another use to argue for the ability to create the required program.)

4.15 A PARTIAL RECURSIVE FUNCTION WITH NO TOTAL RECURSIVE EXTENSION

Programmers are often impatient with partial recursive functions as the semantic element of a language. The contention that such functions do not capture the way in which programs work can be answered—neither do they restrict it, and a proper theory might be constructed in the same way, perhaps using the full computations at all arguments as semantics. (For a beginning of such a theory, see Section 10.4.) The more usual contention is that the operation of minimalization is unsatisfactory: it is the source of all failures of definition, and seems to add nothing of interest to programmers. After all, who writes programs not to work at certain arguments? In view of the essential role one minimalization plays in the Kleene normal-form theorem, it might be wise to investigate further before refusing to minimalize. It is probably not an unfair statement of the programmer's position to say that he has nothing against minimalization, even using it himself, but never if there is a chance that the search will not terminate; he sees no use for a function which is undefined somewhere. Why not simply eliminate lack of definition, at least where programming is concerned, by considering only programs in which a default value is computed whenever the partial recursive function would have been undefined? In this form we can prove that the position is hopeless, since there are functions to which the suggestion cannot be applied, and in Section 5.6 we shall see that there is no effective means (accepting Church's thesis) of identifying all programs for these functions.

Theorem

There is a partial recursive function ψ which cannot be completed to a total recursive function; that is, there exists a partial recursive ψ such that for each total recursive f there is an argument n such that ψ is defined at n, but $f(n) \neq \psi(n)$.

Proof

The argument is a kind of diagonal one, and it needs the enumeration theorem to make it precise: we construct ψ as different from all recursive functions by making it

$$\psi = \varphi_x(x) + 1 = E(x,x) + 1.$$

Suppose that some total recursive f completed ψ. This function has programs, suppose that one is p, $\varphi_p = f$. Then consider $\varphi_p(p)$, which is defined since f is total. By the definition of ψ we have $\varphi_p(p) = \varphi_p(p) + 1$, proving that there is no such f. ∎

EXERCISES

4.1 If you have access to an implementation of SNOBOL, write a function definition with the prototype call

YIELD (I. D., PROGRAM)

which returns the instantaneous description resulting from the description input as I. D. on the Turning machine PROGRAM. If it should happen that PROGRAM could not apply to I. D., give a failure return. (A reasonable notation to use for keypunching machines and instantaneous descriptions is indicated in Section 4.6; feel free to devise your own.)

4.2 Even if you cannot use SNOBOL, explain how to use the result of Exercise 4.1 to create a simulator for Turing machines. If you have the YIELD function implemented, go on to finish the simulator, and give it debugging facilities which permit tracing Turing programs. (Such an implementation is particularly impressive on a timesharing system with a display screen terminal on which the computation can be shown taking place just a little too fast to follow.)

4.3 If the scanned square in an instantaneous description is at the end of a tape and the transition is a move toward the interior, and the scanned symbol was a blank, then there is no need to retain it as part of the tape since if ever needed it would be created again. Modify the definition of "yield" in Section 4.2 so that such end blanks are removed. (If you did Exercise 4.1, make appropriate changes in the YIELD function. Or did you write it that way to begin with?)

4.4 Two variants on the Turing machine with only "semi-infinite" tape do not permit the addition of a new blank (say) to the left. Instead, one version halts if this is attempted, while the other "tests" for the end condition so that a program can detect that it is about to go off the tape. Modify the definition of "yield" in Section 4.2 to reflect these variants respectively. [*Hint for the second variant:* Make a quadruple of the form q_i a $q_j q_k$ mean that a left move is attempted, and if not at tape end, succeeds with q_k the next state. But if at tape end there is no move, and q_j is entered.]

4.5 There is a sense in which Turing machines with tape alphabet A and those with tape alphabet B are equally powerful when A has the same cardinality as B. Give a careful definition of this idea. Do the same when the cardinalities are different but the smaller alphabet contains at least one nonblank symbol. Using your definition, prove that the power of a Turing machine does not depend on the size of its tape alphabet (beyond two symbols).

4.6 In a fashion analogous to Exercise 4.5, prove that whether the tape may be extended in both directions (as in the definition of Section 4.2) or not (as in Exercise 4.4) does not affect Turing machine power.

4.7 Write out a complete formal description of a Turing machine S_L which performs the computations indicated by

$$b1^x b \to b1^x b.$$
$$\underset{i}{\uparrow} \quad \underset{f}{\uparrow}$$

4.8 Give quadruples for a Turing machine which computes the addition function according to the definition of Section 4.3. Suppose the coding of numbers were changed to the conventional binary without leading zeros. Write an adder for such a code.

4.9 Using all the machinery of juxtaposition of component machines from Section 4.4, specify a machine that computes the multiplication function (according to the definition of Section 4.3), and give a short argument that your program works.

4.10 Consider the Turing machine

$$A: \ S_R^{(2)} LBS_L OL \begin{smallmatrix} 1 \\ b \end{smallmatrix}$$

with some care. What is Ψ_A^1? What is Ψ_A^2? What is Ψ_{AA}^3? What is $\lambda x \lambda y \lambda z\, [\Psi_A^1(\Psi_A^3(x,y,z))]$?

4.11 Prove that $\Psi_{AB}^1 \neq \lambda x [\Psi_B^1(\Psi_A^1(x))]$ for the machines given below

A: $i\, b\, R\, q_0 \quad i1Lf \quad q_0\, b\, Lf \quad q_0 1 R\, q_0$

B: $i\, b\, b\, f \quad i1Li$.

4.12 A function g defined by *bounded minimalization* from a function f, written

$$g = \lambda x_1 \ldots \lambda x_n [\mu y \leq x_i [f(x_1, \ldots, x_n, y) = 0]], \quad 1 \leq i \leq n,$$

is to agree with minimalization if the proper y exists and is no larger than x_i, but if not, then g takes the value 0. Prove that if f is primitive recursive, then g is primitive recursive, using much the same trick as for the bounded quantifiers of Section 4.7.

4.13 Prove that bounded quantification of Section 4.7 does not lead outside the primitive recursive class without actually using a definition by primitive recursion. Instead employ bounded minimalization (Exercise 4.12), proper subtraction, addition, and multiplication.

4.14 Consider Turing machines as acceptors by agreeing that a machine accepts an input if it halts scanning a nonblank symbol, and otherwise does not accept. Now imagine applying the procedure used to minimize finite-state acceptors (Section 2.12) to Turing acceptors. Is the result the same, that there is a unique minimum machine for each language accepted?

4.15 What is the smallest integer z_0 which is the number of a Turing machine? What is φ_{z_0}?

4.16 Call two integers *twin programs* if both are numbers of Turing machines, and they are successive. Given a Turing program number, has it always a twin? Explain.

4.17 According to the definitions of Section 4.7, which of the following hold?

0 *BEG* 0,   0 *BEG* 1,   1 *BEG* 0,   1 *BEG* 1,   1 *BEG* 10
0 *END* 0,   0 *END* 1,   1 *END* 0,   1 *END* 1,   0 *END* 10

4.18 Modify the concatenate predicate of Section 4.7 so that there may be no internal zero digits in any concatenate, hence none of 10, 103, etc. would be anything concatenated with anything.

4.19 Modify the concatenate predicate so that internal zeros are of no consequence; for example

$$407 = 4\,\&\,7 \quad \text{and} \quad 102003 = 1\,\&\,(2\,\&\,3).$$

104 Turing Computability

4.20 Make a short table of what *CODES* what, continuing until it is no longer interesting.

4.21 Let p_b be the number

$$4121215114131215$$

for the program which simply prints a single blank (it was called **B** in Section 4.4). Give the values of y,u, and the least x_1 such that $COMP_1(p_b,x_1,y,u)$ holds. Give y,u, and the least x_1,x_2 such that $COMP_2(p_b,x_1,x_2,y,u)$ holds. (If there are no such values, explain why.) What is $U(\mu y[t_1(p_b,1,y) = 0])$? How about $U(\mu y[t_2(p_b,1,1,y) = 0])$?

4.22 Give a set of arguments such that each of the following predicates holds, or explain why there are none:

$$C(y,u) \wedge \sim COMP_1(z,x,y,u)$$
$$COMP_1(z,x,y,u) \wedge COMP_2(z,x,x,y,u)$$
$$\sim COMP_1(z,x,y,u) \wedge U(y) = 0.$$

4.23 What value(s?) does the function U which recovers computed values from a computation sequence of instantaneous descriptions (Section 4.9) assume when its argument is not the number of such a sequence?

4.24 Write an explicit universal Turing machine using the techniques of Sections 4.4 and 4.5. Choose between coding quadruples in our "unary" numerical codes, or using a larger alphabet, only after examining Exercise 4.5.

4.25 The method of Sections 4.6 through 4.10 proving that each Turing-computable function is partial recursive might be described as assigning a partial recursive derivation to each Turing program. Explain the statement that denumerably many derivations are assigned to each machine, yet there are derivations not assigned to any machine.

4.26 The most difficult part of correctly defining the predicates leading up to the Kleene T-predicates is excluding cases in which things hold unexpectedly for pathological reasons. Suppose that an error of this kind is contained in the presentation of Sections 4.6 through 4.10, with the result that T_n holds for two different values of the last argument, the other arguments being the same. Discuss the possible effects of such an error on the proof that each Turing-computable function is partial recursive.

4.27 Prove that the function d defined at the end of Section 3.5 is recursive. Do not arithmetize the primitive recursive derivations and give an explicit derivation. Does the same argument apply to the function $\lambda x[r_x(x) + 1]$ defined at the end of Section 4.11?

4.28 The closure definition using the unrestricted μ-operator

$$\psi = \lambda x_1 \ldots \lambda x_n [\mu y [\theta(x_1,\ldots,x_n,y) = 0]]$$

may omit the restriction that θ be total. It is then necessary to specify what happens when θ fails to be defined. With the definition

$\psi(x_1, \ldots, x_n) = y$ iff   each of $\theta(x_1, \ldots, x_n, 0), \theta(x_1, \ldots, x_n, 1), \ldots,$
$\theta(x_1, \ldots, x_n, y-1)$ is defined and nonzero,
and $\theta(x_1, \ldots, x_n, y) = 0$,

the operation may be used to define the partial recursive functions. With the definition

$\psi(x_1, \ldots, x_n) = y$ iff $\theta(x_1, \ldots, x_n, y) = 0$
and for each $y' < y$,
$\theta(x_1, \ldots, x_n, y')$ is undefined or nonzero,

the class resulting from closure strictly contains the partial recursive functions. Call the class of partial recursive functions defined in Section 3.7 P, the class defined with the first convention above P', and the one defined with the second convention above P''. Prove that $P = P' \subseteq P''$, and explain why the proof that $P = P'$ fails if P'' replaces P'.

4.29 How many integers are there which are numbers for any given Turing machine? How many integers are there which are numbers for Turing machines computing any given partial recursive function? Between the extremes of numbers for a fixed machine and numbers for a fixed function lies a natural class of Turing machine numbers. Describe such a class.

4.30 Define the *partial interative functions* as the smallest class of number-theoretic functions containing base functions

constants (with any number of arguments)
projections U_m^n
addition
proper subtraction
multiplication
base-10 exponentiation $\lambda x[10^x]$

and closed under minimalization of total functions and composition. Prove that this class is really the partial recursive functions. (*Hint:* See Exercise 4.13 and look over the arithmetization of Sections 4.6 through 4.10.)

4.31 Do Exercise 4.30, but without including base-10 exponentiation in the list of base functions.

4.32 Using an adequate alphabet and the methods of Section 4.4, specify a Turing program for the function S_1^1 of Section 4.13, thus eliminating the use of Church's thesis in the parametrization theorem.

4.33 Prove that there is a recursive function G with the properties $G(x) > x$ and $\varphi_{G(x)} = \varphi_x$ for each Turing program x. What does the existence of such a function imply about the Turing programming language?

4.34 What bearing does Exercise 4.11 have on the proof of the syntactic composition theorem of Section 4.14?

REFERENCES

Details of the formal presentation of Turing machines are largely from notes of R. W. Ritchie [12], although the arithmetization there uses dyadic coding, and is more carefully carried out. Davis [10] is a self-contained treatment of similarly defined Turing machines using a Gödel numbering more like those of Gödel. As an immediate application of the S-m-n theorem, the syntactic composition theorem appears in Rogers [2] although not called so there. Kleene's text [13] contains much original work, but is not always easy to read. The discussion of syntax and semantics of programming languages arises in part from personal experience with the ambitious Burroughs' attempt to build an ALGOL machine in the B5500 [14], and in part from formal syntax which attempts to capture the notion of the *de facto* syntax an implementation imposes. Probably the most successful such attempt is the Stearns and Lewis discussion of symbol tables [15].

5
SETS OF NATURAL NUMBERS

5.1 RECURSIVE, RECURSIVELY ENUMERABLE SETS

From the study of algorithmic functions (according to Turing) we turn to a subject which is mathematically very little different: sets which can be in some sense mechanically determined. A function may be identified with its graph—the set of pairs of argument and functional value—so a theory of sets should be constructable from the Turing theory. Intuitively, sets are very different from functions, however. A function computed by a program is concisely described by that program, which is finite even when the function has infinitely many values. A set is an entity which simply exists without a solid tie to the process of listing or recognizing its elements. The study of sets must therefore begin with a somewhat artificial association of recognition procedures, unneeded for functions. Perhaps this first counterintuitive requirement is the reason that despite some technical advantages and an historical start which actually preceded Turing's work, sets are neglected for functions in studying computability.

It is typical of the technical superiority of set theory that in Chapter 4 we were unable to precisely formulate some questions in terms of functions without expending a great deal of effort in the answers. For example, in considering what could not be done effectively, there was a good deal of hand waving in applying Church's thesis essentially. It was asserted (Section 4.11) that listing the total recursive functions is impossible, but the proof involves constructing a list and searching it, operations which are complicated to capture with a recursive function. It was asserted (Section 4.15) that identification of certain unfortunate Turing programs (the ones for a function which was inherently partial, so that its lacks of definition could not be supplied) was impossible, and there was no simple hand-waving argument. These questions are really about sets, and the ability to effectively recognize their members. It seems reasonable to use our idea that recursive functions are the effective ones for a corresponding notion about sets.

Definition

A set of natural numbers is *recursive* iff its characteristic function is (total) recursive. The characteristic function of set S is usually written

$$\chi_S(x) = \begin{cases} 1 & \text{if } x \in S \\ 0 & \text{if } x \notin S. \end{cases} \blacksquare$$

The complete set of natural numbers $\mathbb{N}$ is recursive, since $\chi_\mathbb{N}$ is $\lambda x[c_1(x)] = \lambda x[1]$. (The empty set is also recursive. Why?) For a more complex example, $E = \{x \mid x \text{ is even}\}$ is recursive, its characteristic function being

$$\chi_E = \lambda x[1 \dotdiv (((x+1) \div 2) \dotdiv (x \div 2))].$$

It is sometimes more difficult to construct a characteristic function than to prove that a set is recursive. The effort-saving trick uses Church's thesis with a slight twist: one devises a procedure for deciding whether or not a given natural number is in the set, then adds to that procedure steps to give the correct 1 or 0 value as output; the whole procedure then argues (by Church's thesis, inessentially) for the existence of the necessary recursive function.

The entities discussed in this chapter are sets of natural numbers, so their characteristic functions have a single argument. A complete theory of sets of pairs of natural numbers, triples, etc. can be obtained by using characteristic functions of more arguments. All of the definitions and results stated here generalize in this trivial way, but we save considerable writing of *n*-tuples for arguments by sticking to sets of nunbers alone. We may then also speak of "the empty function", meaning the nowhere defined function of just one argument, distinguished from all those other empty functions which (unsuccessfully) operate on pairs, triples, etc.

The context usually makes clear what kind of set is being discussed, so while assertions made in this chapter using terms like "recursive" strictly apply only to sets of numbers, not pairs, etc. of numbers, the terms are usually used more broadly to cover whatever is under discussion, and there is no harm in taking them that way even here. (In the next chapter we will develop the formal tools for a proof that argument counts are not of much consequence in discussions of partial recursive functions.)

A precise statement about the set of programs for computing ψ being unrecognizable is that the set $\{x \mid \varphi_x = \psi\}$ is not recursive. Note that the passage to the set of programs captures the idea of *uniform*—the recognition is to work on all programs—and the recursive function captures the notion of *effective* based on Church's thesis. Similarly, the question of listing exactly the total recursive functions concerns the recursiveness of $\{x \mid \varphi_x \text{ is total}\}$. These questions are answered in Sections 5.6 and 5.5.

To some, "effective recognition" does not intuitively coincide with the recursive sets defined, because recursive "recognition" is required not only to find set members but also to reject nonmembers. A broader idea is that there is a partial recursive function describing the set whose value is 1 for members, not-1 for nonmembers, but included in the latter case is the possibility that the function may fail to be defined for some (or all) nonmembers. Algorithms which begin unbounded searches known to terminate for members are thus permitted. The formal characterizations of this idea are not all motivated in this way, the closest being:

Definition

A set of natural numbers S is *recursively enumerable* (*r.e.*) iff it is the domain of a partial recursive function. (That is, iff $S = \{x \mid \phi(x) \text{ is defined}\}$ for some partial recursive ϕ.) ∎

The notion is equivalent to what was proposed above, since if we had a function with the 1, non-1 behavior, it would be easy to find another which was undefined instead of non-1; on the other hand, given one which is defined exactly where we want it to have value 1, the output could be properly adjusted. Church's thesis saves us from the details. The name of these "almost recursive" sets requires some further motivation: they are also those which can be effectively listed.

5.2 RELATIONSHIPS BETWEEN RECURSIVE ENUMERABILITY AND RECURSIVENESS

"Recursively enumerable" carries the idea of an ability to mechanically list elements of a set. The name comes from an alternate definition in which the listing entity is a total recursive function:

Definition

The set S is *recursively listable* iff it is empty ($S = \emptyset$) or the range of a total recursive function ($S = \{x \mid (\exists t)\, [f(t) = x]\}$ for some total recursive f). ∎

("Recursively listable" is a name which will disappear as soon as it is shown to be no different than "recursively enumerable.")

Intuitively, the recursive function which lists a set is presented with an input, and from this computes a set member. From another input, it computes another set member, or the same one, and so on for all natural number inputs.

The proof of the theorem that asserts the equivalence of this idea to the one of a partial recursive determination of set membership contains essential ideas about the relationship between recursiveness and recursive enumerability.

Theorem

The recursively enumerable sets are exactly the sets which are recursively listable.

Proof

Suppose given any recursively listable set S. If $S = \emptyset$, then S is the domain of the partial recursive empty function, and hence is r.e. If S is the range of total recursive f, then it is the domain of the partial recursive function which is computed as follows: Given input x, compute $f(0), f(1)$, etc., until the value of f is x, then give as output 1. This function is evidently undefined on arguments not in S, and defined ($=1$) on arguments in S, as required.

On the other hand, suppose given the r.e. set S which is the domain of partial recursive ψ. If ψ is the empty function, $S = \emptyset$ may be recursively listed. Otherwise, we must find a recursive function which lists S from ψ. This requires an important trick to control the partial recursive function so that it does not escape us—no procedure which simply "computes ψ" can hope to describe a total recursive function. Turing machines provide the needed control. Let t be a Turing program which computes ψ, $\varphi_t = \psi$. Since $S \neq \emptyset$, there is at least one element (say) $x_0 \in S$. S is the range of the total recursive function computed as follows: Given input x, use the program t to work out no more than x yield operations of the putative computations of $\varphi_t(0), \varphi_t(1), \ldots, \varphi_t(x)$. If no numerical computation results within x steps, take as output the value x_0. But if one or more numerical computations result within x steps, take as output the successful argument which is the smallest, but which was not taken as output for a smaller input than x. This computation procedure is evidently designed to produce as outputs any and all values at which ψ is defined. The control on ψ comes in never pursuing its computations unsuccessfully for too many steps, "step" being defined by Turing yield operations. ■

It should be apparent that the inessential use of Church's thesis in the first part of the proof is easy to eliminate, while that of the latter part would be very hard to dispense with.

5.3 POST CANONICAL SYSTEMS

At the same time that Turing was attempting to capture the notion of algorithmic function in his machines, E. L. Post was working on the similar problem for enumerating sets. Post's motivation was not so close to computation as

Turing's. As a logician Post was studying the process of mechanically generating proofs of theorems in formal mathematical systems. For our purposes the origin and significance of this problem are too far afield, but it is easy to describe the context. In formal theories the idea of proof is constrained to be an essentially syntactic one: a proof is a string of symbols with certain properties as symbols, and no more. The properties have to do with being formed according to a finite set of rules which treat the string as composed of pieces, each piece following from previous pieces by application of the rules, with a few special pieces permitted to get started. (The preferred starting strings are the axioms of the theory, while the rules for passing beyond the axioms are the rules of inference. A distinguished final part of the proof is the theorem which has been proved. The description omits "well-formedness" as a separate entity. Some of this terminology appears in the definitions below.)

Those familiar with string-manipulation languages such as SNOBOL might view the generation of a proof more in the following terms. An axiom string represents input to a program, and the proof sequence is the series of intermediate strings created from the input by the program, finally resulting in the output string, which represents the theorem proved. (The analogy has some serious weaknesses. Only a very limited set of strings constitutes the axioms, and the rules of inference are similarly restricted. SNOBOL, on the other hand, can permit its programs to take any input whatsoever, and to do almost anything with it.)

Definition

A *Post canonical system* (*P.c.s.*) is a 4-tuple (A,X,V,P) where A is a finite *alphabet*, $X \subseteq A^*$ is a finite set of strings from the alphabet, the *axioms*, V is a finite set of *string variables*, and P is a finite set of *productions*, each written as a finite alternation of strings from A^* with string variables on the left, and a similar alternation on the right, but there using no string variables which did not appear on the left:

$$x_0 V_1 x_1 V_2 x_2 \ldots V_n x_n \rightarrow y_0 W_1 y_1 \ldots W_m y_m$$

in which the number of alternations $n \geq 0$ and $m \geq 0$ depends on the production. (It is probably less informative to state that a production is a mapping from $(A^* \times V)^n \times A^*$ into $(A^* \times V)^m \times A^*$ in which the image string variables must be selected from among those of the argument.) ∎

To view a P.c.s. as an active entity requires, as usual, a definition in which we state its purpose, namely, the production of certain special strings by carefully controlled means:

Definition

A *theorem* of a P.c.s. (A,X,V,P) is a string $t \in A^*$ such that there is a *proof* of t: a sequence of strings $s_0, s_1, \ldots, s_k$ such that s_k is t, and for each $i, 0 \le i \le k$, either $s_i \in X$, or s_i results from some $s_j, j < i$, by *application* of a production

$$x_0 V_1 x_1 \ldots V_n x_n \to y_0 W_1 y_1 \ldots W_m y_m$$

in the sense that there is an identification of each V_p, $1 \le p \le n$, with a string of A^* such that $x_0 V_1 \ldots V_n x_n = s_j$, and the same identification applied to the right of the production (since each W is some V) makes

$$y_0 W_1 y_1 \ldots W_m y_m = s_i. \blacksquare$$

One feature of this definition of proof of a theorem which is essential in the original logical context—but embarrassing for present purposes—is that the intermediate steps in a proof are necessarily theorems as well as the last. If the remainder of a proof is deleted following any string of the sequence, the result is a proof of that string. When viewing a proof as a kind of computation this is most awkward, because it means that from one input (axiom) many different outputs (theorems) may result. The final definition circumvents the problem by singling out some symbols of the P.c.s. alphabet to appear in theorems, and uses all other alphabet symbols to disqualify intermediate results in which they appear.

Definition

A P.c.s. *extends* a set of strings $T \subseteq A^*$ over alphabet A iff the intersection between its theorems and A^* is exactly T. $\blacksquare$

To illustrate the use of Post canonical systems, we treat a problem similar to that of specifying a programming language syntax in which it is improper to declare an identifier more than once. The "identifiers" are simplified to strings of the same letter, and "declaration" to listing the sequence of names separated by semicolons. Thus in this language fragment

$$x;xxxx;xxx;xxxxxxx$$

is proper, but

$$xx;xxx;xx$$

is not. The P.c.s. $(\{0,;,:,x\}, \{0:\}, \{A,B,C\}, P)$ whose productions P are

$$A:B \to A0:B$$
$$A0B:C \to AxB:C;Ax$$
$$A:B0xC \to A:BxxC$$
$$A:;B \to B$$

extends the set of such nonrepeating declarations over the alphabet {x,;}. The trick is to keep a "symbol table" at the front of a growing string which contains symbols outside this alphabet, and to update this as new identifiers are added, then permit its deletion to create the final string. The form of the symbol table is a pattern of x and 0, marking positions counting from the left. An x means that the identifier whose count of symbols is the same as the position appears already; 0 means that it does not. A : not only marks the end of the table, but is important in making sure that pattern matches fall in or out of the table. The first production permits addition of 0 symbols at the end of the table as needed. The second adds a new identifier at the end of the forming chain and updates the symbol table. However, the added identifier is not yet all x symbols, since it is a copy of the symbol table itself, and the third production eliminates its embedded 0 symbols. Finally, the fourth production deletes the symbol table, and an unfortunate semicolon which the second production added ahead of the first identifier generated. A proof of the first example above is then

0 :	(axiom)
x : ;x	(production 2, $A = B = C = \Lambda$)
x0 : ;x	(production 1, $A = $ x, $B = $;x)
x000 : ;x	(three more uses of production 1)
x00x : ;x;x00x	(production 2, $A = $ x00, $B = \Lambda$, $C = $;x)
x00x : ;x;xxxx	(two uses of production 3)
x0xx : ;x;xxxx;x0x	(production 2)
x0xx : ;x;xxxx;xxx	(production 3)
x0xx000 : ;x;xxxx;xxx	(three uses of production 1)
x0xx00x : ;x;xxxx;xxx;xxxxxxx	(production 2; three uses of production 3)
x;xxxx;xxx;xxxxxxx	(production 4)

(Strictly speaking this is not a proof because of the combination of steps, but from it a proof could easily be written down in more space.)

The example illustrates a typical situation in which the intermediate steps contain information crucial to proceeding with the proof, expressed in the symbols which take them outside the set to be extended. In the proof which relates the theorems of certain Post canonical systems and r.e. sets, we will see the same thing as a Turing machine's computation is "proved".

Theorem

A set S is r.e. iff a P.c.s. extends $\{1^x | x \in S\}$ over the alphabet $\{1\}$.

Proof

Suppose a P.c.s. extends $\{1^x | x \in S\}$ over $\{1\}$. Since the notion of proof is a mechanical one, it is possible to generate all possible proofs of the P.c.s., and to determine which theorems stay within the alphabet $\{1\}$. The following function is therefore partial recursive by Church's thesis:

$$\psi(x) = \begin{cases} 1 & \text{if } 1^x \text{ is a theorem of the P.c.s.} \\ \text{undefined otherwise} \end{cases}$$

(If 1^x is a theorem, the mechanical generation will find it; otherwise the never-ending attempt can be used to automatically see that ψ has no value.) The domain of ψ is S, which is therefore r.e.

On the other hand, suppose that S is r.e. We use the result that either $S = \emptyset$, or S is the range of a total recursive function. In the former case, any P.c.s. with no axioms has the correct theorems (none), and thus is also the required extending system. This leaves the case in which S is the range of a recursive function, say g. There is a Turing program for computing g, and the required P.c.s. mimics all possible computations by this machine. Whenever the machine halts at the end of a numerical computation, it leaves a tape of the form b...b1^xb...b for some x, and since it is computing g, we have that $x \in S$. That is, a P.c.s. which proves all possible successful computations will extend $\{1^x | x \in S\}$ over $\{1\}$ if we see to it that just following a halt the surrounding blanks are deleted. The P.c.s. $(\{b, 1, i, f, q, /\}, \{i\}, \{A,B\}, P)$ can mimic the computations of a Turing machine whose states other than i and f are written as strings of q symbols, if its productions P are

$$iA \to i1A$$
$$iA \to /i/bAb$$

to create from the axiom any possible input configuration which might be part of a beginning instantaneous description, in the notation of Section 4.6, and

$$bAfB \to AfB$$
$$/fAb \to /fA$$
$$/f/bA \to A$$

to remove blanks from around a terminating instantaneous description, and then the final state name itself. (But note that an improper final tape cannot be stripped down to all ones by these productions.) The remaining productions must transform the string for a beginning instantaneous description to that of a terminating one if the Turing machine permits. Different quadruples of the Turing program give rise to different productions. A quadruple which specifies printing, of the form $q_c a_s a_p q_n$, requires

$$A/q_c/a_s B \to A/q_n/a_p B$$

while a right move $q_c a_s R q_n$ requires

$$A/q_c/a_s B \to A a_s/q_n/B$$
$$A/q_c/a_s \to A a_s/q_n/\text{b}$$

to cover the case interior to the tape and at its right boundary, while a left move $q_c a_s L q_n$ requires

$$A\text{b}/q_c/a_s B \to A/q_n/\text{b} a_s B$$
$$A1/q_c/a_s B \to A/q_n/1 a_s B$$
$$/q_c/a_s B \to /q_n/\text{b} a_s B$$

because of the added complication that both possibilities left of the scanned square must be provided for. These productions are schematic in that the appropriate number of q symbols has been abbreviated by a subscripted q, and the subscripted alphabet symbols are always either b or 1, all taken from the Turing program's quadruples. The P.c.s. thus has one, two, or three productions for each quadruple of the Turing program, plus five other productions. ∎

5.4 NONRECURSIVE SETS. THE TURING HALTING PROBLEM

With a few exceptions, interesting sets which are recursive or r.e. may be proved so by describing computation of the total or partial recursive functions which characterize them. To prove that a set is not recursive is more difficult. (It will not do, of course, to display something which is not the characteristic function.) Perhaps the best methods are diagonalization and "reduction" of a known nonrecursive set to another. These ideas are nicely illustrated by the solution to the "halting problem" for Turing machines (or rather its nonsolution).

Theorem

$K = \{x \mid \varphi_x \text{ is defined at } x\}$ is not recursive.

Proof

Suppose K were recursive. By Church's thesis the following would then be a recursive function:

$$B(x) = \begin{cases} \varphi_x(x) + 1 & \text{if } x \in K \\ 0 & \text{if } x \notin K. \end{cases}$$

Consider a Turing program b for B, $B = \varphi_b$. It is impossible that $\varphi_b(b) = \varphi_b(b) + 1$, so it cannot be that $b \in K$. On the other hand, $\varphi_b(b) = 0$ would certainly mean that b is an argument at which φ_b is defined, so it cannot be that $b \notin K$. What must be wrong is the assumption that K is recursive. ∎

It is somewhat more graphic to say that membership in K is *undecidable*, or that the problem of membership in K is *unsolvable*.

In considering problems and their uniform effective solution (that is, considering sets which may or may not be recursive), it is usually possible to show nonrecursiveness by assuming that some considered set S, if recursive, would imply that K is also recursive. Church's thesis is used to give the effective membership algorithm which is known not to exist for K, based on the supposed algorithm for the set S which is really under study. The technical name for this is "reduction of K to S," but the name is seldom used because it is too easy to mix up the roles of the sets involved. In any case, the Turing-machine halting problem is one of those to which K can be reduced (and to add to the confusion, which can also be reduced to K). Intuitively, the halting problem for Turing machines concerns deciding, for a given arbitrary machine and a given arbitrary input, whether or not the machine eventually halts. Rather than give any of the shades of meaning between the intuitive statement and a precise one, we immediately pass to the

Theorem

$H = \{(z,x) \mid \varphi_z$ is defined at $x\}$ is not recursive.

Proof

We reduce K to H. Suppose that in fact membership in H were decidable. Then to decide for any z whether or not $z \in K$, use the answer to whether or not $(z,z) \in H$. ∎

The unsolvability of the Turing-machine halting problem does not reflect a weakness in the Turing language, but is rather a feature of every reasonable programming language. The halting problem will be unsolvable for any language in which each partial recursive function has programs, and which possesses an enumeration theorem (interpreter). Since these are hardly restrictive conditions, an unsolvable halting problem is a part of every language.

5.5 FURTHER REDUCTIONS OF K. NON-R.E. SETS

Another reduction will illustrate the power of the syntactic-composition theorem of Section 4.14, and finally provide a precise statement of our long-heralded feeling that the total recursive functions cannot be recognized effectively. (Another way to view this result is as the end of another programmer's pipe dream: to build something like the Turing language, but for the total functions only.)

Theorem

$T = \{x \mid \varphi_x$ is total$\}$ is not recursive.

5.5 Further Reductions of K. Non-R.E. Sets

Proof

Reduce K to T. Suppose that membership in T were decidable. Given any z, proceed as follows: First, find a program for the constant function c_z, say k, $\varphi_k = c_z$. Using the syntactic composition function C, compute $C(z,k)$. Decide if $C(z,k)$ is a member of T; z is a member of K iff it is. The reason is that

$$\varphi_{C(z,k)} = \lambda x [\varphi_z(\varphi_k(x))]$$

by definition of C, and the inner function takes the constant value z. Therefore the composite function is either the constant function of value $\varphi_z(z)$, or the empty function, and in the one case is total, in the other, is not. ∎

(The proof also establishes that the constant-function programs are not a recursive set.)

In K we have a nonrecursive set. But K is r.e., since it is the domain of $\lambda x [E(x,x)]$. There are non-r.e. sets, just as there are non-partial-recursive functions, by the argument that the number of sets of natural numbers (number-theoretic functions) is nondenumerable, while the r.e. sets (partial recursive functions) have the same cardinality as the set of Turing programs, that of the natural numbers. Displaying a non-partial-recursive function explicitly isn't very satisfying since the definition cannot in any way give a rule for computing its values (essential use of Church's thesis). For sets we can do a little better, since nonrecursive r.e. sets have complements which are not r.e., and although a non-r.e. set is almost as hard to imagine as a noncomputable function, the slightly more tenuous connection with algorithmic procedures for sets is an advantage. The proof below can be applied to the complement of any non-recursive, r.e. set, but we use K to give an ersatz concreteness.

Theorem

$\overline{K}$ is not r.e.

Proof

We know that K itself is r.e. Suppose that $\overline{K}$ were also. Consider the following function-computing procedure, which makes use of the two recursive functions f and g which list the elements of K and $\overline{K}$ respectively (neither set is empty): given input x, compute $f(0), g(0), f(1), g(1), \ldots$, examining each value as it is computed. When x turns up, the output value is 1 if x was a result using f, but is 0 if x resulted from g. Since each x is in either K or $\overline{K}$, but no x is in both, this procedure is well defined, and by Church's thesis computes a total recursive characteristic function. Of what set? K. Contradiction. ∎

The sets we have considered above, K, H, and T, contain only Turing programs, since the defining conditions involve functions computed by Turing programs. $\overline{K}$ therefore contains not only those programs which are not defined on their own input, but also all natural numbers which are not Turing programs at all. The non-r.e. nature of $\overline{K}$ is not due to the inclusion of non-Turing-program numbers because the proof is almost unchanged if "Turing programs not in K" is substituted for "$\overline{K}$" throughout. The reason is that we have an effective procedure for deciding if a natural number is a Turing program, the primitive recursive function *tm* of Section 4.8.

5.6 RICE'S DECISION THEOREM

One asserted impossibility remains from Section 4.15: why is there no way to effectively find all Turing programs for certain unfortunate functions? The difficulty does not lie with the function, but with the variety of programs for any partial recursive function:

Theorem

$F = \{x | \varphi_x = \psi\}$ is not recursive for any nonempty partial recursive function ψ.

Proof

To reduce K to F we must fall back on the parametrization theorem, because tricks with syntactic composition would involve a function with two arguments (for which such a theorem could be proved—using parametrization). Suppose then that F were recursive. Given any Turing program z, we define a function which is ψ just when $z \in K$. Start by defining

$$X = \lambda x \lambda y \begin{bmatrix} \psi(y) & \text{if} & \varphi_x \text{ is defined at } x \text{ (i.e., } x \in K) \\ \text{undefined} & \text{if} & x \notin K \end{bmatrix},$$

which is partial recursive by Church's thesis. (Compute $\varphi_x(x)$ and if there is a result, discard it and compute $\psi(y)$; if φ_x is undefined at x, the computation will not terminate.) Let t be a Turing program for this function, $\varphi_t^{(2)} = X$. For the particular program z, the S-1-1 theorem gives

$$\varphi_{S_1^1(t,z)} = \lambda y [\varphi_t^{(2)}(z,y)] = \begin{cases} \psi & \text{if} \quad z \in K \\ \text{the empty function} & \text{if} \quad z \notin K. \end{cases}$$

Recall that ψ is not the empty function, so that the function with program $S_1^1(t,z)$ differs, depending on whether or not $z \in K$. If in fact $z \in K$, the program is one for ψ; if $z \notin K$, the program is for some other function. But this allows us to use F to decide membership in K: $z \in K$ iff $S_1^1(t,z) \in F$. Thus F is not recursive after all.

5.6 Rice's Decision Theorem

(The restriction to nonempty functions is essential to the proof; a similar result is easier to prove for the special case of the empty function using the syntactic composition function.)

It is possible to twist the essential idea of the theorem into a much more general form, which permits trivial solution to the problem of deciding whether many sets of programs are recursive. The rule is: certain sets of programs are never recursive if there exists one program in the set, and another not in the set. The restriction on application of this rule is that not all sets are the "certain" kind to which it applies. That kind are the sets of programs which contain all possible programs for each function if they contain one for it.

Definition

A set of Turing programs is *complete* iff for all programs p and q, if p is in the set and $\varphi_p = \varphi_q$, then q is in the set. ∎

Theorem (*Rice's Decision*)

A complete set is recursive iff it is empty or all Turing programs.

Proof

The empty set is recursive (membership decision: no), and so is the set of all Turing programs (characteristic function is $\lambda x [1 \dotminus tm(x)]$).

Suppose on the other hand that A were a nonempty recursive complete set which is not all Turing programs. Reduce K to A. There exist two programs $a \in A$ and $b \notin A$, which are necessarily for different functions because A is complete. One of these functions is not the empty function, then, suppose φ_a. As in the previous theorem define

$$\varphi_t^{(2)} = \chi = \lambda x \lambda y \begin{bmatrix} \varphi_a(y) & \text{if} \ x \in K \\ \text{undefined} & \text{if} \ x \notin K \end{bmatrix}.$$

Then given any program z, compute $S_1^1(t,z)$ which is a program such that

$$\varphi_{S_1^1(t,z)} = \varphi_a \quad \text{iff} \quad z \in K.$$

Because A is complete, this means that to decide membership of z in K requires only deciding membership of $S_1^1(t,z)$ in A, so A is not recursive after all.

It might have happened that the program a was for the empty function, however. In that case, using $\varphi_b \neq \emptyset$ proves that the set of all Turing programs not in A is not recursive. But that also contradicts the assumption that A is recursive, because a membership test for the complement of a set can be constructed from one for the set itself. ∎

Rice's decision theorem characterizes at least some recursive sets in a striking way. It often applies to sets of programs, because the interesting collections of programs often happen to be complete. Characterizations also exist for r.e. sets, similarly useful when discussing sets of programs. Another "Rice theorem" can be used to show that the set of programs which compute the same function is not r.e. as well as not recursive. Non-r.e. sets are almost literally intuitively unimaginable, since no procedure can be associated with them. It is possible, however, to grasp non-r.e. sets a little more firmly than non-partial-recursive functions, as illustrated by the set of programs which compute the empty function. The set is not r.e., but its complement is r.e. (but not recursive). This information about the set can be paraphrased as follows: for some non-r.e. sets it is possible to make a kind of unpredictable list of what isn't of interest. It is difficult to imagine anything farther out on the fringes of intuitive computability.

EXERCISES

5.1 Prove that the set $\{0,1\}$ is r.e. by exhibiting a partial recursive function which has it for domain, and again by exhibiting a total recursive function which lists it.

5.2 Use the definition of recursive listing to prove that every recursive set is r.e. How difficult is it to avoid inessential use of Church's thesis?

5.3 An argument which claims to prove that an infinite set is r.e. by outlining a procedure for listing its elements so that as the procedure is followed, the elements listed eventually include any member of the set, can be shown to rely on an inessential use of Church's thesis. Describe exactly the relation among such a procedure, the definition of an r.e. set, and Church's thesis.

5.4 Give a precise definition of an "r.e. set whose elements can be enumerated in order," and prove that such a set is recursive.

5.5 Suppose that the total recursive function f lists a set which is known to be finite. Consider the following instructions for computing the characteristic function of the set: on input x, compute $f(0), f(1), \ldots$, until the value x is obtained, then give output value of 1; if x does not appear, give the output value 0. Explain why it is improper to cite Church's thesis and this procedure to prove that the set is recursive. Is the set recursive?

5.6 The definition of a P.c.s. permits any number of string variables. Explain why in one sense there is never a need for more than two.

5.7 Write out the P.c.s. of the theorem in Section 5.3 in the case that the Turing program **N** for the zero function (Section 4.4) is being simulated, and give the proof of the theorem 1^0 starting from input 3. What other proofs can you give with this particular P.c.s.?

5.8 Consider the ICECHIP programming language (which resembles part of SNOBOL), in which programs are finite sequences of P.c.s. productions, thought of as being "executed" in order. An input string is presumed to exist at the beginning, being successively transformed to the output string at the end. If a production does not apply, the string remains unchanged. Give a natural definition of what it means for an ICECHIP program to compute a number-theoretic function of one argument. Prove that there are primitive recursive functions which are not ICECHIP-computable.

5.9 If a "test and branch" construction is added to the ICECHIP language of Exercise 5.8 to define (say) ICE9CHIP, perhaps by conditioning the branch on whether or not the production of the test step applies to the string, give a rough outline of a proof that now the functions computed are exactly the partial recursive functions.

5.10 In the proof of Section 5.4 that K is not recursive, inessential use was made of Church's thesis. Remove this fault from the proof.

5.11 Without using Rice's decision theorem, prove that the following sets are not recursive:

$$\{x | \varphi_x \text{ is any constant function}\},$$
$$\{x | \varphi_x \text{ is the particular constant function n}\}.$$

5.12 Prove that the following sets do not have recursive characteristic functions:

$$\{(x,y) \ | \varphi_x = \varphi_y\},$$
$$\{(x,y,z) | \varphi_x(y) = z\}.$$

5.13 Prove that for any fixed x, y, $\{p | \varphi_p(x) = y\}$ is r.e.

5.14 Prove that $\{x | \varphi_x \text{ is the empty function}\}$ is not recursive, without using Rice's decision theorem. Prove that $\{x | \varphi_x \text{ is not the empty function}\}$ is r.e. [*Hint*: Dovetail all possible Turing computations at all possible arguments for all possible numbers of steps.] Use these two facts to show that the set of programs for the empty function is not r.e.

5.15 Why doesn't Rice's decision theorem prove that the set of Turing programs

$$\{x | x < 99999999999999\}$$

is not recursive?

5.16 Use Rice's decision theorem to verify all the results about nonrecursive sets in Sections 5.4 and 5.5.

5.17 In the proof of Rice's decision theorem (Section 5.6) two functions φ_a and φ_b appear, and a function X is defined in terms of one of them. Why is it incorrect to simplify the argument by defining

$$X = \lambda x \lambda y \begin{bmatrix} \varphi_a(y) & \text{if} & x \in K \\ \varphi_b(y) & \text{if} & x \notin K \end{bmatrix}?$$

REFERENCES

The model for the presentation of recursive enumerability is Rogers [2]; some of Rogers' exercises are the source of the proof for Rice's theorem. Minsky [16] and Davis [17] are largely responsible for recent interest in Post's early work with canonical systems. The theory of enumerability also has current research interest, typified by Young's paper [18]. Further "Rice theorems" may be found in Rice [19] and Hamlet [20].

6
ARGUMENT COUNTS. COMPUTABLE NUMBERS

6.1 PAIRING FUNCTIONS

The two apparently unrelated topics of this chapter resolve two fundamental questions about programming. In fact we have assumed the answers to these questions starting in Chapter 3, but are now in a position to clearly state what has been assumed, and to argue its intuitive correctness. The questions concern the importance of argument counts in programming languages (answer: they are not of fundamental importance), and the basic entities with which computation should deal (answer: the natural numbers).

To discuss the problem of argument counts, the data we have are roughly this:

A. The Turing language takes no syntactic notice (as the predicate *TM* of Section 4.8 specified the limits of syntax) of how many arguments are being considered, so this information must be supplied in the semantics.

B. Most high-level procedural languages do make argument lists explicit in syntax. The partial-recursive-derivation language suggested in Section 4.1 also has explicit arguments.

C. It is very convenient (as in Sections 5.4–5.6) to deal with functions of just one argument, but there are occasions on which at least two arguments are essential (as in the enumeration theorem, Section 4.10).

There are some exceptions to item B in languages which permit only one argument to a procedure, but allow that argument to be some complex kind of "list" which really may incorporate many intuitively diverse values. The idea is similar to the coding of Turing machine entities, and is the heart of the argument that one-argument functions are really adequate for a fundamental theory, thus reconciling the data above. (Of course, no one would deny the utility of multiple-argument procedure for efficiency and documentation purposes in practical programming languages. This utility need not obscure the result that all ideas are contained in one-argument procedures, with a considerable simplification of the theory.)

The agent of the proof that one argument is enough is a kind of general two-argument-to-one coding function:

Definition

A *pairing function* is a recursive, one-to-one, onto mapping from pairs of natural numbers to natural numbers. ∎

Any pairing function has a pair of inverses, which are themselves recursive functions of a single argument. They create from a paired value the first and second elements of the pair, respectively. (The existence of inverses in a consequence of the pairing mapping being one-to-one and onto. Why are the inverses recursive?)

The discussion to follow concerns the theoretical significance of pairing-function use. It makes everything easier to say if we can use a particular pairing function and its two inverses, so that we can write down pairs and the parts of pairs explicitly. Which pairing function we use is not of much importance, so we choose a common one based on the Cantor diagonal correspondence. Imagine the natural numbers written down in a square tableau starting at the upper left, then filling in successive diagonals. It is certainly effective to make such a tableau up to any given maximum number. If the rows and columns are labeled with the natural numbers, we have specified a pairing function as shown in Fig. 6.1. We read a paired value from the row-column intersection, and inverses by going back from the entry to the row (first-position inverse) or column (second-position). For example, Fig. 6.1 allows computation of ten values of the pairing function, and the circled example shows that 2 pairs with 1 to give 7. The notation for our standard pairing function is $<x,y>$, and for the inverses it is π_1 and π_2, so that in general

$$\pi_1(<x,y>) = x, \quad \pi_2(<x,y>) = y, \quad \text{and} \quad <\pi_1(z),\pi_2(z)> = z.$$

For example,

$$<2,1> = 7, \quad \pi_1(7) = 2, \quad \pi_2(7) = 1.$$

	y				
	0	①	2	3	...
0	0	2	5	9	
1	1	4	8		
②	3	⑦			
3	6				
⋮					

x labels the rows.

Figure 6.1

6.2 EQUIVALENCE OF ONE- AND MULTI-ARGUMENT PARTIAL RECURSIVE FUNCTION THEORIES

A pairing function combines two values into one; the process can be iterated to combine any multiple argument into a single one, an *n*-tuple requiring $n - 1$ successive pairings.

Theorem

Consider the relation between functions ψ and θ displayed by

$$\psi = \lambda x_1 \ldots \lambda x_n [\theta(< \ldots <<x_1,x_2>,x_3>,\ldots,x_n>)].$$

Given any partial recursive θ of one argument, and any n, the ψ of the display is partial recursive; given any partial recursive ψ (of n arguments, say), there is a partial recursive θ for which the display holds.

Proof

A Church's thesis argument for computing ψ from θ is evident in the display. To be precise would require the definition of $n-1$ auxiliary functions starting with pairing, and proceeding by composition until θ may be used. When ψ is given, the necessary θ is a succession of the inverses π_1 and π_2 properly composed with ψ. For example, the last argument for ψ is obtained from a single given natural number with π_2, the second last with π_2 composed with π_1, etc. ∎

In view of this result, a common way to present partial recursive function theory is entirely in one-argument functions, casting the enumeration and parametrization theorems into one-argument form using pairing. This approach is used in Chapter 8.

6.3 EQUIVALENCE OF PARAMETRIZATION AND SYNTACTIC COMPOSITION IN THE PRESENCE OF ENUMERATION

In Sections 4.13 and 4.14 it was more difficult to give an intuitive meaning to the process of parametrization than to that of combining programs to compute composition. Similarly, in Sections 5.5 and 5.6, the arguments involving composition are easier to understand than those which use parametrization. In Section 4.14 it was shown that syntactic composition is a consequence of the S-2-1 theorem (and the enumeration theorem). We now indicate how to prove S-m-n theorems from syntactic composition. We have already proved the parametrization theorem; now we wish to give a different proof, one which indicates the S-m-n functions may be formed from "composing functions" for programs.

We verify that the function S_1^1 may be written as a program created by syntactic composition functions. The needed functions are C_n^m such that for all Turing programs $z, x_1, \ldots, x_m$

$$\varphi_{C_n^m(z,x_1,\ldots,x_m)}^{(n)} = \lambda y_1 \ldots \lambda y_n [\varphi_z^{(m)}(\varphi_{x_1}(y_1,\ldots,y_n),\ldots,\varphi_{x_m}(y_1,\ldots,y_n))];$$

that is, they create from programs for any composition a composite-function's program. (In Section 4.14 we established the existence of C which is C_1^1, in this notation.) Recall that the definition of S_1^1 requires that for all Turing programs z and all x,

$$\varphi_{S_1^1(z,x)} = \lambda y [\varphi_z^{(2)}(x,y)].$$

The form of the two-argument function on the right permits application of the composer C_1^2; the inner functions must be the constant function of value x and the identity function, that is,

$$\varphi_z^{(2)}(x,y) = \varphi_z^{(2)}(c_x(y), U_1^1(y))$$

to better indicate the composition. Certainly U_1^1 has a Turing program, say u, $\varphi_u = U_1^1$. c_x also has Turing programs, but that is not enough: we require that these programs be uniformly obtainable from x. But since c_x is precisely x compositions of the successor function with the zero function, if a is a program for adding unity, and b a program for the zero function, we have

$$c_x = \lambda y [\underbrace{\varphi_a(\varphi_a(\ldots \varphi_b(y)\ldots))}_{x \text{ times}}] = \varphi_{\underbrace{C(a,C(a,\ldots C(a,b)\ldots))}_{x \text{ times}}}$$

using C_1^1. If we write

$$H = \lambda x [(\underbrace{C(a,C(a,\ldots C(a,b)\ldots))}_{x \text{ times}})],$$

then

$$\varphi_z^{(2)}(x,y) = \varphi_z^{(2)}(c_x(y), U_1^1(y))$$
$$= \varphi_z^{(2)}(\varphi_{H(x)}(y), \varphi_u(y))$$
$$= \varphi_{C_1^2(z,H(x),u)}^{(2)}(y)$$

so it is evident that

$$S_1^1 = \lambda z \lambda x [C_1^2(z,H(x),u)].$$

We have thus indicated how an *S-m-n* function may be obtained from syntactic composing functions, just as syntactic composers are obtained from parametrizations. Hence the ideas are equivalent as complements to the enumeration theorem for the Turing programming language.

6.4 COMPUTABLE NUMBERS

The values used in any actual computation have finite representations, and hence (in view of pairing functions) are at most a finite segment of the rational numbers. However, it is not impossible that computations might deal with real numbers (and by pairing, complex ones) in the sense that although no irrational numbers were ever used during the computation, some desired result might be irrational, and the computation might provide arbitrary precision in return for a sufficient investment of running time. Without loss of generality, we consider only the interval [0,1), and express numbers as "decimals" beginning with "." and containing a sequence of "digits," although any radix would do just as well. It is assumed that the positional notation is well understood so that nothing need be proved about it.

Definition

The real number r, $0 \leq r < 1$, is *computable* iff there is a total recursive function f_r whose value at input i is the ith digit following the point in the decimal representation of r. That is, if $r = \cdot d_0 d_1 \ldots$, then $f_r(0) = d_0, f_r(1) = d_1, \ldots$. The function f_r is called a *generator* for r. ∎

The definition may seem artificial, and concerned only with output, but of course the output ability is the minimal one required to deal with numbers. Furthermore, the definition captures the intuitively correct result for rational numbers.

Theorem

The rational numbers in [0,1) are computable.

Proof

The characteristic property of a rational number expressed in positional notation is that after a finite initial set of digits, it repeats a finite pattern. The generator may then use a built-in table for the intial digits, and modular arithmetic with a table to produce the repeating group. Church's thesis justifies omitting details. ∎

6.5 UNCOMPUTABLE REALS

If a similar result held for arbitrary real numbers, it would be wise to question the definition as too weak. The rather surprising case is that it does not.

Theorem

There are real numbers which are not computable.

Proof

In any radix, the number whose n^{th} "digit" is 1 if φ_n is defined at n, and 0 otherwise, cannot possibly be computable, for if it were, any generator would be a recursive characteristic function for the nonrecursive set K. ∎

Examples such as the one in the theorem seem phony, but this is as much the fault of trying to display something undisplayable (if one accepts Church's thesis) as of diagonalization.

To summarize, it is inaccurate to say that computation produces rational approximations to real numbers without the qualification that some reals may not be approximated arbitrarily closely by a single program. Rather, to obtain added precision in some computations requires a succession of different programs.

EXERCISES

6.1 The pairing function of Section 6.1 has the closed form

$$<x,y> = \frac{(x + y)^2 + x + 3y}{2}$$

Prove that the formula is correct.

6.2 Write ALGOL 60 typed procedures for the two inverses of the pairing function of Exercise 6.1.

6.3 State the enumeration and S-1-1 theorems in a form which uses pairing to eliminate all mention of two-argument functions.

6.4 Rational numbers are sometimes defined as pairs of integers (p,q) to represent p/q (if $q \neq 0$), with such special properties as

$$(p_1,q_1) \cdot (p_2,q_2) = (p_1 p_2, q_1 q_2).$$

Using such a definition, give a suitable definition of computability, and prove that the rationals in $[0,1)$ are computable.

6.5 Prove that there are computable irrational numbers by displaying one and giving an algorithm for its generator.

6.6 Consider any uncomputable real number r. Suppose a Turing machine, on input n, were to compute the first n digits of r, then halt. Prove that there can be no such machine.

6.7 Suppose a program in any language computes roots of polynomial equations if their coefficients are given. Can such a program be expected to provide any level of precision in its results, given sufficient time to compute?

6.8 Is the set $\{x | \varphi_x$ is a generator for a computable real$\}$ recursive? Is this set related to the question of whether or not the computable reals may be effectively recognized?

REFERENCES

Argument counts are part of the standard fare of recursion theory, for example in Rogers [2]. P. R. Young suggested the equivalence of parametrization and syntactic composition. The presentation of computable real numbers is after Minsky [16]; the subject has been neglected since Turing [3].

7
REGISTER MACHINES

7.1 AN IDEALIZED COMPUTER AND ITS ASSEMBLY LANGUAGE

In this chapter we consider a different model of a computer than the human being which was at the heart of Turing's work. This computer is a simple abstraction of the single-address machines which have come to be called after J. von Neumann. The purpose is threefold. First, to study such machines by formalizing them; second, to again study the process of characterizing the partial recursive functions; and third, to provide another precise language for use in a discussion of language translation.

Description of computation by machines executing a program of simple instructions sequentially, in the process affecting a finite list of registers, seems very like a conventional digital computer. If each register can record only a finite range of values, the model is very like a processor and memory in fact. But the restriction to model actual memories poses some difficulties if all partial recursive functions are to be computed, since there can then be no bound on input or output values. (Perhaps a convention could bring the input under consideration serially, a digit at a time, and produce output in the same way. It is more convenient to imagine input magically appearing in a special register, to be replaced by output when the computation terminates. Even with the serial conventions, it would be a good guess that for finite memory, the computer model would look like a giant finite-state device, and have the same limitations.) A solution to these difficulties is to remove the bound on register storage capabilities, and hence consider what can hardly be called a register, but is better thought of as a repository for an arbitrary natural number.

"Unlimited registers" of this kind, if addressed as the realizable ones are, are not so foreign to actual computers. Many machines have "decimal arithmetic" packages in which arbitrary precision is available, limited only by the available total memory size. Some systems permit "virtual memory" usage, in which the programmer may pretend that memory is larger than in fact it is, the extra space being actually placed on some sort of rotating storage device. Some rotating storage units (disk packs, for example) have replaceable recording surfaces. Combining these elements with an automatic operation system, and a system of manufacturing disk packs and mounting them as needed, would realize an unlimited register machine. There appears to be little to choose between a finite number of unlimited registers, or an unlimited number of finite registers; we shall see that the former can accomplish everything imaginable.

What elementary operations should be permitted in a computer trying to model computing? Most programmers would feel that arithmetic, testing, and branching form a minimal set. The fewer instructions there are, the less will have to be proved when we come to compare the power of the model with Turing machines, and the simpler the form of a compiler will be. Most of the complexity of index registers, logical operations, etc., is generally agreed to add only to the convenience and efficiency of programming and programs; we will consider such frills in Chapter 9 (where we will prove correspondingly less).

The final question concerns the form of programs themselves, and here we can adopt the full conventions of a typical basic assembler with its labels, operation codes, and addresses. The format of the coding lines will not be of great importance since no arithmetization is contemplated.

The instruction repertoire is represented in the usual mnemonic form shown in Table 7.1.

With the convention that A0 is the preferred register which is assumed to contain input, and which is taken for output when the END is reached, the program (later called MUL2) of Fig. 7.1 multiplies its input by two.

What is being done here should be clear to anyone who has ever used an assembler, and we could now immediately define what it intuitively means for such a machine-language program to compute a function of one argument, using the i/o register as in the example. Instead, we try to adapt the formal definitions of Turing computation to apply to the new model.

Table 7.1

SETZ A	Set the contents of register A to zero.
INC A	Add 1 to the contents of register A.
JZDEC A,L	Test the contents of register A; if zero, continue at the label L; otherwise, subtract 1 from the contents.
END	"Pseudo-operation" serving only to place the exit label at which the program terminates.

7.2 FORMAL REGISTER MACHINES

If formalism is a good thing, then it is always worth practicing the art of creating it, capturing diverse ideas as continual reassurance that it can be done. A careful definition of a register machine can be viewed as a sort of formalism

```
              SETZ A1              Clear A1, A2 to use in
              SETZ A2              unconditional branches, counting.
LOP:          JZDEC A0,GONE        Is input zero yet?
              INC A2                  No, so bump up a copying register,
              JZDEC A1,LOP            and try again.
GONE:         JZDEC A2,EXIT        First time here, A2 has copy of the
                                      input. Is it zero yet?
              INC A0                  No, so bump up the answer...
              INC A0                  twice,
              JZDEC A1,GONE           and continue.
EXIT:         END                  That's all—answer in A0.
```

Figure 7.1

drill in addition to supplying precise information concerning what we are talking about. Assembly languages are so widely used that it is almost always enough to write the programs and ignore the formal definitions with no danger of misunderstanding. However, there is a difference between not using a definition and not having one, which is all-important in careful work.

Definition

A *register machine* is a 6-tuple (S,L,i,m,e,s) where S is a nonempty finite set of *registers*, L is a nonempty finite set of *instruction labels*, $i \in S$ is the *input/output register*, $e, s \in L$ are the *exit* and *start labels*, and

$$m: L - \{e\} \to S \times (\{°,+\} \cup L) \times L$$

is the *transition function*. An *instantaneous description* of a machine with k registers $s_1,\ldots,s_k$ is a $(2k+1)$-tuple $(s_1,r_1,\ldots,s_k,r_k,j)$ where $r_1,\ldots,r_k$ are natural numbers, the registers' *contents*, and $j \in L$ is the *current instruction label*. The instantaneous description $X = (s_1,r_1,\ldots,s_k,r_k,j)$ yields instantaneous description Y on the machine iff one of the following obtains:

1. $m(j) = (s_p,°,t)$ and $Y = (\ldots,s_p,0,\ldots,t)$,
2. $m(j) = (s_p,+,t)$ and $Y = (\ldots,s_p,r_p + 1,\ldots,t)$,
3. $m(j) = (s_p,n,t)$ and $r_p = 0$ and $Y = (\ldots,n)$,
4. $m(j) = (s_p,n,t)$ and $r_p \neq 0$ and $Y = (\ldots,s_p,r_p - 1,\ldots,t)$.

A *numerical computation on argument* x *with value* y is a finite sequence of instantaneous descriptions each yielding the next. The first instantaneous description has the start label s as final element, and the contents of the input/output register is x, all other registers with contents zero. In the last instantaneous description the contents of the input/output register is y and the current instruction label is the exit label *e*. A register machine *computes* a partial function ψ (of one argument) iff for each x: if ψ is defined at x, then there is a numerical computation on argument x with value $\psi(x)$; if there is a numerical computation on argument x with value y, then $\psi(x) = y$. ∎

Because this indigestable wad attempts to capture something like a real single-address computer, it is worth pointing out some of the correspondences to the assembly-language notation. The labels are the possible control positions, and each instruction has one (we don't write the ones to which we don't branch, but of course in the machine all are in existence anyway). The machine "runs" by knowing where it is (unless at the exit, when it runs no more), and passing to a new place after an instruction involving a register is performed. The affected register is the first component of the transition mapping, and the type of the instruction is specified by the second component: ° means zero the register, + means add 1, and if a label appears, it means do the JZDEC operation, that label being the place to go if the register contains zero. An important abbreviation in the usual assembly-language program is that there is a default value for the new label to use following an instruction: if none is indicated, the next in line is implied, so the order becomes of importance, as it is not in the formalism.

The formal specification of the program MUL2 for doubling in Section 7.1 would be

({A0,A1,A2},{L0,L1,LOP,L3,L4,GONE,L6,L7,L8,EXIT},A0, *m*, EXIT, L0),

m being given by Fig. 7.2.

L	$m(L)$
L0:	(A1,°,L1)
L1:	(A2,°,LOP)
LOP:	(A0,GONE,L3)
L3:	(A2,+,L4)
L4:	(A1,LOP,GONE)
GONE:	(A2,EXIT,L6)
L6:	(A0,+,L7)
L7:	(A0,+,L8)
L8:	(A1,GONE,EXIT)

Figure 7.2

MUL2 computes the function $\lambda x[2x]$. One way to prove this is to analyze numerical computations such as the one on argument 1 with value 2 as displayed in Fig. 7.3.

(0,1,1,0,2,0,L0)
(0,1,1,0,2,0,L1)
(0,1,1,0,2,0,LOP)
(0,0,1,0,2,0,L3)
(0,0,1,0,2,1,L4)
(0,0,1,0,2,1,LOP)
(0,0,1,0,2,1,GONE)
(0,0,1,0,2,0,L6)
(0,1,1,0,2,0,L7)
(0,2,1,0,2,0,L8)
(0,2,1,0,2,0,GONE)
(0,2,1,0,2,0,EXIT)

Figure 7.3

It is not hard to see the pattern, and to see that it is really the same for any input. (Strictly speaking we need not zero registers A1 and A2, since the definition presumes them zero, but good programming practice trusts the local loader and operating system less than a formal definition. Does the existence of some presumed-zero registers make the SETZ instruction unnecessary in general?)

The formal exercise is now at an end. Perhaps it has established the idea that we could proceed for register machines just as we did for Turing machines, and if the model is up to it, prove again that exactly the partial recursive functions are computed. Indeed that is what we want to prove, but there is a much easier way now that we have done the thing once.

The royal road makes use of a compiler which has register machines as its source language, and Turing machines as its object language (for the proof that every register machines computes a partial recursive function), and another which goes the other way (to prove that every partial recursive function is computed). The definitions restrict us to one-argument functions, but in view of the theorem on pairing in Section 6.2, there is no loss of generality in this simplification.

7.3 COMPILATION OF TURING PROGRAMS TO REGISTER PROGRAMS

Whenever we consider the equivalence of a new programming language to one we already know, the most interesting part of the discussion lies in proving that the new language can do whatever the old could do. This part of the equivalence proof provides the opportunity to write programs in the new language. When we translate Turing programs to register programs the object language is like the machine languages into which most compilers translate. The source language of Turing programs is a little unusual, because of its nonprocedural nature. As it happens, the worst difficulty is the difference in "peripheral equipment:" the Turing tape does not easily go into registers.

Theorem

Each partial recursive function of one argument is computed by some register machine.

Proof

By constructing a register machine computing the same function as any given Turing machine. In doing this, the major problem is keeping the tape in such a way that it is easy to read and change the scanned square. Of course, it is immaterial how this is done, so long as the register machine does what the Turing machine does relative to their respective input/output conventions.

Suppose that we are given the quadruples of any Turing program. The register program to be compiled will use registers as shown in Table 7.2. The "binary" used for tapes codes back into numbers the strings which represented numbers on Turing tapes. We consider each 1 on a tape as an "on" bit, and each b as an "off" bit of a binary number. Such numbers are not the ones coded by the Turing tape strings, however. If 1^n appears on a tape it codes n, and in a register the number is $2^n - 1$. The tape to the left of the scanned square may contain an arbitrary number of leading blanks, but these are not significant as leading zeros of the binary in a register. Also, the part of tape left which is changed when the Turing machine makes a transition is the least significant part of the register binary. To acquire these same advantages for the tape to the right of the scanned square requires that it be coded in reverse with the most significant bit at the right. The register machine we compile will need some initial instructions to code the given input into this reverse binary, and some final instructions to decode the result of computing.

Table 7.2

A0	Input/output register.
A1	Contents of the tape to the left of the scanned square, in "binary" (see below).
A2	Contents of the tape to the right of the scanned square, in "reverse binary."
A3	Scanned symbol in "binary."
A4	A register always zero, for branching.
A5	Temporary register.

This disadvantage is more than compensated for by the ease with which the simulated tape is "moved," which amounts simply to multiplication and division by 2 on A1 and A2.

It happens that the "multiply by 2" register program was used in Section 7.1 as an example (Fig. 7.1). In compilation it will be needed with various registers instead of A0 for the input/output, and A1 and A2 must instead be A4 and A5 respectively (not initially zeroed; that will be done in the initialization code). The best way to think of all this is to assure that the routine above can be generated by a "macro" of the form MUL2 Ax to arrange to multiply the contents of register Ax by two, using A4 and A5. The "macro" capability must include "local label generation" so that legitimate programs will result when the macro is used several times in the same program.

A similar divide-by-2 macro is needed, and it is convenient to obtain the remainder at the same time. At different times the contents of different registers must be divided by 2, but it happens that the remainder is always needed in A3, and A4, A5 can be used as for multiplication. (A5 is initially zero; it is the business of any user to see that it is returned to zero.) The division marco will be supplied in the conventional form of Fig. 7.4.

```
           DEFINE  D2R3  X
TOP:       JZDEC   X,REM0           Is the input zero yet? Decre-
           JZDEC   X,REM1              ment, and again. Zero now?
           INC     A5                   No, so add one to the
           JZDEC   A4,TOP               answer and go around
                                        again.
REM1:      INC     A3                Remainder was 1; put in A3
                                        (was 0).
REM0:      JZDEC   A5,OUT            Must clean up A5. Zero?
           INC     X                    (Also get answer in correct
                                        place.)
           JZDEC   A4,REM0           Loop until A5 copied to X.
OUT:       END
```

Figure 7.4

The macro call is then of the form D2R3 Ax to divide the contents of register Ax by 2, leaving the remainder in A3. (The macro convention for its END pseudo-operation is evidently that a branch to the exit label means a branch to the instruction which follows the macro-generated code.)

The initialization routine which will be compiled at the front of each object program, independent of the Turing machine which is to be compiled, is given in Fig. 7.5. The bare label at the end is evidently to be placed on the next instruction to be compiled. To illustrate the "binary," note that if the input in register A0 happens to be 5, then at the end of the initialization routine, A2 will contain 31 ($=2^5-1$). Because A3 is zero, a blank is being scanned, and to the right of

7.3 Compilation of Turing Programs to Register Programs

this square is a 1 (the remainder on dividing 31 by 2) while to the left is a blank (remainder on dividing contents of A1—zero—by 2). Note also that the suggested conditions on A4 and A5 are met.

```
       SETZ   A1              You knew
       SETZ   A2                 that this code
       SETZ   A3                    was initializing all
       SETZ   A4                       the registers without this
       SETZ   A5                          comment, didn't you?
INIT:  JZDEC  A0, I           Is the input exhausted yet? Decrement,
       MUL2   A2                 if not, and shift A2 one bit,
       INC    A2                 adding in a bit,
       JZDEC  A4, INIT           and continue.
I:                            Input conventions have been met.
```

Figure 7.5

Now the given Turing program must be considered in detail, and code generated to complete the register program. For each pair of quadruples whose current state is the same a segment of the form given in Fig. 7.6 will be required, in which STATE is replaced by a unique name identifying the current state (perhaps QQQQQ for the state qqqqq, etc.), ZERO is strictly local to this segment, and NEXT identifies the next state from the quadruple uniquely (and hence occurs in the segment generated for that state's pair of quadruples). The "implementation" portions of the code depend on what actions the quadruples specify. Note that in any case A3 contains zero, as required by the divide macro.

```
STATE:   JZDEC  A3, ZERO      Scanned a zero? Jump.
           :                  Implementation for the 1 quad-
           :                  ruple.
         JZDEC  A4, NEXT      Continue with another quadruple
                              pair.
ZERO:      :                  Implementation for the b quad-
           :                  ruple.
         JZDEC  A4, NEXT      Continue with another quadruple
                              pair.
```

Figure 7.6

For a "print" quadruple, nothing need be compiled if b is printed—A3 is already zero. If a 1 is printed, the "implementation" code is just

```
         INC    A3      Now scanning a 1.
```

for the proper contents of the scanned square.

138 Register Machines

For a "move right" quadruple, Fig. 7.7 gives the code. The instruction marked (*) in Fig. 7.7 is included only in the implementation for the 1 quadruple. The "move left" implementation is exactly the same with all A1 and A2 references reversed, and comments adjusted to appropriately interchange left and right.

MUL2	A1	Shift to the right, lengthening the left tape.
*INC	A1	Append the formerly scanned 1.
D2R3	A2	Shorten the right tape, and scan its rightmost bit (A3).

Figure 7.7

After treating all quadruples of the given Turing machine in this way, there will be one undefined label in the register program that has been generated, which corresponds to the name of the final state of the Turing machine. A branch to this label will occur should the machine halt, so the code to return the result to register A0 can be placed there. Perhaps the Turing machine will not reach its final state; then the register machine will not reach this ultimate label. However, another case poses a difficulty: we must be certain that a halting Turing program is scanning a number properly on its tape, since the register program has nothing corresponding to the strange Turing terminating conventions, and must not reach its exit if the Turing tape was garbaged. The finalization code arranges to loop in that case as Fig. 7.8 shows.

FINAL:	JZDEC A3,PASS1	Are we scanning a blank? Jump.
FAIL:	JZDEC A4,FAIL	Bad news; die.
PASS1:	JZDEC A1,PASS2	Is tape to the left all blank? Jump.
	JZDEC A4,FAIL	No; die.
PASS2:	JZDEC A2,PAST	Is the remaining tape all blank?
	INC A2	No, add back the one subtracted.
	D2R3 A2	Split out the last square to A3.
	JZDEC A3,FAIL	If it is a blank, it is embedded, so die.
	INC A0	Nonblank, increase output tally.
	JZDEC A4,PASS2	Continue.
PAST:	END	

Figure 7.8

The complete register machine computes exactly the same function as the given Turing machine, completing the proof of the theorem. ∎

A compiler might be described as an effective mapping between syntaxes which preserves semantics. It is therefore instructive to examine the roles of syntax and semantics in the compilation specified by the above proof. Half of the syntax problem was simply omitted there: no check was applied for a correct Turing program. The function *tm* of Section 4.8 would fill this gap, and it was tacitly assumed that all matters it judges are correct. If, for example, the source program has missing quadruples, the compiled object program will come up with undefined labels. This example illustrates what should be called syntax and what should be called semantics for register programs. Certainly syntax must specify proper operation codes and instruction formats. But it is also part of syntax to see that every label is defined if used, and that none are defined more than once. Our compiler of the theorem then necessarily generates correct register programs from correct Turing programs. What of semantics? The compiler in no sense decides which partial recursive function is computed by the source program and then creates an object program for that function. In Section 5.6 we proved that such a design cannot be implemented. Rather, the compilation is extremely local. To each quadruple the compiler assigns a fragment of register program, in such a way that the two pieces of syntax do the same thing. The proof that the compiler does not bend semantics then proceeds upward to the full source program from its elements.

7.4 COMPILATION OF REGISTER PROGRAMS TO TURING PROGRAMS

Assembly languages are seldom translated except into internal loading codes, but of course they can be easily compiled into many forms.

Theorem

Each register program computes a partial recursive function of one argument.

Proof

By constructing a Turing program which computes the same function as any given register program. The Turing program computes a partial recursive function, hence so does the given register machine.

Think of any register program of $n + 1$ registers in its assembly-language form. The Turing program will keep track of the registers needed as an $(n + 1)$-tuple on its tape, using the usual b and 1 symbols, with the input/output register placed first. The initial tape contains just the input value, which corresponds to all other registers initially zero. (This brings the input conventions into line.) The quadruples of the Turing machine will be obtained in groups, corresponding to each instruction line of the register machine. These groups will have the same effect (on the tape-represented registers) as the instruction does, and the Turing machine will always position itself at the beginning of the tape (scanning the input/output register's tape code). A final convention is that the registers are named in the tape order by integers $0, 1, \ldots, n$ so that in the compiled Turing program we can easily specify the proper register to update.

If the instruction is SETZ Ak, compile the quadruples represented by Fig. 7.9. The algorithm by which the kth tape-register is zeroed is a bit at a time from the right. The difficult part of this operation is moving the registers lying to the right of the kth toward the left in compensation, but a tricky use of the F

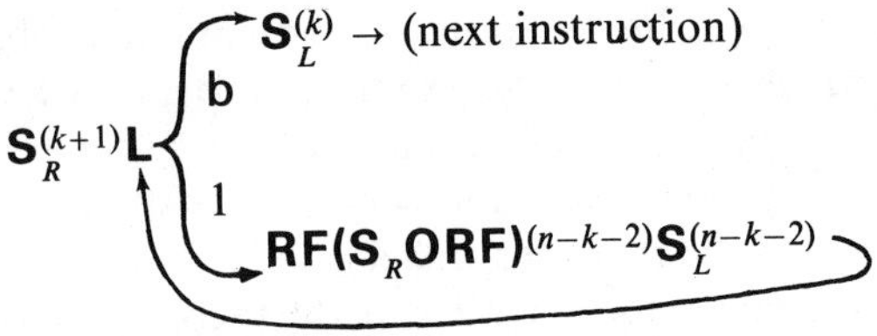

140   Register Machines

$$S_R^{(k+1)}L \begin{cases} \to S_L^{(k)} \to \text{(next instruction)} \\ b \\ 1 \\ \to RF(S_R ORF)^{(n-k-2)} S_L^{(n-k-2)} \end{cases}$$

Figure 7.9

machine in which it is led to believe that the last bit of numbers is the "marker" bit which it erases is of some help. The phrase "(next instruction)" indicates where to attach the quadruples to be compiled from the next line of the assembly code.

If the instruction is **INC A**k, the code is

$$S_R^{(k)} X_{n+1-k} OLBS_L^{(k)} \to \text{(next instruction)},$$

in which the **X** machine is used to add and shift all registers to the right.

If the instruction is **JZDEC A**k,P, the generated segment is shown in Fig. 7.10, using the same trick as zeroing (but not so many times). Here, how-

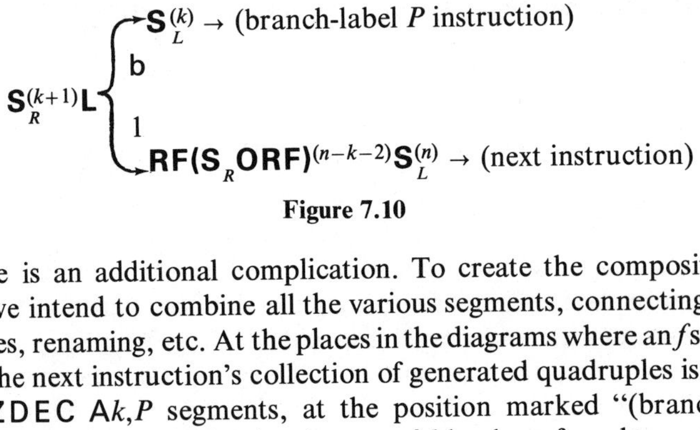

$$S_R^{(k+1)}L \begin{cases} \to S_L^{(k)} \to \text{(branch-label } P \text{ instruction)} \\ b \\ 1 \\ \to RF(S_R ORF)^{(n-k-2)} S_L^{(n)} \to \text{(next instruction)} \end{cases}$$

Figure 7.10

ever, there is an additional complication. To create the composite Turing program we intend to combine all the various segments, connecting final and initial states, renaming, etc. At the places in the diagrams where an f state name remains, the next instruction's collection of generated quadruples is attached. In the **JZDEC A**k,P segments, at the position marked "(branch-label P instruction)" the "branch" is taken because **A**k has been found to contain zero. The code segment attached there is the one which results from translating the instruction at label P.

There is a final complication which occurs at the **END** line (exit label) of the register program. The compiled code then exists to faithfully simulate the registers, which will all have their correct values on the tape. But to ensure that there is a legal Turing computation all but the first must be deleted. (By changing the definition of a register-machine numerical computation to insist that all except the input/output register be left zero, this step could be avoided.) The code required is

$$S_R X_n N^{(n)} F S_L$$

(but omit the **X** and **F** if $n = 0$). ∎

(Some efficiency could be gained if the compiler in the proof had an optimization pass which arranged to keep track of tape position so that things like $\mathsf{S}_R^{(5)}\mathsf{S}_L^{(3)}$ were replaced by $\mathsf{S}_R^{(2)}$.)

There are many variations on the register machine which differ inessentially from the one used here. To give two examples, the SETZ instruction is not required if a particular register is assumed to be initialized to zero in all programs. In that case JZDEC (with that register) can be used to count down other registers. For a second, more drastic change, the JZDEC could be replaced by other test forms which skip instructions (say) instead of jumping, or which perform different tests. More fundamental changes are considered in Chapter 9.

Given the definition of register programs and experience with assembly-language systems, it is tempting to replace compiling to Turing programs with an argument of the following kind: accepting Church's thesis, any intuitively effective process computes partial recursive functions; the register programs are such a process. There are two reasons why full details on compilation were given: (1) Such a specification of translation can be used as a semantics for a language. That is, instead of describing what register programs themselves do, we could give the Turing equivalents, and assert that they do that, by definition. (A good name for such a scheme would be "object-code semantics;" it is extensively used with FORTRAN and von Neumann-style object code.) (2) A careful specification of Turing compilers allows a proof of the enumeration and parametrization theorems without appeal to the language structure. That is, when translation is possible, the syntax and semantics of a language have these important properties automatically. Full details are provided in the next chapter.

EXERCISES

7.1 Suppose that register machines were defined with the instructions

JUMP L   Continue at label L
SKIPZ A   Test the contents of register A; if zero, skip the next instruction, otherwise subtract 1 from the contents

but lacking the JZDEC and SETZ instructions. Argue informally that such machines are exactly as capable as those described in Section 7.1. Make appropriate changes in the formal definition of Section 7.2 to describe the altered machines. Is it possible to do without both JZDEC and JUMP if you have SKIPZ?

7.2 Describe precisely all the ways a register program may fail to compute any result for a given input in terms of what happens in the machine. Suppose that the definition of computation were changed to require that each computation begin and end with at most the input/output register nonzero. How would this change the function computed by a given machine?

7.3 Informally define an *oracle machine* as a register machine with an associated set of natural numbers, its *oracle set*, and an instruction

    JORC A,L Test the number contained in register A; if it is a member of the oracle set, continue at the label L.

Write an oracle program which computes the characteristic function of its oracle set. Can oracle machines compute non-partial-recursive functions? What about Church's thesis?

7.4 Classify the following ideas about register programs as "syntax" or "semantics" according to the criteria indicated in Section 4.8 for Turing programs:

One of the instructions is SEZT A.
There is no END line to the program.
The register designated as the input/output register does not appear in the program.
The program does not execute its END line for certain values placed in the input register.
Labels are used in JZDEC which are never placed.
The same label is placed more than once.
Labels are placed but never used in any JZDEC.

7.5 Discuss the consequences of allowing a register program to contain the label irregularities of Exercise 7.4 for the compiler in the proof of the theorem of Section 7.4.

7.6 What does it prove that exactly six registers were used in the register machine simulating any Turing machine in Section 7.3? Can fewer registers be used?

7.7 At the end of Section 7.4 it was indicated that optimization might improve the code generated by the register-machine-to-Turing-machine compiler, by eliminating canceling combinations of shifts. Describe a similar kind of optimization which would benefit the Turing-machine-to-register-machine compiler of Section 7.3.

7.8 Suppose that we agree to write ρ_x for the partial recursive function computed by register program x in some suitable Gödel numbering. State a syntactic composition theorem for register programs and prove it with a Church's thesis argument.

7.9 Using the notation of Exericse 7.8 and a pairing function, state an S-1-1 theorem for register programs, and prove it with a Church's thesis argument.

7.10 Prove that the problem of deciding whether an arbitrary register machine ever alters the contents of any register at all for an arbitrary input is solvable or unsolvable, as the case may be.

REFERENCES

The informal discussion of register machines is based on Minsky [16], but the formal definition is somewhat different from the one originally presented by Shepherdson and Sturgis [21].

8
ABSTRACT PROGRAMMING LANGUAGES

8.1 PARTIAL RECURSIVE FUNCTION CHARACTERIZATIONS

Whenever a precise description of a programming language has been given, its syntax and semantics can be arithmetized, as in Sections 4.6-4.9 for the Turing language. It is very common to distinguish between recognition of program syntax (as with the predicate *TM* of Section 4.8) and specification of a semantic computation sequence (as with the Kleene T-predicates of Section 4.9). Unfortunately the process is always tedious, the more so the "higher-level" the language. The reason is that a high-level language which is easy and economical to use for complex programming has many "constructions" which are difficult to recognize syntactically, and which have involved semantics, so the predicates becomes very complicated. Furthermore, repeating the process for even unusual languages yields a very small return in fundamental insights, since most of the effort goes into specialized tricks.

However tedious the process may be, it has been carefully carried out for many low-level languages (Chapter 7 register programs for one), always with the result which supports Church's thesis: the functions computed are exactly the partial recursive functions. The detailed presentations have the same overall appearance. There is an enumeration theorem and a parametrization or syntactic composition theorem as a consequence of the interplay between syntax and semantics.

Study of full details of syntax and semantics is essential in language specification, and to a smaller degree in learning and using a language. For fundamental theory the details of T-predicates even for low-level languages are forbiddingly complex. The abstract approach to programming languages is therefore based on the most important properties derived from the details, the enumeration and parametrization theorems of the language. These certainly hold for reasonable languages, and are sufficient to say a good deal about unsolvable problems and language translation.

8.2 NUMBERINGS (ABSTRACT PROGRAMMING LANGUAGES)

Our goal is to obtain use of the notation φ_p for the partial recursive function computed by a program p without giving its definition in terms of details of p or its computations.

Definition

An *abstract programming language* is a pair (L,φ) where L is a recursive set of *programs*, and φ maps L onto the partial recursive functions (of one argument), the *semantic mapping*. L is sometimes loosely called the *syntax*, or even "the language." The notation for the image $p \in L$ under φ is φ_p, the function computed by p. Another notation for the language is $\{\varphi_p\}_{p \in L}$. An abstract programming language is also called a partial recursive function *numbering*, or *indexing*. ∎

The recursive syntax of the definition provides an effectively recognizable domain for the semantic mapping. Since the map is onto the partial recursive functions, the definition requires that exactly the algorithmic functions according to Church's thesis will be computed. The restriction to one-argument functions is convenient, but inessential as shown in Section 6.2.

What is missing from the definition concerns connections between syntax and semantics. For example, nothing forbids use of the natural numbers as syntax and assignment of partial recursive functions in a completely haphazard way from being an abstract programming language. However, we feel that such a syntax-semantics connection is too loose. These matters were handled in the arithmetization that created syntax and semantics from language details, and have been lost to abstraction. There is nothing to do but put them back as further abstractions.

8.3 ACCEPTABLE NUMBERINGS (ABSTRACT PROGRAMMING LANGUAGES WITH INTERPRETERS AND COMPOSERS)

The properties which we want to add to abstract programming languages are precisely those called enumeration and parametrization or syntactic composition theorems for characterizations in which full details were available. In the abstract setting there is no hope of proving such theorems, since it is just the necessary details which have been eliminated. We therefore add the theorems as defining "properties" an abstract programming language may possess. (We rename the enumeration property.)

Definition

An abstract programming language (L,φ) has the *interpretation* property if there is a partial recursive function I (the *interpreter*) such that for all $p \in L$,

$$\lambda x[I(<p,x>)] = \varphi_p.$$

The language (L,φ) has the *composition* property iff there is a total recursive function C (the *composer*) such that for all $p, q \in L$,

$$\varphi_{C(<p,q>)} = \lambda x[\varphi_p(\varphi_q(x))].$$

With both properties a language (numbering) is also called *acceptable*. ∎

These forms should be familiar from Sections 4.10 and 4.14, except for the presence of pairings which convert all functions to single arguments. The pairing function is arbitrary, but fixed for the discussion.

Existence of language interpreters certainly seems a necessity if the syntax is to be structured well enough to carry the semantics. The need for composition is less obvious, and should be judged when we discuss an example of a language which lacks it, in Section 8.5.

The parametrization property for an abstract programming language follows from the composition property in much the same way as in Section 6.3. However, the pairing function introduces new technical details which are fairly typical of work in the abstract setting, so the result will be repeated.

Theorem (*Parametrization*)

For any abstract programming language (L,φ) with the composition property there is a recursive function S such that for all $x \in L$ and all y,

$$\varphi_{S(<x,y>)} = \lambda z[\varphi_x(<y,z>)].$$

Proof

The particular pairing function of Section 6.1 is a very natural one, since it counts the "distance" to a point in a square matrix from the upper left corner, along successively deeper corner cuts. The distance to the end of the corner cut prior to position (x,y) is

$$1 + 2 + \ldots + (x+y) = \frac{(x+y)(1+(x+y))}{2},$$

and the additional distance along the final corner cut to the point is just y, so

$$d(x,y) = \frac{(x+y)^2 + x + 3y}{2}$$

is the "natural" pairing function. If its inverses are b_1 and b_2, then for an arbitrary pairing function,

$$<x,y> = p(d(x,y))$$

where p is the recursive function $\lambda z [<b_1(z),b_2(z)>]$.

We now show that a special case of the theorem holds for the pairing function d: there is a recursive S_d such that for all x,

$$\varphi_{S_d(x)} = \lambda y [d(x,y)].$$

A more convenient form is

$$d(x,y) = ((2y + (2x + 3))^2 - (8x + 9))/8,$$

which indicates the algorithm in y: double, add 1 ($2x + 3$) times, square, subtract 1 ($8x + 9$) times, and divide by 8. Each operation (not including the repetitions) has a program in L, so $\lambda y[d(x,y)]$ is a ($10x + 15$)-fold composition of functions each of one argument, and $S_d(x)$ can therefore be created by a ($10x + 15$)-fold application of the composer C for L to the individual programs. S_d is recursive because C is.

Returning to the theorem, we have for all $x \in L$, all y, z:

$$\varphi_x(<y,z>) = \varphi_x(p(d(y,z))) = \varphi_x(\varphi_t(\varphi_{S_d(y)}(z))),$$

t being any program for the function p, so that using the composer twice gives

$$\lambda z [\varphi_x(<y,z>)] = \varphi_{C(x,C(t,S_d(y)))},$$

almost in the correct form. It remains only to write in the pairing inverses to produce a one-argument function:

$$S = \lambda z [C(\pi_1(z), C(t, S_d(\pi_2(z))))],$$

the single-argument abstract equivalent of the S-1-1 function. ∎

Of course, we could have assumed the parametrization theorem and proved the existence of the composer (with less difficulty) much as was done in Section 4.14. The justification for the approach used here is that composition is the more intuitively correct property, while parametrization seems only a technical trick. It is appropriate to prove the correctness of technical tricks at some length.

8.4 COMPILERS. ROGERS' TRANSLATION THEOREM

For pairs of abstract programming languages the most interesting entity is the translator, which can be defined as soon as syntax and semantics are defined.

Definition

A *compiler* from *source language* (L_1, φ) to *object language* (L_2, ψ) is a recursive function $T: L_1 \to L_2$ such that for each $p \in L_1$, $\varphi_p = \psi_{T(p)}$. ∎

It is important to keep in mind that for abstract programming languages nothing whatsoever is assumed about the details of the semantic mapping. The function φ_z in our discussion of Turing programs could be "worked out" (or at least an attempt made), since z coded an intuitive machine whose operation could be imagined. In an abstract language, φ_z is a function about which we know nothing except its name. What function is it? The one which is computed by program z. What is that computation like? We cannot say. It is therefore somewhat surprising when we can give a complete answer to some important language questions entirely in abstract terms.

Theorem (*Rogers' Translation Theorem*)

Given any two abstract programming languages (L_1, φ) and (L_2, ψ):
1. If L_1 has the interpretation property and L_2 has the composition property, then there is a compiler from L_1 to L_2.
2. If L_1 has interpretation and a compiler exists from L_2 to L_1, then L_2 has interpretation. If L_1 has composition and compilers exist in both directions, then L_2 has composition.

Proof

1. Since the interpreter for (L_1, φ) is a partial recursive function, it has programs in L_2; suppose one of these is i: $\psi_i = I$. If the parametrization function for (L_2, ψ) is S, we have

$$\varphi_p = \lambda x [\psi_i(<p,x>)] = \psi_{S(<i,p>)},$$

which shows that the required compiler is $T = \lambda p[S(<i,p>)]$.

2. Let I be the L_1 interpreter, and T' the compiler from L_2 to L_1. For a given L_2 program p, translate and then interpret:

$$\psi_p = \varphi_{T'(p)} = \lambda x [I(<T'(p),x>)].$$

The last function in this chain, considered as depending on p and x, is the desired L_2 interpreter, but there is some technical problem placing it in the form of a function of $<p,x>$, solved by application of the inverse pairing functions. All requirements are met by

$$I' = \lambda z [I(<T'(\pi_1(z)), \pi_2(z)>)].$$

In addition to T', suppose T compiles L_1 to L_2, and C is the composer in L_1. To perform composition of p and q in L_2, translate to L_1, compose, and

translate back:
$$\lambda x [\psi_p(\psi_q(x))] = \lambda x [\varphi_{T'(p)}\varphi_{T'(q)}(x)]$$
$$= \varphi_{C(<T'(p),T'(q)>)} = \varphi_{T(C(<T'(p),T'(q)>))}.$$

The same technical problems are overcome in the same way, with the result
$$C' = \lambda z [T(C(<T'(\pi_1(z)), T'(\pi_2(z))>))]. \blacksquare$$

Part 2 of the theorem applies to register machines, because in Sections 7.3 and 7.4 we displayed compilers in both directions with the Turing language. Therefore the register language has both the interpretation property and the composition/parametrization property, without a single T-predicate in sight.

The translation theorem also indicates something of the difficulty of the semantic part of compilation: it is not difficult, amounting to minor technical modifications of the source-language interpreter.

8.5 SEPARATION OF SYNTAX AND SEMANTICS

As an application of the abstract approach, we consider again the boundary between syntax and semantics of programming languages. The interpretation and composition properties express enough of the relation which must hold between the essentially recursive (syntax) part of a language and the nonrecursive (semantics) part to forbid improper connections.

Theorem

No abstract programming language with the interpretation and composition properties has a unique program which computes each partial recursive function.

Proof

Suppose that the theorem is false, and that (L,φ) is the magic language. Recall that $T = \{p \in L \mid \varphi_p \text{ is total}\}$ is not a recursive set. (Section 5.5 for the Turing language. Why does the result hold for an abstract language with interpretation and composition properties?) Nevertheless, we solve membership in T as follows: suppose that n is the program for the zero function in L. Given any $z \in L$, calculate $C(<n,z>)$. This program computes either the zero function, if the inside function is everywhere defined, or some other function, if not. That is, a test for membership of z in T is precisely whether or not $C(<n,z>) = n$. Evidently there is something wrong, namely that such a language exists. $\blacksquare$

Intuitively, the languages forbidden by the theorem would not permit easy modification and debugging of programs. To make a minor change in meaning might require seeking a radically different syntax for the sole program with the new semantics.

The theorem also provides considerable insight into the necessary role of composition as a programming language property. R. M. Friedberg has constructed a numbering with the interpretation property which has exactly one program for each partial recursive function. Hence his language necessarily lacks the composition property. (*Friedberg numbering* has been suggested as a name for such a language, where an acceptable numbering is also called a Gödel or Rogers numbering.) Friedberg's language is not a reasonable programming language, because the syntax-semantics connection is too weak by conventional standards. The Friedberg interpreter works not by attempting a computation of a given program on a given argument, but by systematically examining all possible actions of all programs of the language on all arguments, and watching for the correct program and argument to appear. The construction is difficult, and its difficulty seems to lie in the fact that the syntax is so weak that an interpreter must use the entire language in order to discover the semantics of a single program. In practical terms, one could only program in such a language by guessing a program, then testing whether or not it had desirable properties with the interpreter, and if not, making a new guess, with little direction provided by the mistaken earlier try. The syntactic-composition property eliminates the need to founder about in this way, and so might be taken as the property of a language which forces programs to be "individually interpretable," in the way practical interpreters do their work. Since programmers also operate in this way when writing and debugging, syntactic composition is a far more important property than it seems at first sight. Perhaps the reason why all reasonable languages have the property, and why it is often so easy to prove it, is that programming without syntactic composition is hopeless, even if very few programmers make explicit use of the composer function to actually combine programs.

This excursion back into recursive function theory perhaps appears more promising than it should. Compilation is probably the idea whose expression in the theory is best, but it seems that Rogers' theorem exhausts almost all that can be learned without adding to the language "properties" assumed. All questions about the way in which programs work, and hence about compiler optimization, "faithfulness," etc., cannot be stated in the abstract terms given in this chapter, since the only semantic idea is that of the function computed by a program. However, there are some promising extentions to the abstract approach which we consider in Sections 10.2 and 10.4.

EXERCISES

8.1 Outline an arithmetization of register machines described in Section 7.1 by devising some detailed numerical codings of the assembly-language-form programs, but stop short of giving predicates for syntax and semantics.

8.2 Which theorems of Chapters 4 and 5 are true not only for the Turing language, but for any abstract language with the interpretation and composition properties?

8.3 Verify that the class of ALGOL 60 procedures with a single argument, considered as a partial recursive function characterization as in Exercise 3.11, has the composition property, by a Church's-thesis argument.

8.4 Write out the function S_d of the parametrization theorem of Section 8.3 explicitly in terms of the composer C.

8.5 In programming language terms describe how to turn an interpreter into a compiler following the suggestion of Rogers' translation theorem.

8.6 Using as many abstract programming languages as necessary, give the abstract equivalent of the obvious result that if a compiler written in any language is compiled (perhaps by another compiler, perhaps by itself) into any other language, then the object program resulting from the first compiler remains a compiler for its original two languages. Comment on how difficult it might be to verify a statement of this kind for a particular group of programming languages.

8.7 Consider a pair of abstract programming languages (L_1, φ) and (L_2, ψ), and compilation from the source language L_1 to object language L_2. Intuitively, a compiler is *self-compiling* if it has a program in the source language. Prove that every compiler is self-compiling. Comment on why some actual programming language compilers are called self-compiling and some are not. Imagine starting with an arbitrary compiler and translating the self-compiling compiler source program, then using the resulting object program to translate that source again, and so on repeatedly. Prove that after the second iteration the object program cannot change.

8.8 Give an abstract version of the argument about "test inputs" in Exercise 1.4 which shows that this idea is not proper for an abstract programming language with interpretation and composition properties.

REFERENCES

Mendelson [9] includes a careful presentation of two partial recursive function characterizations not mentioned here: Markov algorithms and Herbrand-Gödel-Kleene sets of equations. The abstract approach is largely due to Rogers [22, 2]. Friedberg's paper [23] contains deep results of recursion theory, and the discussion by Pour-el [24] is only a beginning of the application to numberings.

9
RANDOM-ACCESS MACHINES

9.1 FURTHER IDEALIZATIONS OF SINGLE-ADDRESS COMPUTERS

The register machines presented in Chapter 7 have two deficiencies as a model of a digital computer. First, the limitation to a finite number of registers forces complex data coding and devious means to perform operations which would be straightforward if data were not so compressed. Second, the range of operation codes is very small. The latter is not a fundamental limitation, since a larger order code could be defined by extending one component of the transition function. Many operations can be easily described as sequences of those already specified, an analogy to language extension by assembler macro-operations (if you prefer software) or of micro-programming of instructions (if you prefer hardware). On the other hand, the shortage of distinct addressable memory is more serious. On the surface, programs working with a small number of registers, spending most of their instructions coding and decoding the contents, are not very like programs for a computer with a relatively large memory. In actually programming we by and large assume that the registers (memory locations) have no limit to the values they can contain, but we also assume that there is no limit to the number of registers. (We know that both assumptions betray us, but leave it to the various arithmetic traps and the system software to catch transgressions when they occur.) It would be relatively easy to alter our definition of a register machine to include infinite memory—allow the set of registers to be infinite. Such an approach fails to answer the criticism above: indeed, reference to unlimited memory is then available, but not within one program. For, since to reference a register requires naming it in an instruction, finite collections of instructions use finite sets of registers. Intuitively, it will not do to allow the set of labels to be infinite also; one does not begin key-punching infinite programs.

How does a von Neumann-style assembly-language program address a large amount of memory? Two methods immediately come to mind: (1) index registers and (2) program address modification. (The historical order of machine development was roughly from external programs dissociated from the memory, to stored programs which could modify themselves, to index registers and disuse of program modification for reasons of sharing code. The formal models for indexing turn out to be easier than those for self-modifying programs.) Corresponding to an index-register machine is the formal random-access machine (RAM), while the computer von Neumann conceived is modeled by a random-access stored-program machine (RASP).

9.2 RANDOM-ACCESS MACHINES (RAMs). INDEX REGISTERS

Following the assembly-language presentation of Section 7.1, use of index registers might be typified by an instruction

$$\text{INC} \quad \text{A3(A1)}$$

which specifies that unity be added, not to A3, but to a register whose name is computed: it is the one whose distance from A3 is currently contained in register A1. Suddenly it is very awkward not to have simple numerical values for the registers, making the "distance" between them apparent. Registers will therefore be assigned numerical names $0, 1, 2, \ldots$, called the register addresses. The example instruction then might appear as

$$\text{INC} \quad 3(1)$$

and if the contents of address 1 happened to be 4, it would be address 7 whose contents is incremented. Evidently the same kind of index modification can be applied to the registers of each kind of instruction, with the same intent.

If we permit indexing of all instructions, but otherwise do not extend the instruction repertoire of the register machines of Chapter 7, the new model captures address calculations without requiring much new formal apparatus in the definition. In addition to the INC instruction, the indexed form of the test and branch (for example)

$$\text{JZDEC} \quad 3(1), \text{L}$$

has exactly the same address calculation: the contents of register 1 plus the number 3 is the number of the register to be tested. If that register contains zero, the jump occurs to label L, otherwise the contents are decreased by one. For the SETZ instruction, it seems best not to use indexing. The problem with universal indexing is that it is difficult to get started: how can any register be addressed, if the contents of none is known? Address calculations would always then have one unpredictable element. By retaining (for example)

$$\text{SETZ} \quad 3$$

as simply clearing register 3 (no indexing), the initialization problem is short-circuited. The SETZ is not strictly necessary for computing functions, since as for register machines, the definition will assume that all registers other than the input/output register start out containing zero, but the tie to real assembly languages where the loading and memory initialization are less predictable is weakened unless we program as if registers had to be cleared before use.

The indexed machine can be formally defined by examining the register-machine definition of Section 7.2, and adjusting it to handle the expanded memory. A register machine is a 6-tuple (S,L,i,m,e,s) of register names S, instruction labels L, a preferred i/o register i, transition mapping m, and exit and start labels e and s. For the indexed machine, S has been replaced by the natural numbers, but L remains unchanged, as do i, e, and s (although now i is just a natural number). The transition mapping now involves two register addresses: first the base and second the index, in addition to the operation code and next-instruction label(s). An instantaneous description is now required to include an element of varying size—the contents of the registers which the program has "used" in its computation, so must be something like a pair (D,j) in which D is a finite set of ordered pairs of integers, the first element being a register address, and the second its contents. (The cardinality of this set grows as the program runs and register-contents pairs are added to D. It is assumed that registers whose names do not appear in D have contents zero, and the INC instruction may cause D to expand.) Finally, the yield operation, for example in INC 3(1), authorizes an instantaneous description with register-contents set $\{(0,c_0),(1,c_1),\ldots,(k,c_k)\}$ in which the $k+1$ registers $0,1,\ldots,k$ have respective contents $c_0,c_1,\ldots,c_k$ to yield the instantaneous description with register-contents set $\{(0,c_0),(1,c_1),\ldots,(3+c_1,c_{3+c_1}+1),\ldots,(k,c_k)\}$.

Definition

A *random-access machine* (RAM) is a 5-tuple (L,i,m,e,s) where L is a nonempty set of *instruction labels*, $i \in \mathbb{N}$ is the *input/output location*, $e, s \in L$ are the *exit* and *start labels*, and

$$m: L - \{e\} \to ((\mathbb{N} \times \mathbb{N} \times ((\{+\} \cup L)) \cup \mathbb{N} \times \{°\})) \times L$$

is the *transition function*. An *instantaneous description* of a RAM is a pair (D,j) where D is a finite set of pairs of natural numbers, each pair a *location* and its *contents*. No two distinct pairs of D have the same first element. Finally, $j \in L$ is the *current instruction label*. The instantaneous description $X = (D_X, j)$ *yields* instantaneous description $Y = (D_Y, t)$ on the RAM iff one of the following obtains:

1. $m(j) = (a, °, t)$ and one of:
$$(a, 0) \in D_Y$$
$$(a, -) \notin D_Y$$

("$(a,-) \notin D_Y$" is an abbreviation for "no pair in D_Y has a as first element.")

2. $m(j) = (a,x,+,t)$ and one of:

$(x,y) \in D_X$	and	$(a+y,b) \in D_X$	and	$(a+y,b+1) \in D_Y$,
$(x,y) \in D_X$	and	$(a+y,-) \notin D_X$	and	$(a+y,1) \in D_Y$,
$(x,-) \notin D_X$	and	$(a,b) \in D_X$	and	$(a,b+1) \in D_Y$,
$(x,-) \notin D_X$	and	$(a,-) \notin D_X$	and	$(a,1) \in D_Y$.

3. $m(j) = (a,x,n,t)$ and one of:

$(x,y) \in D_X$	and	$(a+y,b) \in D_X$	and	$b \neq 0$
	and	$(a+y,b-1) \in D_Y$,		
$(x,-) \notin D_X$	and	$(a,b) \in D_X$	and	$b \neq 0$
	and	$(a,b-1) \in D_Y$.		

4. $m(j) = (a,x,t,n)$ and $D_X = D_Y$ and one of:

$(x,y) \in D_X$	and	$(a+y,b) \in D_X$	and	$b = 0$,
$(x,y) \in D_X$	and	$(a+y,-) \notin D_X$,		
$(x,-) \notin D_X$	and	$(a,b) \in D_X$	and	$b = 0$,
$(x,-) \notin D_X$	and	$(a,-) \notin D_X$.		

A *numerical computation on argument x with value y* is a finite sequence of instantaneous descriptions, each yielding the next. The first instantaneous description has the start label as current instruction and the i/o register contains x, all other registers containing zero. (The instantaneous description $(\{(i,x)\},s)$ satisfies these conditions, but other registers may appear if they contain zero.) The last instantaneous description of the sequence is at the exit label and its register-contents set contains (i,y). A RAM *computes* a partial function ϕ iff for each x: if ϕ is defined at x, then there is a numerical computation on argument x with value $\phi(x)$; if there is a numerical computation on argument x with value y, then $\phi(x) = y$. ∎

The new feature which should be evident in this definition is the way in which the instantaneous descriptions handle the finite number of registers which are of interest at any instant of a computation, yet permit the number of registers which may be used to be unlimited: the yield operation adds to the set of register-contents pairs as locations with nonzero contents appear. (In the first part of the definition, why is the range of the transition mapping so complex?)

The RAMs defined have no limit on the size of the natural numbers which can be stored in each location, but by observing a limitation on location capacity one can model the way a finite-word-size computer is required to operate when large numbers are involved. We provide an example of part of an "extended arithmetic" package in which collections of locations represent a large number, each location containing a number of limited size. With the given instruction set, it is best to limit the word length to one bit, so that numbers are represented by consecutive locations each containing 1, as many locations as one more than the number stored, with a zero location at the end of the string. (Why do we use one more 1-containing location than the number represented?) The sample program is an "input routine" which creates such a data structure starting in location 13 from a number which is presumed to be in location 1, given in Fig. 9.1. (Why can't a SETZ be used to replace the instructions at LOOP and LOOP + 1? If the formal definition were applied to this example RAM with i/o register 1, start label START, and exit label STOP, what function does it compute?)

START:	SETZ 0	Initialize branching register.
	SETZ 2	Initialize index register.
	SETZ 13	Clear first location of the structure.
LOOP:	JZDEC 14(2), CLEAR	Clear the flag location at the end of
	JZDEC 0(0), LOOP	structure so far, by repeated decrement.
CLEAR:	INC 13(2)	Plant the next one in the structure.
	INC 2(0)	Bump the index.
	JZDEC 1(0), STOP	Quit if the input is exhausted, otherwise
	JZDEC 0(0), LOOP	proceed.
STOP:		Exit label.

Figure 9.1

No one doing (for example) data reduction, sorting, or symbol-table processing would question the value of index registers, not only for program running speed, but even in simplifying the programming effort itself. We can see an example of this in the programs of Section 7.3 simulating Turing machines. That task is much easier on a RAM than on a register machine. Recall that the reason for simulation was to prove that all partial recursive functions could be computed by the register machine. It is enough to simulate only Turing machines which compute their functions positively, since all partial recursive functions have such Turing programs. To simulate a Turing program, use the ideas of Section 7.3 but with a different data structure. Place the simulated tape one symbol per register in the unbounded set 5, 6, 7, . . . (saving 0 through 3 for other work), and keep track of the scanned square with the contents of register 4. This will eliminate the need for the multiply and divide macros, and speed up the running of the simulator greatly. (Does such a simulating RAM compute any interesting function?)

We would not need the simulation of a Turing machine using indexing to show that RAMs can compute all partial recursive functions, since a RAM can do anything a register machine can do, by simply not using indexing. (As we have defined the machine, it must do that by always using an index register containing zero.) To go the other way, to show that all RAM-computed functions are partial recursive, we could use Church's thesis. If the "infinite memory" seems to cast doubt on the effectiveness of RAM operations, note that in each actual computation only a finite amount can be used, since to address arbitrarily large registers requires first the storage of the address in the indexing register. For those who must do a simulation to be sure of Church's thesis arguments, perhaps the easiest path is to simulate a RAM with a Turing machine carrying the registers in code on its tape. The simulation can also be carried out with register machines; it is outlined here.

A simulating register machine must keep track of the RAM memory, and perhaps the most straightforward way is with a pair of unlimited registers, one for the addresses, and one for their contents, maintained by techniques used in tag sorting (the addresses are the tags). The idea also has roots in the list-structure treatment of sparse matrices, since only the nonzero (used) registers of the RAM are coded. For concreteness, suppose that the address register is A1 and the contents register is A2 in a register machine simulating a RAM. We use the "binary" coding in which k is coded as $2^k - 1$, and the spacer between numbers is 0. Then, for example, if the RAM used registers 2, 3, 6 with contents 5, 1, 2 respectively, the register machine would have in its registers:

$$A1: \quad 11111101111011_2$$
$$A2: \quad 110101111_2$$

The algorithm for simulating a RAM instruction with address $n(m)$ then has the following steps:

1. Look up the contents of register m in A2 (it is zero if m itself is not in A1). Add the value obtained to n to form the address actually required.
2. Look up the contents of the register whose address was calculated in step 1. Further action depends on the operation being simulated:
   a. If JZDEC, simulate the jump if the step 1 address was not in A1; otherwise decrement the corresponding contents in A2. Should the result be zero, delete the corresponding address from A1.
   b. If SETZ, do nothing if address not in A1; otherwise delete address from A1 and corresponding value from A2.
   c. If INC, insert the address if it was not in A1, and place a corresponding 1 in A2; if it was in A1, add one to the contents in A2.

The involved part of this algorithm is the operations of searching, inserting, and deleting in A1 and A2. An appeal to Church's thesis should now seem very reasonable.

Each time we expend theoretical effort on a model it seems necessary to question its worth. Perhaps this is a hangover from programming, where in the process of coding it is important to be ready to scrap the plan that is being implemented if the details go bad, and start over to eliminate the design flaws. The question that must be asked about the RAM (and the same one later for the RASP) is whether or not it is much of a step beyond the register machine. Indeed it is a little closer to existing digital computers, but is the theoretical complication of the idea worth it? Considering only computation of the partial recursive functions, no. The register machines can always manage. What then is the theoretical excuse for the RAM? The answer is that the RAM is a good model to study the speed with which computations can be performed, because unlike the Turing machine and the register machine, it does not need to spend most of its time in bookkeeping. This topic of the "complexity" of computations is a modern successor to the 1930's problem of what is computable, and is touched on in Chapter 10.

9.3 RANDOM-ACCESS STORED-PROGRAM MACHINES (RASPs). PROGRAM MODIFICATION

In both the register machine and the RAM, there is a clear distinction between the program of the machine and the data on which the instructions of the program operate. It was von Neumann's idea that if the program were to be placed with the data, in a suitable coded form, it would extend the power of the machine. (It is generally believed that the ability to modify a stored program is equivalent to existence of index registers to adjust addressing. Indeed, in the study of complexity which we introduce in Chapter 10, a proof that the two schemes are equally good can be given for a somewhat extended RAM.) There are many decisions to be made about what the numerical representation of the stored program will be, most only a matter of taste or formal convenience. In real computers, such decisions are part of the "system architecture," and may have important economic consequences in that an unfortunate hardware design choice may be expensive or unreliable, or may adversely influence the design of software (making it expensive or unreliable). That computer architecture is an art is proved by the observation that most designs are poor; there are many artists, but only a few have talent.

When we described register machines and RAMs (and Turing machines, for that matter) we encouraged a confusion between the machine and its program. In each case a component of the definition was a transition function which determined the actions of the machine for a given input. Intuitive symbolization of the transition function described the programs which were our main interest. This viewpoint is really a hangover from the discussion of finite machines, where the mechanical device being modeled is an actual physical unit, and to perform different actions, one really does get a new device. The partial-recursive-function-computing "machines" can also be viewed this way—Turing machines, register machines, and RAMs can all be thought of as having the program (transition function) wired in—but such an interpretation does not match well with practical digital computers in which the machine is unchanging, and programs come and go. In the stored-program machine, we can no longer be sloppy about the hardware/software distinction, which is both a virtue and a failing of the model. It gets at the way digital computer hardware

9.3 Random-Access Stored-Program Machines (RASPs). Program Modification 159

really works, but, as we shall see, it requires programs with almost no syntactic structure, so that information about programming languages does not naturally enter the discussion. To further compound confusion, when formal stored-program devices were first defined, the definition permitted the "hardware" part to have a range of actions. This is analogous to real machines in which microcode is used to implement the gross instructions which a programmer sees, but the additional formal complexity is considerable. Our stored-program devices therefore use fixed "hardware." We proceed to the "system architecture."

There is no question but that a stored-program machine must have an unlimited memory, and be capable of reaching arbitrarily large portions of it with one program. Since address modification alone permits this reach with a fixed-length program, we can choose not to permit indexing. Further, there will be no immediate instructions, and no indirect addressing. All of these features could be incorporated in the model without any difficulty other than the complication of detail. (It is worth noting that if indexing were included it might be best done through a single register, for much the same reason that a single accumulator is used.) Perhaps the most difficult question to answer is whether or not the program for a machine is restricted to a finite portion of the memory. Our choice will be to avoid the restriction, because such a bound is not useful in allocating a fixed-size "address field" for jump instructions unless it limits all programs ever to be written, and because one technique for gaining extreme execution speed at the cost of storage is the generation during execution of massive straight-line programs which would not be permitted if there were a fixed bound. Finally, we choose to have some instructions which are strictly unnecessary, but which simplify programming, particularly address modification.

Informally, our stored-program machine has an unlimited set of memory locations ("registers" is a less common name), named by their addresses $0, 1, 2, \ldots$ each of which can contain an arbitrary natural number as contents. Two special registers exist in addition to the memory, the accumulator AC and the program counter PC. These also have no content limitation. The PC controls the use of a stored program, since it indicates a memory location whose contents are to be obeyed as an instruction. For this purpose the value stored in the location is to be thought of as a decimal nonnegative integer, the rightmost digit of which is the "operation code", and the rest of the integer (that is, the value divided by 10) as the "address". Representing the associated location as x, and using "()" to mean "contents of", the operation codes are shown in Table 9.1.

In addition, each operation increases (PC) by 1 just before the other actions are taken. Thus if PC is set to a location containing code, the instructions will be executed sequentially, barring surprises caused by JUN and JAZ instructions, or unexpected changes in instructions caused by themselves or others.

Table 9.1

Operation Code	Mnemonic	Description
0	HLT	Terminate the operation of the RASP.
1	LOD x	Place (x) in AC, destroying previous contents.
2	LAD x	Place the address part of (x), that is, $(x)/10$, in AC, destroying previous contents.
3	STO x	Place (AC) in memory location x, destroying the previous contents.
4	STA x	Place (AC) in the address part of x, destroying that part, but leaving the op code part unchanged.
5	JUN x	Place x in PC, destroying previous contents.
6	JAZ x	If (AC) is zero, JUN x; otherwise no action.
7	ADD x	Replace (AC) by (AC) + (x).
8	SUB x	Replace (AC) by (AC) $\dot{-}$ (x).
9	-	Not used; HLT until hardware is modified.

There is probably no need to belabor the intuitive details of the model; except for the operation codes at the right (required by the arbitrary-size addresses) and the absence of many details, the machine is like the 700/7000-series computers which IBM used to make large-scale scientific computing common. We belabor the details of the formal definition instead. We might try to adapt the register-machine definition as we did for the RAM in Section 9.2. We could substitute AC for the special input/output register, eliminate the exit label because there is a HLT instruction, and agree to initially set PC to zero so that a start label is unnecessary. If we agree not to mention AC and PC, a formal transition function would be

$$m: \mathbb{N} \to \{0, 1, \ldots, 8\} \times \mathbb{N},$$

the domain representing current locations whose (instruction) contents are indicated by the range of an operation code and affected memory location. Such a definition does caputre the idea of a RASP before it begins its computation. But once instructions begin to be executed, the "program" may no longer be described by the function m, if PC is set to a location which has been modified previously. It is not a very good formal description of a program to call it a "changing function", nor is it particularly good to call its initial configuration a function at all, since it may have almost nothing to do with later operations. Formally, a program appears to have almost no syntactic structure: it is a finite sequence of natural numbers $i_0, i_1, \ldots, i_k$ presumed to be associated with locations $0, \ldots, k$ as contents. This lack of structure is characteristic of the model, since programs cannot have restrictions if they are permitted to modify themselves. What would happen if the modifications did not follow the rules?

9.3 Random-Access Stored-Program Machines (RASPs). Program Modification

Instantaneous descriptions for stored-program machines are not so different from those of register machines, except that it is not a fixed program which authorizes a "step" of execution, but part of the instantaneous description itself. The state of the machine is specified by a triple in which the contents of AC and PC are the first two elements, followed by a set of address-contents pairs as for a RAM. The instantaneous description

$$(a,p,\{\ldots,(p,10q + 7),\ldots\})$$

therefore not only tells that the machine is executing its current instruction at location p, but also includes that instruction (an **ADD**), and therefore yields $(a + (q), p + 1, \{\ldots\})$. Similarly

$$(a,p,\{\ldots,(p,10q + 5),\ldots\})$$

is executing a **JUN**, and yields $(a,q,\{\ldots\})$, while

$$(a,p,\{\ldots,(p,10q + 4),\ldots,(q,x),\ldots\})$$

is a **STA**, and if the remainder on dividing x by 10 is x', yields

$$(a, p + 1, \{\ldots,(q, 10a + x'),\ldots\}).$$

A computation by a program $i_0, \ldots, i_k$ begins with $(i, 0, \{(0, i_0), \ldots, (k, i_k)\})$ and ends when PC indicates a **HLT**. Functions are computed by assuming input in AC at the beginning, and output there at the end. For example, the program consisting of zero alone computes the identity function; perhaps it should be written

$$\textbf{HLT}$$

instead. For the zero function, on the other hand, we might use something like

$$\textbf{STO 20}$$
$$\textbf{SUB 20}$$
$$\textbf{HLT}$$

which is the sequence 203,208,0. (Evidently the 20 is arbitrary, any other number but 1 or 2 would do.)

Definition

A *random-access stored-program machine* (RASP) is a set of *operation codes* $\{0, \ldots, 9\}$ (informally we write the mnemonics **HLT**, **LOD**, etc. given above), and a *transition mapping*

$$t: \mathbb{N} \times \mathbb{N} \times 2^{\mathbb{N} \times \mathbb{N}} \to \mathbb{N} \times \mathbb{N} \times 2^{\mathbb{N} \times \mathbb{N}}$$

(defined below). A triple (a,p,D) of the domain or range of t is an *instantaneous description* (or *processor state*) of the RASP, in which $a \in \mathbb{N}$ is the *contents of the accumulator*, $p \in \mathbb{N}$ is the *contents of the program counter*, and the finite $D \subseteq 2^{\mathbb{N} \times \mathbb{N}}$ is the *memory*, a pair $(r,v) \in D$ specifying the *contents* (or *value*) v of *location* (or *address*) r. No two pairs in D have the same first element. The transition mapping is defined as follows:

$t(a,p,D)$ is undefined if $(p,i) \in D$ has i mod $10 = 0$ or $= 9$ or no location in D is p. (The RASP executes a HLT; it *halts*.)

$t(a,p,D) = (v,p+1,D)$ if $(p,i) \in D$ has i mod $10 = 1$ and $i \div 10 = q$ and either $(q,v) \in D$ or no location in D is q and $v = 0$. (The RASP *executes a* LOD; it *loads v into the accumulator*.)

(Definitions of the LAD and STO operations are omitted.)

$t(a,p,D) = (a,p+1,D')$ if $(p,i) \in D$ has i mod $10 = 4$ and $i \div 10 = q$ and $(q,(a \div 10) \cdot 10 + (u \bmod 10)) \in D'$ where either $(q,u) \in D$, or no location in D is q and $u = 0$. (The RASP executes a STA.)

$t(a,p,D) = (a,q,D)$ if $(p,i) \in D$ has i mod $10 = 5$ and $i \div 10 = q$. (The RASP *executes a* JUN; it *branches* or *jumps* to q.)

(Definitions of the JAZ, ADD, and SUB operations are omitted.) ∎

The transition function corresponds to our earlier definitions of the yield operation. However, note that the RASP does not judge what it finds (or fails to find) in its memory; every case is provided for, and one instruction after another is executed until a HLT is encountered, or the "illegal operation code" 9. The definition would be adequate to test the hardware of a RASP, although of course in practice that might prove impossible, since the number of cases covered by the definition is not finite (corresponding to the possibilities for memory sets). Next the software:

Definition

A RASP *program* is a pair (P,s) where $P = i_0, i_1, \ldots, i_k$ is a finite sequence of natural numbers (the *instructions*, P is also loosely called the program), and $s \in \mathbb{N}$, $0 \leq s \leq k$ is the *starting address*. ∎

It remains to permit the software to run on the hardware, and to say what is accomplished thereby:

Definition

A *numerical computation on input x with value y* by the RASP program (P,s) is a finite sequence of instantaneous descriptions $(a_0,p_0,D_0), \ldots, (a_k,p_k,D_k)$ such that $a_0 = x$, $p_0 = s$, $a_k = y$, and the RASP executes a HLT in the final instantaneous description, but does not halt inside the sequence. The instructions of the

9.3 Random-Access Stored-Program Machines (RASPs). Program Modification

	JUN OVER	Skip over three locations of data.
ONE:	LOD 0	(really constant 1)
I:	HLT	(really temporary location)
T:	HLT	(ditto).
OVER:	LAD L	Pick up the address to be modified.
	STO I	Save for later restore.
	ADD 13	Compute new address
	STA L	and put it where it will be used.
L:	LOD 5	Get the old data.
	ADD ONE	INC in the AC.
	STO T	Save temporarily, while AC is busy.
	LOD I	Reclaim original address
	STA L	and restore it.
	LAD S	Begin the address modification again.
	STO I	
	ADD 13	
	STA S	Completed.
	LOD T	Get back the data loaded from 5(13), after INC.
S:	STO 5	Put it back in 5(13).
	LOD I	Fix
	STA S	address.

Figure 9.2

program are initially in consecutive memory locations; that is, if $P = i_0, \ldots, i_n$, then for some $r \geq 0$, $\{(r, i_0), \ldots, (r + n, i_n)\} \subseteq D_0$. The program *computes* a partial function iff it performs a proper numerical computation with the correct value just in case the function is defined. ∎

The definitions make it apparent that even though there is a good distinction between hardware and software in the RASP and its programs, the software part is not very interesting because it has so little structure. The hardware can literally run any program, so that all programming blunders are detected only at the semantic level when the program fails to work. The proper function of syntax—catching typing errors and things the programmer could not have meant—is missing.

Again, we are now in a position to carry out the proof that RASP programs compute exactly the partial recursive functions, a position we will again fail to exploit. As usual, the most interesting part of the proof would be the opportunity it provides to simulate another model with a RASP. It gives an indication why index registers and program modification can be similarly used to indicate how a RASP program could replace a RAM. Consider the fragment of RAM program

INC 5(13)

in which one is added to memory location 5 + (13), to confuse two notations which do not conflict. The RASP program fragment of Fig. 9.2, if placed far away from actual locations 5 and 13, does the simulation of the RAM instruction INC 5(13). "Far away" from 5 and 13 means that the RASP program itself must not lie in these locations, nor in location 5 + (13). This can be arranged by off-setting all the RAM addresses below the complete simulating RASP program, although it was not done in the example. If this seems too many RASP instructions to simulate just one RAM instruction, part of the rules for comparing diverse computing systems is that any constant factor is immaterial. Here this means that if the RASP hardware happened to operate 18 times as fast as that of the RAM, the two would be equally good at indexing.

We have presented only the barest outline of the RAM and RASP models, largely as an exercise in formalization. A glimpse of their usefulness appears in Section 10.3.

EXERCISES

9.1 Modify the formal definition of a RAM (Section 9.2) so that no zero registers ever appear in the set of register-contents pairs. In the definition, what corresponds to a Turing machine adding blanks at the ends of its tape?

9.2 Many computers with index registers have optional "index modification". When an index register is used, the instruction may specify that after use its value is automatically changed. (This is useful in moving down tables, for example.) Suppose that a RAM instruction of the form

$$\text{INC } 5(13\&)$$

indicated adding one to register 13 after it had been used to index register 5, but before adding to the resulting address. Indicate the necessary modifications in the formal definition of a RAM to incorporate this idea.

9.3 In assembly-language form specify a RAM program which does output conversion on the one-bit-word data structures of the example of Section 9.2. Construct a program to add the numbers represented by two such structures and place the answer in the same form. Combine the input routine, your adder, and your output routine to create a program which computes $\lambda x[2x]$ (in a very difficult way, but using one-bit registers to handle arbitrary inputs).

9.4 Using the divide and multiply macros of Section 7.1 and 7.3, implement the algorithms outlined in Section 9.2 for simulating a RAM with a register machine.

9.5 Consider a Turing program, a register program, and a RASP program, each designed to recognize $\{0^n 1^n | n \geq 0\}$ (a Turing program is given in Section 4.2). Make a rough count of how many "steps" are used by each program to accept $0^{10}1^{10}$ using any straightforward algorithm. What fraction of these would you call "bookkeeping" in each case?

9.6 Fill in the gaps in the formal definition of a RASP of Section 9.3. According to the definition, does the size of the memory set ever decrease?

9.7 Most computers permit some kind of "immediate" instructions in which data for the instruction, instead of being in a memory location which the instruction addresses, are stored in the address portion of the instruction location itself. Suppose that a RASP instruction of the form

$$\text{ADDI } x$$

instead of adding the contents of location x to AC, added x itself. Indicate the necessary modifications in the formal definition of a RASP to incorporate this idea for all appropriate instructions.

9.8 "Indirect addressing" (to one level) for a RASP might be indicated by instructions like

$$\text{JUN @}x$$

which instead of placing x in PC placed (x) in PC, and

$$\text{STO @}x$$

instead of storing AC in location x, stored it into location (x). Make necessary modifications in the definition of a RASP to incorporate this idea.

9.9 Imagine a RASP which has immediate instructions (Exercise 9.7), indirect addressing (Exercise 9.8), and also index registers. Specify the yield operation which describes some meaning for something like

$$\text{ADDI @}23(7).$$

9.10 Write a RASP none of whose instructions is actually obeyed except the one in location zero, yet which contains no jump instructions.

9.11 Explain why forcing a syntax structure on a RASP which requires labels to be properly placed and used (as for a register machine) is not useful.

9.12 Prove that the problem of whether or not an arbitrary RAM has a bound on the number of locations it will ever reference for an arbitrary input is unsolvable. Prove that the problem of whether or not an arbitrary RASP program will ever cause an arbitrary instruction to be executed for arbitrary input is unsolvable. (Assume the unsolvability of some standard problem for these languages.)

9.13 Consider how a RAM might simulate a RASP within a constant time factor. Can it be done if the RAM does not possess better add and subtract operators?

REFERENCES

The RAM model is due to Cook [25], whose machines usually do not follow register machines as closely as here. The RASP presentation is based on Hartmanis [26], but the formal treatment is less general than the original of Elgot and Robinson [27].

10
BEYOND THE PARTIAL RECURSIVE FUNCTIONS

10.1 PROGRAM COMPLEXITY

Church's thesis that the intuitively algorithmic functions are exactly the partial recursive functions can never be formally established, but the evidence of many diverse notions of "intuitively computable" leading to the same class is convincing. There is one sense in which Church's thesis is too easy to support: subclasses of the partial recursive functions based on computing power are difficult to define. The situation is that from the most rudimentary computing devices the full class of partial recursive functions results. It is possible to capture the primitive recursive functions in a natural programming language, and other "subrecursive" languages exist. But mathematically it would have been much more interesting if there were some nice measure of power built into the intuitive devices which gave an infinite hierarchy of classes of functions computed. For example, it would be interesting if register machines had been able to compute more functions using more registers. One feels that there is something lacking in a theory which makes no distinction between (say) ALGOL 60 and the Turing language, since both are examples of acceptable numberings of the partial recursive functions.

One way to reopen the questions about computability is to add a qualification—to consider not what can be computed at all, but rather what can be computed under some artificial, imposed limitation. The right sort of limitation would lead to the kind of detailed substructure that the mathematician believes is essential to understanding. It should also lead to practical results, if the limitations imposed on a program reflect real digital computer limitations. The most obvious such qualification to computability is that of "run time", which translates formally into the count of the number of steps in a formal computation. Another limitation measure is the "storage" used by a program, but this idea is not quite as good as run time, partly because it occurs differently in each formalism (tape used for Turing programs, registers for a RAM, etc.), and partly because while run time is always unbounded when a sequence of instantaneous descriptions has no end, the storage used need not be. (How can this happen for a Turing machine? A register machine?)

The name used for the quantity of time or storage a program needs is "complexity". The idea is a semantic one, and does not refer to the difficulty of recognizing syntax (except when parsers are the programs investigated). In the study of complexity there is still an interest in the partial recursive function computed by a program, but the semantics also includes something about the time required to compute it at various arguments. This suggests that complexity theory might be extended to some sort of "algorithm" theory, in which semantics was made still stronger to include something of the "way" in which the program computed its function. This would permit study of compiler "faithfulness," for example, and of "patentability" of programs, in the abstract setting where the myriad of details is stripped away.

Complexity can be studied in two ways: parallel to detailed arithmetization, and through its abstraction. In the former, a particular computing model is assigned a measure of its programs' computing time, for example, the number of yield operations involved in a computation. Using full details of the model, this measure is studied. The abstract approach starts with an abstract programming language, and defines the program complexity as a second semantic function associated with each program, substituting a few general properties of this function for the lost detail.

10.2 ABSTRACT PROGRAM COMPLEXITY

In this chapter we can give only a hint of the developing complexity theory. It is therefore appropriate to present topics in the reverse historical order of abstract approach before concrete. It is a virtue of abstractions that when only a little can be said, they often say it best.

The basis of the abstract approach is that the semantic T-predicates contain more information that the contents of the final tape (input/output register, etc.). A recursive function is able to pick the value computed from the complete computation, but another recursive function could extract the number of steps of the computation—the "run time". (And the full computation must somehow include the formal equivalent of "way" of computing, to which we return in Section 10.4.) Thus in exactly the way we defined the function φ_p for Turing program p in Section 4.10, we could have defined a different function (say) Φ_p at inputs for which a computation takes place (the program eventually halts), to count the number of yield operations involved. This function is an additional piece of semantics assigned to a program, based on the syntax as the function computed is. There is one crucial difference between the semantic ranges $\{\varphi_p\}$ and $\{\Phi_p\}$ for all programs p of a language. In neither case can we predict in general the outcome for a given program and a given input—that is, given arbitrary p and x there is no effective means of deciding whether a computation will ensue, and hence no means of similarly finding its value or run time. The same situation holds with respect to the problem: given arbitrary p and x and y, to decide if $\varphi_p(x) = y$. Giving a proposed value helps not at all in solving the halting problem. But for the run time it is another matter. Given p, x, y, there is an algorithm for deciding if $\Phi_p(x) = y$. Namely, begin the computation of φ_p at input x, and count the number of yield operations. When the count reaches y, stop and see if the sequence of $y + 1$ instantaneous descriptions is in fact a computation (that is, if it terminates correctly), and if so, $\Phi_p(x) = y$, otherwise not.

It turns out that the two properties of the discussion in the previous paragraph are good ones to assume in an abstraction: first, for any program p, that the number-of-steps function Φ_p is defined exactly where the function computed φ_p is defined; second, that deciding if the step count is a given value for a given input is a mechanical problem.

Definition

An abstract programming language *with complexity* is a triple (L, φ, Φ) where (L, φ) is an abstract programming language with interpretation and composition, and the *measure function* Φ maps L into the partial recursive functions (of one argument), the image of $p \in L$ being written Φ_p. The measure function has the following properties:

1. For all $p \in L$, the domain of φ_p is the same as the domain of Φ_p.
2. $\{(p, x, y) | p \in L \text{ and } \Phi_p(x) = y\}$ has a recursive characteristic function. ∎

To indicate the scope and character of the abstract theory we state two theorems without proof. The first is something like the translation theorem of Section 8.4 in that it concerns compilers, and is an "obvious" result, surprising only because it is obtained from such abstract hypotheses.

Theorem

For any source language with interpretation and composition (L, φ) and any object language with complexity (M, ψ, Ψ) and any compiler T between them, corresponding to any object program $i \in M$ there is a source program $j \in L$ such that $\varphi_j = \psi_i$ but $\Psi_i < \Psi_{T(j)}$ whenever these are defined. ∎

The paraphrase of the theorem is that any compiler botches certain programs in comparison to any object program chosen. It is obvious in that it follows from the inability of the compiler to recognize all programs for a given function, and thus to ignore atrocious coding in the source language. For some truly awful source program the compiler cannot see the forest for the trees, and performs a faithful translation, thus creating an inferior object program. The theorem certainly does not assert anything about the superiority of "high-level" or "low-level" languages, since it does not specify in which direction the compilation takes place.

The second theorem is deeper, and is one of the triumphs of the abstract theory, for it presents information unsuspected by most programmers.

Theorem (Speed-up)

For any abstract programming language with complexity (L,φ,Φ) there is a total recursive function f such that given any program $p \in L$ for f, f has another program $q \in L$ such that $\Phi_q(x) < \Phi_p(x)$ for all but a finite number of inputs x. ∎

The paraphrase is that there are functions which have no best program in the sense of least run time. The exception of a finite number of input values is essential, since in most languages there is a fastest way to compute any function for a finite input set, usually involving some form of table lookup. On that set there is no hope of improving the run time. Note that the theorem does not assert that all programs can be speeded up, nor that some program for any function may be speeded up. The unusual object it proves to exist is a function which is a programmer's nightmare—no matter how well he does with it, there is a better way. (It is perhaps some consolation that a better way cannot be mechanically found: no recursive function exists to create the faster program from the slower; this is also a deep result.)

10.3 CONCRETE PROGRAM COMPLEXITY

The important part of the abstract approach to program complexity is isolation of the "machine-independent" (meaning "programming-language-independent") ideas and their consequences. However much the intuitive work relies on T-predicates and details of programming, one must always be careful that what he does follows from the abstract properties. The concrete approach instead selects a language, defines it carefully, and pursues detailed investigations of program complexity with no holds barred. The first such work used Turing machines, and forced consideration of theories in which a machine could use several tapes at the same time. Multitape Turing machines are quite efficient computers, since the burden of copying and marking is eliminated by availability of "scratch" tapes. A more recent theory uses a RAM or a RASP as the basic machine model, because these correspond closely to existing digital computers, and because algorithms for such machines can be written in "natural" ways, without bookkeeping which is not intuitively essential. (Perhaps the ability to write natural programs explains why most digital computers are like RAM/RASPs; however, this argument would lead to computers with high-level machine languages, and these are not often built despite some evidence that they can and should be.)

10.3 Concrete Program Complexity

A RAM with more instructions than those of Section 9.2 is perhaps the best model of a modern von Neumann digital computer. For its "steps" to be like those of a real machine, the RAM must have arithmetic beyond adding 1 to a register, and this is most generally done by using two-address instructions, which may use both addresses to get data for the operation, but store the results at only one address. Index modifications may be applied only to one address. This set of decisions outlines a machine whose memory is entirely composed of general-purpose registers of unlimited size. Associated with each instruction is its execution time. To make the model reflect actual computers whose locations are not of unlimited size, execution times vary with the size of numbers contained in the locations. The appropriate measure is roughly the logarithm to the base of the largest one-location number for machines which are memory-cycle limited. We leave the base unspecified, and write $\lg[x]$ for $\log(x + 1)$, with value zero for argument zero. "(x)" is the contents of register x. Table 10.1 specifies the RAM in the usual computer-manual fashion.

Table 10.1

Instruction	Execution time	Action
SET r,n	$\lg[n]$	Place the natural number n in register r (note: immediate-type instruction, no indexing).
STO $r,n(x)$	$\lg[(x)] + \lg[n]$ $+ \lg[(r)]$	Calculate an address by adding the contents of register x to the base address n, then store the contents of register r there.
ADD $r,n(x)$	$\lg[(x)] + \lg[n]$ $+ \lg[(n+(x))]$ $+ \lg[(r)]$	Calculate an address by adding the contents of register x to the base address n, then add the contents of that calculated address to the contents of register r, result in register r.
SUB $r,n(x)$	(Same as ADD)	Similar to ADD, but using proper subtraction: $(r) \leftarrow (r) \dotminus (n+(x))$.
JZ $L,n(x)$	$\lg[(x)] + \lg[n]$	Calculate the indexed address, and if its content is zero, continue at label L.

The SET instruction allows easy initialization of registers without having to worry about indexing. The more general STO permits information to be moved from any place in memory to any other (although a sequence such as

    SET 3,0
    ADD 3,$n(x)$
    STO 3,$m(y)$

must be used to move $(n(x))$ to $m(y)$.) **ADD** and **SUB** provide the arithmetic power which almost all computers have (with the proper expense based on memory cycle time as the limiting factor). **JZ** serves as an unconditional branch as well as a test and branch, by the familiar trick of using a test location which has been set to zero.

The execution times require some justification. The model distinguishes between a "register" of the assembly language, and the implementation of that register in hardware where information can be accessed only at a fixed rate. The language registers have no storage size limitation, but real information is delivered from fixed-word-length memory, with delivery time proportional to the number of words actually required for the information. Thus the **STO** instruction requires that the contents of its index register be added to the fixed base address, and the sizes of these numbers count. Then the contents of a register must be moved, another expense. Of the other instructions, only **JZ** may seem too cheap: we do not count **JZ** $L,n(x)$ as

$$\lg[(x)] + \lg[n] + \lg[(n + (x))]$$

because in the zero test we can arrange the information which is actually examined in such a way that only the most significant word need be delivered to make the decision.

The careful formal definition of a RAM given in Section 9.2 applies to these augmented RAMs, with only straightforward changes in the yield operation. (For example, the old **SETZ** and the new **SET** are very similar; the new **JZ** is the same as part of the old **JZDEC**; etc.) With this machinery we can define a precise limitation on the way partial recursive functions will be computed by the new RAMs:

Definition

The *run time* $R(x)$ of a RAM program which performs a computation on input x whose k steps (yield operations) are justified by instructions with respective execution times $t_1,\ldots,t_k$ is

$$R(x) = \sum_{i=1}^{k} t_i.$$

If the program performs no computation on input x, then $R(x)$ is undefined. Now let f and T be recursive functions of one argument. A RAM program *computes f in time T* iff it computes f, and there are constants k_1 and k_2 such that for each input x,

$$R(x) \leq k_1 T(x) + k_2. \blacksquare$$

For a given input, the execution times of instructions of a program are complicated functions of the input, since those times depend on the contents of various registers used, and those in turn depend on the input and previous instructions' actions. The linear adjustment to the time function ensures that no constant factors in instruction timings will influence what can be computed in that time. Instruction timings (to a constant factor) are a matter of taste in formal theory, and a matter of technology in digital computers; both change, but without changing results based on this definition.

The following theorem stated without proof shows that time-bounded RAM computations define complexity classes of recursive functions with a fine structure.

Theorem

Given any recursive T_2 which is computable by some RAM in its own time and such that $T_2(x) > x \lg[x]$ for each x, there is a recursive g such that g is computed by a RAM in time T_2, but for any recursive T_1 such that

$$\liminf_{n\to\infty} \frac{T_1(n)}{T_2(n)} = 0,$$

no RAM computes g in time T_1. ∎

The ratio of time functions with limit zero is a way of asserting that the bound in the numerator is more stringent than that in the denominator for sufficiently large inputs. Thus for a given time bound there are functions which require at least that much time to compute, and a series of growing bounds defines a sequence of functions harder and harder to compute. For example, the bounds $\lambda x[x^n]$ for $n \geq 2$ give such a sequence.

10.4 FORMAL COMPUTATIONS

Much of the "theory of computing" presented in the preceeding sections is really a "theory of partial recursive functions." This is not to say that we have penetrated very far into the part of mathematics with that name, but rather to indicate that the emphasis was placed on what was being computed (the function) instead of on the specification for the computation (the program). In discussing the algorithmically computable functions it is necessary to mention the algorithms, but only in passing. We cannot in fact give a definition of "algorithm" which is intuitively satisfactory. It would be precise to define each program of a language as an algorithm, but would fail to capture the intuition that many programs might use the same algorithm. It is incorrect to take all programs of a language computing the same function as an algorithm because there are intuitively many algorithms for each function. The intuition which must be captured is that an algorithm is a "way" of computing something, and is therefore related to the computation performed by a program. This approach does not answer all objections; for example, because computations in different languages are different, it fails to allow algorithms spanning many languages. Still, it seems a good possibility for a formal theory of programming.

For the Turing language, the T-predicate contains more information than was extracted for either the function computed or the complexity measure. In fact, the full computation as a semantic range might be appropriate. To a program p we could assign as semantics the function $\lambda x[\,\mu y[t_1(p,x,y) = 0]\,]$, that is, the computations by p (if any). If we write this "semantic computation function" for program p as C_p, much as we used φ_p and Φ_p, we have implied a language-independent idea. In words, we even appear to have captured such an idea. C_p is the function whose value is the full sequence of instantaneous descriptions which constitutes a computation on any input (if there is one—otherwise C_p is undefined). But the words hide the fact that in different languages the computations are very different, since they necessarily involve the details of the particular language (tapes, registers, accumulator, program counter, etc.). It is not at all obvious what "properties" should be taken to replace all this detail in an "abstract computation." Nevertheless, we can use C_p as if it were defined, and fall back on the Turing language for which we have full details should they become important.

We reconsider some of the questions answered for the function computed by a program, as instead applied to the computation of a program.

Some questions make no sense without adequate abstract definition for "computation." For example, we cannot discuss a "faithful" compiler until we can assert that it preserves the computation of the source program as well as the function computed. This is exactly what we may not do because of the different details. How might a Turing-to-RAM compiler preserve a sequence involving tapes, scanned squares, and states in one involving registers and current instructions, for example? There is an obvious connection, but its statement is peculiar to this pair of languages, and does not define "faithful" in general.

Other ideas are not really different for computations and functions computed. An interpreter exists for computations as well as functions computed, and in fact our Turing interpreter worked by producing the computation, then extracting the computed value from it. It is certainly true that enumeration and parametrization are not sufficient to authorize interpreting computations, but the former could be replaced with a "computation-enumeration" property.

Finally, some ideas are different. The computation-function semantics which assigns C_p as the meaning of program p is like that of a complexity measure in that $\{(p,x,y) | C_p(x) = y\}$ is recursive, for the same reason: one can examine steps which might make up the desired computation, and has a bound at which to give up when it does not terminate. The set $\{p | C_p = C_{p_0}\}$ might be said to be a good candidate for defining "algorithm," since it is the set of programs which have a fixed computation—all compute in exactly the way

p_0 does. (Most programmers would call the conception too narrow, but it is better than many attempts.) The corresponding set for functions computed is not only not recursive, but not even r.e. Strangely enough, whether or not $\{p | C_p = C_{p_0}\}$ is recursive depends on the program p_0 whose computations are to be duplicated. One way of stating this result uses the "patentability" of program p_0. If the set of programs with the same computations is recursive, then there is an effective infringement test if what is protected by patent are the computations. On the other hand, if the set of programs is not recursive, a patent attempt would involve disputing Church's thesis in court. It probably is in the spirit of the United States Patent Law to permit a computation patent if an infringement test exists, although a recent Supreme Court decision denies program patentability.

To see why $\{p | C_p = C_{p_0}\}$ may be either recursive or nonrecursive, we can give a relatively machine-independent argument. Consider programs computing the function which is identity except for a failure of definition at input zero. The ALGOL 60 procedure

integer procedure u(n); value n; integer n;
u := if n = 0 then u(0) else n

specifies computations of roughly: "test argument for zero and return it" for nonzero inputs. At zero, no computation results because of the nonterminating recursive procedure designation. This program is not patentable in the sense that the set of programs with the same computations is not recursive (in fact, it is not r.e.). The difficulty is that in the computations no information is provided about actions at input zero. Any statements could be inserted in the **then**-clause without changing the computation, so long as they do not yield a value. By suitable use of an interpreter program, one could insert as **then**-clause an instance of the question "Is $\varphi_z(z)$ defined?" for any particular ALGOL program z. The resulting program may or may not have the computations we seek to patent. If it does, then in fact $\varphi_z(z)$ is undefined; if it does not, it is because $\varphi_z(z)$ is defined. Thus the patentability of one program provides a membership test for the nonrecursive set K, showing that the given computations are not patentable.

On the other hand, the computations of

integer procedure u(n); value n; integer n; u := n

are exactly: "return argument" for all inputs. The function computed is recursive, there is a definite computation for all inputs, and there is no way to insert the general halting problem without altering the existing computation. (Furthermore, the proper test statements cannot possibly already exist in a program for a recursive function, because some instances of the halting problem involve nondefinition.) Thus all programs for recursive functions have patentable computations. But the dichotomy is not so simple, as another program for the almost-identity function shows. The idea of

integer procedure u(n); value n; integer n; u := n ↑ 2/n

(if the compiler does not optimize it away) is that for every argument but zero, the multiplication and division cancel each other; at zero some sort of fault occurs, and there is no computation. But we cannot insert the halting-problem code—any attempt to create an explicit test for zero will alter the computation at other inputs. The program's computations are patentable, since it is certainly effective to see if a computation is "return square of the argument divided by the argument."

EXERCISES

10.1 For an abstract programming language with complexity (L, φ, Φ) prove that there is a recursive function B such that $\Phi_p = \varphi_{B(p)}$ for all $p \in L$. What does this imply about the existence of a "complexity interpreter" for L?

10.2 Imagine a "two-tape Turing machine" which can move and write the tapes independently. (That is, the transition function includes two move/print outputs, and depends on a state and two scanned symbols.) Give the algorithm by which such a machine might accept the set $\{0^n 1^n \mid n \geq 0\}$ much more efficiently than the one-tape machine of Section 4.2.

10.3 What is the run time of the RAM program in Fig. 10.1 whose i/o register is 1, start label **START**, and exit label **STOP**:

```
START:    SET   0,0           Initialize useful register.
          SET   5,1           Another.
          SET   2,0           Trial value initialized.
   TRY:   STO   2,4(0)        Save original trial value.
          STO   2,3(0)        Again, to count with.
SQUARE:   JZ    TIRED,3(0)    Counter exhausted?
          ADD   2,4(0)        No. Increase 2 by original contents.
          SUB   3,5(0)           Bump down counter,
          JZ    SQUARE,0(0)      and loop.
 TIRED:   SUB   2,1(0)        (Here 2 contains trial square.) Deduct input.
          JZ    PAST,2(0)     Gone too far?
          SET   2,1           No. Restore trial value,
          ADD   2,4(0)           plus 1,
          JZ    TRY,0(0)         and go around again.
  PAST:   SET   1,0           Place previous trial value
          ADD   1,4(0)           in output register
          SUB   1,5(0)           and quit.
  STOP:
```

Figure 10.1

What function does this program compute? Does it do so in time $\lambda x[x^2]$?

10.4 Assign some intuitively correct execution times to the RASP instructions described in Section 9.3. (Be careful about "charging" for the PC and addressing overhead.) State a theorem that a RASP is just as efficient a computing device as the RAM of Section 10.3, using the concept of computation time-bounds.

10.5 Might a reasonable programming language have just one program for each computation? (See Section 8.5.)

10.6 Consider two Turing programs with Gödel numbers as shown:

p_1: i b b q_0 p_2: i b R q_0
      i 1 b f (same
      q_0 b R q_0 as
      q_0 1 L f p_1)

Prove that $\{p | C_p = C_{p_i}\}$ is recursive for $i = 1$, but nonrecursive for $i = 2$.

10.7 The RAM program with i/o register 1, starting at MARCH, exit label HALT, viewed as a program of an abstract language with computation-function semantics

     MARCH: SET   0,0
     DIE: JZ   DIE,1(0)
     HALT:

computes the identity function, except at zero. Show that this program's computations are not patentable in the sense of Section 10.4. Is there a RAM program for the same function whose computations are patentable?

10.8 Is a program which happens to be a compiler likely to be patentable in the sense of Section 10.4?

REFERENCES

The abstract approach to complexity is largely due to M. Blum; the two theorems of Section 10.2 are special cases of ones in the basic papers [28,29]. The first paper also includes an abstract theory of program size. Hartmanis and Hopcroft [30] is a recent summary of abstract complexity. The RAM of Section 10.3 is adapted from Cook and Reckhow [31], where the theorem of that section also appears. The Turing-language form of the material on formal computations appears in Hamlet [20], where the proofs of assertions about patentability may be found, as well as an attempt to begin a machine-independent theory of computations.

SOLUTIONS AND HINTS FOR EXERCISES

CHAPTER 1

1.2 Unlimited storage must be used in interpreting $[P](P)$, because there is no bound on the storage used by all programs P of the language.

1.4 In the imprecise intuitive form this exercise is difficult. Exercise 3.11 defines a better way to relate ALGOL 60 to formal computing, using procedures and their arguments instead of "instring." Chapter 8 provides the formal tools for a careful analysis, and Exercise 8.8 asks the question again. At the present level, one must hit on the right property that "any reasonable language" must have, then exploit it. That property is the ability to examine any two programs of the language, and from their syntax alone, create another program (syntax) which acts as the first two do in composition, that is, as if the output of one were fed to the other as input. ALGOL 60 has this property, and so do other existing languages, but the given modification to ALGOL 60 does not have it. Suppose it did. Here is a method for discovering if an arbitrary program P does or does not have output when given its own source string as input:

> Consider two programs. First, the one which always gives **P** as output:
> **if** instring = 'TEST' **then** outstring('P')
> **else begin** outstring('P') **end**

Second, P itself. Now since the supposed language permits construction of a program for any two programs acting in sequence, the second on the output of the first, perform this construction with these two programs, using P second. The composite program, on input **TEST**, thereby does $[P](P)$. But because the composite program is in the language, it must have the "test input" property, and by examing its syntax immediately following the required first phrase "**if** instring = 'TEST' **then**" the decision about output can be made: if the next word is **outstring** then the original P did have output on input **P**; if the next word is **for** then it did not.

This method can be implemented with a program, and that program is the forbidden T of Section 1.5. Therefore the supposed language cannot have both the "test input" property and the ability to mechanically compose programs.

Part of the justification for any reasonable language to have the latter property is that it is essential in combining independently written modules of a large program.

CHAPTER 2

2.1 The state diagram is

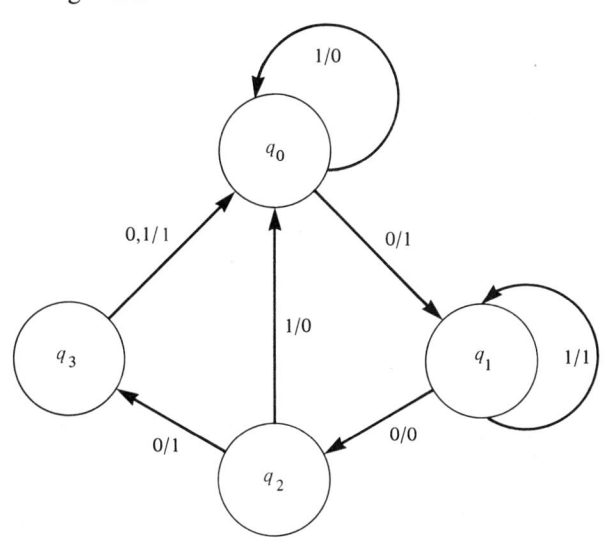

2.3 Two symbols σ_1 and σ_2 are output equivalent iff for any two strings of the input alphabet x and z, $\hat{\omega}(q,x\sigma_1 z) = \hat{\omega}(q,x\sigma_2 z)$ for all states q. In fact, there is a bound on the length of strings that must be so considered (why, and what is it?). It is difficult to frame the definition in terms of the state transition function δ, unless the machine is first converted to one with a minimum number of states (Section 2.12). If that has been done, then symbols are output equivalent iff

$$\omega(q,\sigma_1) = \omega(q,\sigma_2) \quad \text{and} \quad \delta(q,\sigma_1) = \delta(q,\sigma_2)$$

for all the states q of the reduced machine. (Why isn't the latter definition the same as the first given when the machine has not been minimized?)

2.7 It is easy to write a finite acceptor which accepts just one-digit constants, and one for numbers under seven digits can be constructed by properly stringing six such machines together. Intuitions that the thing cannot be done are perhaps based on inability to do it in a concise, revealing way; one may then not think of the pedestrian approach.

2.8 The transducer $(\Sigma, Q, \{Y, N\}, \delta, \omega, q_0)$ *accepts* a set $S \subseteq \Sigma^*$ iff for each $x \in S$, $\omega(q_0,x) = zY$ for some $z \in \{Y,N\}^*$, and $\omega(q_0,x) = yN$ for some $y \in \{Y,N\}^*$ for each $x \notin S$. Suppose given any acceptor $A = (Q,\Sigma,\delta,q_0,F)$ accepting L, which does not contain Λ. Then $T = (\Sigma, Q, \{Y,N\}, \delta, \omega, q_0)$, where $\omega(q,\sigma)$ is Y if $\delta(q,\sigma) \in F$, otherwise is N, accepts L also, since it mimics the transitions of A exactly, and arranges its outputs to correspond to the final states correctly.

2.12 A proof about equality of sets described by a regular expression is like any proof about set equality: it proceeds by assuming an element is in one set, then showing that it is in the other, then the reverse. $S(\Lambda)$ is not defined, since in our treatment "Λ" is not defined as a regular expression. (Many definitions do include both "Λ" and "$\emptyset$" as regular expressions.)

2.13 (a)·(a)★; (a)★·(b)★; ((a)·(a))★; $\emptyset$★.

2.14 The only way in which the null string may enter is in a Kleene closure. However, care must be taken not to eliminate it from both members of a set product simultaneously. The following algorithm is expressed in an ALGOL-60-like language which applies to expressions, and includes as a basic operation the ability to isolate the "main connective" in an expression as part of its test for equality:

expression procedure bar (R); value R; expression R;
bar: = **if** $R = E_1$ v E_2 **then** bar (E_1) v bar (E_2) **else**
  if $R = E_1 \cdot E_2$ **then** bar $(E_1) \cdot E_2$ v $E_1 \cdot$ bar (E_2) **else**
  if $R = E$★ **then** bar $(E) \cdot E$★ **else** R

2.17 Given L accepted by $M = (Q, \Sigma, \delta, q_0, F)$, construct M' to accept L^R using:

q'_0 a new state not in Q, take $Q' = Q \cup \{q'_0\}$.
F' be $\{q_0\}$ if $\Lambda \notin L$, otherwise $\{q_0, q'_0\}$.
For each $\sigma \in \Sigma$, $q \in Q$, take

$$q \in \delta'(q'_0, \sigma) \quad \text{iff} \quad \delta(q,\sigma) \in F,$$

and

$$q \in \delta'(q', \sigma) \quad \text{iff} \quad \delta(q,\sigma) = q' \; [q' \neq q'_0].$$

2.19 The algorithm is roughly to first output a zero no matter what input is seen, then copy the input in a "one-bit-delayed" fashion. The insight to be gained is that multiplication by a fixed constant is not beyond the finite machine, since it can remember up to any length (here one bit) by using its internal states; but it cannot remember an arbitrary length, hence the multiplicand and multiplier may not both be inputs whose length is arbitrary.

2.21 One cannot permit the nondeterministic transducer to try many output sequences, and then assert that it has computed some function if any one of them was correct. There must be some equivalent of the final/nonfinal state to distinguish the good computations from the bad. A convenient way to do this is to insist that the transducer output some kind of "certification symbol" at the end of a computation that should be accepted, and that there be only one output string so ending for each input. With such a convention, the power is no different than that of a deterministic transducer. The nondeterministic transducer is not a very useful idea.

2.22 The proof that multiplication cannot be computed is essentially that any fssm has a longest string of ones it can output in one step, yet to multiply $n \cdot m$ requires $n \cdot m$ ones to result from only $n+m+1$ transitions; there exist pairs of numbers too large for the longest string of any fssm to compensate for the discrepancy between the product and the sum.

CHAPTER 3

3.1 $Z_n = \lambda x_1 \ldots \lambda x_n [Z(U_1^n(x_1,\ldots,x_n))]$ (Base functions Z, U_1^n; composition.)

(The justifications will be omitted; they are easy.)

$P = \lambda x \lambda y \lambda z [S(U_3^3(x,y,z))]$,
$p = \lambda x \lambda y [U_1^1(x) \text{ if } y = 0, \quad P(x,y-1,p(x,y-1)) \text{ if } y > 0]$,
$M = \lambda x \lambda y \lambda z [p(U_1^3(x,y,z), U_3^3(x,y,z))]$,
$m = \lambda x \lambda y [Z(x) \text{ if } y = 0, \quad M(x,y-1,m(x,y-1)) \text{ if } y > 0]$,
$c = \lambda x [S(Z(x))]$,
$T = \lambda x \lambda y \lambda z [S(U_2^3(x,y,z))]$,
$G = \lambda x \lambda y \lambda z [m(T(x,y,z), U_3^3(x,y,z))]$,
$F = \lambda x \lambda y [c(x) \text{ if } y = 0, \quad G(x,y-1,F(x,y-1)) \text{ if } y > 0]$,
$f = \lambda x [F(U_1^1(x), U_1^1(x))]$.

3.2 In a slightly abbreviated form,

$$f' = \lambda x \lambda y [c_n(x) \text{ if } y = 0,$$
$$g(S(U_2^3(x,y-1,f'(x,y-1))), U_3^3(x,y-1,f'(x,y-1))) \text{ if } y > 0]$$

is primitive recursive. Then

$$f(x) = f'(x,x)$$

is primitive recursive by an explicit transformation. This f is the required function because f' was constructed to ignore its first argument and follow the definition of f otherwise.

3.3 Although a primitive recursion is the most obvious way to proceed, the following illustrates some nice tricks:

$$f = \lambda x [(1 \dotdiv x) \cdot g(x) + (1 \dotdiv (1 \dotdiv x)) \cdot h(x)].$$

3.7 f mu-recursive $\Rightarrow$ f nu-recursive by induction on the length of any derivation for f.

Case 1. f's derivation has a single line:

f must then be a base function, and since these are common to the mu- and nu-classes, f is nu- if it is mu-recursive.

Case. 2. f mu-recursive $\Rightarrow f$ nu-recursive for all derivation lengths less than n, $\Rightarrow f$ mu-recursive with derivation length $n \Rightarrow f$ nu-recursive.

Since the base functions and closure operations are common to the two classes, the only possible problem occurs when there is a restricted minimalization in the derivation of f. But if so, the function minimalized has an embedded derivation shorter than n, and is hence nu-recursive, say $g(\mathbf{x},y)$. (Write $\mathbf{x}$ for $x_1,\ldots,x_n$.) Define the relation

$$R = \{(\mathbf{x},y)|g(\mathbf{x},y) = 0\}$$

with characteristic function $X_R(\mathbf{x},y) = 1 \dot{-} g(\mathbf{x},y)$, which is nu-recursive since proper subtraction and g are.

3.8 The function is Z in disguise under the given assumptions. Without them the formula is nonsense, since the function minimalized the second time may not be total.

3.9 The first line must be a base function; the second cannot employ primitive recursion or composition since these require two component functions to have been previously defined (if the first line defines a 1-ary function it could be composed with itself). The second line can always employ minimalization of the first-line function. The projection base U_m^n has two parameters, so the derivation starting with a projection is schematic, and there are really denumerably many derivations. Programmers might not be very happy with restrictions on the form of their identifiers, which is the analogy to standardized variables in derivations. However, some languages do restrict the choice, notably BASIC, in which identifiers can only be a letter, or in some cases a letter followed by a digit.

3.10 Primitive recursion is tricky to use when matters of nondefinition are at stake, because it is easy to make a mistake which makes the function everywhere undefined. Instead,

$$\psi = \lambda x[c_{13}(\mu y[(1 \dot{-} y) + (y \dot{-} x) + (x \dot{-} 1) = 0])]$$

will do.

3.11 The base functions are easy—the procedure bodies are all a single line. Composition is a matter of declaring the procedures to be composed inside another which composes them for its value. Primitive recursion is illustrated by **fact** listed in Section 3.2. Minimalization uses a **for** loop which saves its index and exits when the proper condition is met. Actual ALGOL implementations fall short of really computing composition, minimalization, the successor function, or even projections, because variable values are stored in memory words of a bounded length. Primitive recursion is not actually available because there is a restriction on the number of times a procedure may invoke itself before there is a "stack overflow" in the storage allotted to saving return information. The Burroughs B5000/6000 machines have a machine language which is closely related to ALGOL, but subject to both kinds of difficulties. The SYMBOL machine built by Fairchild (and not, alas, in commercial production) does better for its ALGOL-like language: it has a virtual memory which makes it appear that numbers have unlimited size, and stacks arbitrary depth. The ultimate limit is the fixed size of the paging drum and the address field of the instruction words, but there are other rotating storage devices with expandable recording surfaces, and different schemes of addressing which might have been used. ALGOL might be thought to be too powerful because it has many more constructions than strictly needed for computing partial recursive functions, and it might be true that a wider class of functions is computed. This is not so, but most of Chapter 4 is devoted to proving a similar result for an easier language.

3.13 The solutions indicated above are already in the correct form which specifies the derivation.

3.14 Although it is very unlikely, f need not be primitive recursive; "complete information" implies a procedure for obtaining the value of f, which would necessarily make it total recursive. (There are non-partial-recursive functions, but they are believed to be intuitively uncomputable.)

CHAPTER 4

4.2 If the simulator is to accept a string of symbols which represents a tape as input, and produce another such string as output, then it is only necessary to create from the input an initial instantaneous description, call YIELD repeatedly until it fails, then analyze the last instantaneous description returned to determine the cause. If it is a bad symbol on the tape, a message is appropriate. Otherwise, the failure must be the result of the machine entering its final state, and the last instantaneous description can be converted into the tape form for output.

4.5 So long as the alphabets are of the same size, whatever a machine can do with one alphabet can be done by some machine using the other alphabet, but with a code correspondence agreed upon between the alphabet characters. When one alphabet is larger, the same thing applies to machines using the larger alphabet. Those machines using the smaller alphabet can use a code in which groups of symbols represent single symbols, and so make up the size discrepancy. There must be at least two symbols in the smaller alphabet so that one can serve as delimiter for groups of the other.

4.10 $\Psi_A^1 = S.$ $\Psi_A^2 = \lambda x \lambda y [S(x) \text{ if } y = 0; \ x + y \text{ if } y > 0].$

4.13 The function corresponding to the bounded universal quantification $\forall y \leq x_i [F(x_1,\ldots,x_n,y)]$ where f corresponds to the predicate F is

$$\lambda x_1 \ldots \lambda x_n [f(x_1,\ldots,x_n,0) + \mu y \leq x_i [1 \dotminus f(x_1,\ldots,x_n,y) = 0]].$$

The first term is required to avoid a confusion if $F(x_1,\ldots,x_n,0)$ happens to fail.

4.14 In Chapter 5 an unsolvable problem will be displayed which minimization of Turing acceptors would solve. The construction fails because the equivalence groupings cannot be defined as they were for finite acceptors. The difference between a Turing acceptor and a finite acceptor is the former's ability to keep making transitions without ever repeating an instantaneous description exactly. It can do this by creating a constantly changing (hence expanding) pattern on the tape. One can never be sure that a computation is going wrong, but neither can it be seen that the machine will ever halt.

4.16 There are twin programs, since each machine has an f state, which can be placed last, and then replaced by i to form the twin, since the numbers are 4 and 5. For example,

$$i\ b\ b\ f\quad i\ 1\ b\ f$$

has the twin

$$i\ b\ b\ f\quad i\ 1\ b\ i.$$

However, this will not always work, since elimination of the final f may make the quadruples a non-Turing machine (containing no f). For similar reasons, use of the state q_0 (value 6) often fails.

4.22 For $y = /f/bb$, $C(y,0)$ holds, but there are no x, z such that $COMP_1(z,x,y,0)$ holds.
$x = 0$, $y = /i/bbb\sqcup/f/bbb$, $u = 0$,
$\quad z = i\sqcup b\sqcup b\sqcup f\sqcup\sqcup i\sqcup 1\sqcup b\sqcup f.$

For $y = /f/bb$, $U(y) = 0$, but there is no $COMP_1(z,x,y,0)$.

4.25 The denumerable number of derivations results from various imprecisions in the proof of the Kleene normal-form theorem: we have not been careful to pick a preferred set of state names for each machine or to standardize the variable and function names in the derivations. A more subtle problem is that we permit repetition of quadruples in machines, forbidding only inconsistencies. These points can be repaired. Derivations not in the Kleen normal form are never assigned.

4.26 Such an error has no effect whatsoever if the least computation is still the intended one; however, if the smaller is unintentional, the formal work will come up with the wrong function. Uniqueness is just a nice way of seeing that this does not happen.

4.27 The argument of Section 3.5 shows that d is not primitive recursive, yet it is apparent that there is a computation procedure for d (given there). This makes it partial recursive, and since the procedure defines it everywhere, d is total, hence recursive.

4.28 The definitions give the class containments directly; since each is a special case of the next, given any function which meets the more specialized definition, it certainly meets the more general.

All that is required is to prove $P' \subseteq P$. Suppose that we are given any member of P'. The proof presented in Section 4.5 for its Turing computability holds. The only case of possible difficulty is in the machine which implements closure under minimalization. But examination of that machine shows that all it needs is the kind of "up to the answer" definition which is guaranteed by P', so it continues to work. But Turing computable is partial recursive (P) by Section 4.10.

The proof fails because the closure machine fails. It can certainly happen that a function is undefined at argument values before its definition. Attempting to minimalize such a function with the machine of Section 4.5 will not correctly compute the function, since the machine will loop computing at earlier arguments, and never reach the "least argument" where the function is defined. As a concrete example, the function built from Exercise 3.10,

$$\lambda x[\mu y[\psi(y) \dotdiv x = 0]] \qquad (P''\mu)$$

will be incorrectly computed at argument 13—its value should be 1, but our Turing machine will compute a function which is undefined.

The logical position here should not require the explanation that we know the proof must fail if we know that the containment $P' \subset P''$ is strict. We do *not* know that the containment is strict just because one proof fails. In fact, the containment is strict (as one might guess if he does a psychological analysis of the fairness of assigning this exercise).

4.29 The middle-of-the-road answer is $n!$ for n quadruples (because of rearrangements), but other answers which could be defended are: 1 and denumerably many. There is no question but that there are denumerably many machines for each function. An interesting group of machines is those which have exactly the same computation, or the same computation except for a renaming of states.

4.33 A good candidate for G is a proper S-1-1-ing of the enumeration program: $\lambda t[S_1^1(e,t)]$. However, the inequality is not automatic. To gain it, one must be sure that S_1^1 is larger than its second argument; that is, the program it creates must always have a larger Gödel number than the program being assimilated. The trick for accomplishing this is called "padding." Quadruples can always be added to any machine which do not alter the function it computes, but only make it execute some harmless steps (or no steps at all—the states cannot be reached). The S_1^1 function can be made to create such extra quadruples in its programs, but it still remains to show that it can do so in such a way that $S_1^1(e,t) > t$. Trial and error provides the solution: in computing S_1^1, if the

Gödel number of the result is too small, pad the result until it is not. (Why must the number assinged to a padded program eventually grow as large as may be required?)

CHAPTER 5

5.5 The "procedure" is not really effective, since it cites a possibly non-terminating process, with an "otherwise" which can never be used. But finite sets are recursive.

5.6 Examine the P.c.s. in the proof of the theorem in Section 5.3.

5.7 Simulating this program can only prove one theorem in the set restricted to alphabet {1}, but of course lots of other theorems result along the way in the larger alphabet, and many proofs exist because any input may be generated to start the computation.

5.8 The limitation on the language results from the "straight-line" nature of the statements. With only finitely many chances to modify a string, things like multiplication are impossible.

5.9 (After K. Vonnegut, Jr., *Cat's Cradle*, Holt, Rinehart and Winston, New York, 1963.) The partial recursive functions come in with a grand ah-whoom (hence the language name). Even those who do not have SNOBOL as the wampeter of their karass can guess that the language has test and branch features. As to why ICE9CHIP could not compute more than the partial recursive functions, to do so would create a granfalloon of number-theoretic functions, and make foma of Church's thesis.

5.11 Both parts yield to the technique illustrated in the proof of Section 5.5 that T is not recursive. Compose two functions, and make the outer one the constant function n. It is also instructive to try the technique used to prove the first theorem in Section 5.6, but more difficult.

5.12 If the set of pairs of programs computing the same function were recursive, membership in K could be decided as follows: given z, compute the pair $(C(c,C(z,c)),c)$, where C is the syntactic composition function and c is any program for the constant function c_z; $z \in K$ iff the computed pair is in the given set.

Suppose the given set of triples were recursive, with characteristic function X. Then $\omega = \lambda x[X(x,x,0)]$ would also be recursive, and have a Turing program, say w, $\omega = \varphi_w$. But $\varphi_w(w)$ is 0 iff it is 1, impossible.

5.15 The set is not complete.

5.17 A line like the second case in this definition is thoroughly noneffective, since to apply it requires knowing that φ_x is not defined at x, which one can hardly learn by starting to compute. Thus Church's thesis cannot be used to prove X partial recursive as needed for the theorem.

CHAPTER 6

6.1 See Section 8.3.

6.2 Trial and error applied to an exhaustive search procedure is not hard to program in ALGOL, but is not the best algorithm.

6.3 See Section 8.3.

6.5 $\sqrt{2} - 1 = 0.414\ldots$ is in the proper range, and irrational by a proof dating back to Pythagoras. The following ALGOL 60 procedure computes its generator in the sense of Exercise 3.11.

```
integer procedure Oxen(d); value d; integer d;
   begin
   integer temp, i;
   if d = 0 then Oxen := 4
   else
      begin
      temp := 1 × 10 ↑ (d + 1);
      for i := 0 step 1 until d − 1 do
         temp := temp + Oxen(i) × 10 ↑ (d − i);
      for i := 0 step 1 until 10 do
         if (temp + i) ↑ 2 > 2 × 10 ↑ (2 × (d + 1))then go to exit;
exit: Oxen := i − 1
      end
   end
```

CHAPTER 7

7.2 The only failure possibility is an unending loop ended by a **JZDEC** on a register which is zero, and unchanged in the loop. If the register convention is changed, then computations which were proper may become improper, so the function for a given machine may suddenly go undefined at some points.

7.3 An oracle machine can compute a non-partial-recursive function using a non-r.e. oracle set, but all it is doing is translating one undecidability into another, not contrary to Church's thesis.

7.5 The syntax errors will cause trouble, but the semantic problems will have no effect until the compiled program runs, at which time things will foul up just as they would have in the source language. Thus another syntax-semantics distinction can be made as follows: syntax is what a compiler must know about in order to preserve semantics. Misspelled words would cause problems in the part of the compiler not described in Section 7.4, the part that parses the source string and isolates the individual instructions to be translated. The lack of an **END** line would cause the terminating code to be omitted, and then the Turing machine might not perform a numerical computation on some arguments where it should have done so. Never-placed labels will result in missing quadruples which are nonetheless called for in other quadruples. Duplicate labels will result in inconsistent quadruples specifying more than one response to a single state and scanned symbol. It is roughly correct to say that syntax errors will compile into syntax errors; the missing **END** is an exception.

7.8 Syntactic composition is not so difficult for register machines as for Turing machines. (It is difficult again for the RAM and RASP extensions of register machines described in Chapter 9. The difficulty of syntactic composition has to do with whether or not temporary storage can be obtained in a way that separates it from storage already used. For Turing machines one has difficulty finding tape that is guaranteed to be free, hence the necessity for a restricted "positive computation." Register machines each specify a finite collection of registers, and others are available for storage which is guaranteed not to be touched by the given machine. RAMs and RASPs can compute register addresses during execution, and again nothing is safe.) To construct a program for the composition function of the functions computed by two given register programs it is sufficient to simply place the programs one after the other, so that the output of the first, upon exit, becomes input to the second. Renaming of registers may be required, and relabeling of instructions, but the technical problems are not difficult, and the process is clearly mechanical.

7.10 The problem is solvable because of details of how a register machine works. The only way it can fail to perform a computation is to loop on a register whose contents of zero is not changed in the loop. In general one cannot tell about that "changed in the loop," since there can be considerable complications with other registers. However, all such complications themselves involve a change in a register's contents, and so need not be considered. A careful argument examines all types of instructions and shows that either the program executes in line, or loops in a detectable way, or changes a register to avoid doing so.

CHAPTER 8

8.2 Except for all the details about the predicates in Chapter 4, all of them.

8.3 Use the two given procedures nested in a procedure.

8.5 The interpreter has some sort of buffer into which it reads the program to be interpreted. A compiler can be provided with a version of the interpreter (in the object language) in which this buffer is large enough to contain whole programs. The compiler then compiles any source into the full code for the interpreter with the source program sitting in the buffer ready to interpret.

8.7 In a real computer system, an important distinction exists between programs that can be written in a language, and ones that actually have been written and seem to work. Only some compilers have actually been written in their own language. (Burroughs ALGOL compilers are probably the most successful present system.)

CHAPTER 9

9.2 First, the range of the transition function must be modified (in the part that handles indexed instructions, not SETZ) to include another set, say $\{\&, -\}$, which selects the decision about auto-increment ("&") or not ("−"). Then the yield must have all the new cases added to cover "&". These new cases all assert that when $m(j) = (\ldots, \&, \ldots)$ then the index register's contents in D_Y is one greater than its contents in D_X. There are the usual troubles with the possibility that the index register does or does not actually appear in D_X.

9.5 The RAM can be substantially faster than either of the other programs. It should copy the input a symbol at a time into registers, then use a pair of index registers to work its way in from the ends. The copy must only be done once, while the other machines must continue to run back and forth across the string.

9.9 Such instructions are most useful if the indexing takes place first, then the indirection, and finally the immediate nature of the instruction. In real computers it doesn't always happen that way, and by examining what does happen it is sometimes possible to determine that a machine was designed partly by (usually unlucky) accident. In the desirable order, ADDI @23(7) would: obtain the contents of location 7, add 23 to that number, then add the address portion of that location to the accumulator. Since addresses must often be manipulated in a RASP program, this kind of processing is heavily used. Things like ADDI 23(7) are also useful (what does this do according to your definition?).

9.10 If the first instruction is

STO 1

then subsequent actions depend on the initial content of AC, which is the assumed input. For input zero the program always halts at location 1. It is difficult to write a program which actually changes several instructions in order.

9.12 Both problems are unsolvable. The RASP problem is an easy reduction of the RASP program halting problem (take the given instruction to be a HLT). The RAM problem is more difficult, because the use of an unlimited number of registers is not the only way for a RAM to fail to perform a numerical computation. To eliminate the possibility of using arbitrary storage confined to a finite number of registers, consider only RAMs which never store more than some fixed number in a register. Such RAMs can fail to halt only by using an unlimited number of registers, or by looping in such a way that a finite pattern of register contents appears and can be detected.

CHAPTER 10

10.1 Use parametrization on a function related to the characteristic function of the set of triples (p,x,y) such that $\Phi_p(x) = y$. To interpret Φ_p, use the function interpreter on $B(p)$.

10.5 No. Such a language would encounter the same problem with the empty function (which has just one computation function, also empty) as does a language with only one program for each function.

10.6 The quadruple q_0 b R q_0 is the key to the difference. In p_1, this quadruple is always used to move over the first place on a tape encoding a number, and hence cannot be altered without changing p_1's computations. In p_2 it is not used unless the tape has a double blank, that is, a zero input, where there is no numerical computation. Thus in p_2 this quadruple enters no computations, and can be changed at will without changing the program's computation function, provided that the change still produces no numerical computation at input zero. This quadruple can therefore be altered to lead to a machine investigating the halting problem, and the problem solved on the basis of whether or not the computation remains unchanged, if the computations-the-same set were recursive.

10.8 The programs for recursive functions are always patentable in the sense of Section 10.5, so compilers should be. Of course, if the compiler includes a bug that causes it to loop for some input, then it may fail to be patentable.

REFERENCES

Books marked with a dagger (†) contain the most useful bibliographies.

1. J. B. Rosser, *Logic for Mathematicians*. McGraw-Hill, New York, 1953.
†2. H. Rogers, Jr., *Theory of Recursive Functions and Effective Computability*. McGraw-Hill, New York, 1967.
3. A. M. Turing, On Computable numbers, with an application to the Entscheidungsproblem. *Proceedings of the London Mathematical Society Ser. 2* **42** (1936), 230–265. (Reprinted in Davis [17].)
4. A. M. Turing, Computing machinery and intelligence. *Mind* **59** (n.s. 236, 1950), 433–460. (Reprinted in J. R. Newman, *The World of Mathematics*, as "Can a Machine Think?")
5. T. L. Booth, *Sequential Machines and Automata Theory*. Wiley, New York, 1967.
†6. J. E. Hopcroft and J. D. Ullman, *Formal Languages and Their Relation to Automata*. Addison-Wesley, Reading, Mass., 1969.
†7. A. Salomaa, *Theory of Automata*. Permagon, Oxford, 1969.
8. E. Landau, *Foundations of Analysis*. Chelsea, New York, 1960.
†9. E. Mendelson, *Introduction to Mathematical Logic*. D. Van Nostrand, Princeton, 1964.
†10. M. Davis, *Computability & Unsolvability*. McGraw-Hill, 1958.
11. A. R. Meyer and D. M. Ritchie, The complexity of loop programs. *Proceedings of the 22nd ACM National Conference*, Academic Press, London, 465–469.
12. R. W. Ritchie, Notes for C. Sci. 532, University of Washington, 1969.
13. S. C. Kleene, *Introduction to Metamathematics*. D. Van Nostrand, Princeton, 1952.
14. Burroughs Corporation. *B5500 Extended ALGOL Language Manual* (1028024). Detroit, 1966.
15. R. E. Stearns and P. M. Lewis, Property grammars and table machines. *Information and Control* **14** (1969), 524–549.
†16. M. L. Minsky, *Computation: Finite and Infinite Machines*. Prentice-Hall, Englewood Cliffs, N.J., 1967.
17. M. Davis, ed., *The Undecidable*. Raven, Hewlett, N.Y., 1965.
18. P. R. Young, Towards a theory of enumerations. *JACM* **16** (1969), 328–348.
19. H. G. Rice, On completely recursively enumerable classes and their key arrays. *JSL* **21** (1956), 304–308.
20. R. G. Hamlet, A patent problem for abstract programming languages: machine-independent computations. *Proceedings of the Fourth Annual ACM Symposium on Theory of Computing*, Denver, 1972, 193–197.

References

21. J. C. Shepherdson and H. E. Sturgis, Computability of recursive functions. *JACM* **10** (1963), 217–255.
22. H. Rogers, Jr., Gödel numberings of partial recursive functions. *JSL* **23** (1958), 331–341.
23. R. M. Friedberg, Three theorems on recursive enumeration. *JSL* **23** (1958), 309–316.
24. M. B. Pour-el, Gödel numberings vs. Friedberg numberings. *Proc. Am. Math. Soc.* **15** (1964), 252–256.
25. S. A. Cook, Linear time simulation of deterministic two-way pushdown automata. *Proceedings of IFIP Congress 71*, Foundations of Information Processing. North-Holland, Amsterdam, 1972, 75–80.
26. J. Hartmanis, Computational complexity of random access stored program machines. *Math. Sys. Theory* **5** (1971), 232–245.
27. C. C. Elgot and A. Robinson, Random-access stored program machines, an approach to programming languages. *JACM* **11** (1964), 365–399.
28. M. Blum, On the size of machines. *Information and Control* **11** (1967), 257–265.
29. M. Blum, A machine-independent theory of the complexity of recursive functions. *JACM* **14** (1967), 322–336.
30. J. Hartmanis and J. E. Hopcroft, An overview of the theory of computational complexity. *JACM* **18** (1971), 444–475.
31. S. A. Cook, and R. A. Reckhow, Time-bounded random access machines. *J. of Comp. and Sys. Sci.* **7** (1973), 354–375.

INDEX

An attempt has been made to cite only those pages on which the indexed item is an important topic, or might serve to locate a section mislaid. Page numbers in parentheses ( ) indicate an exercise (but only if there is something important there).

abstract computation 174
abstract programming language 145, 148–9, 168–9
acceptable numbering 146, 167
acceptance 20–2, 64, (103), (164)
accumulator 159, 162
adder 16–7, (102)
addition 47, 50
address field 159–60
address modification 152, 158, (165)
address 160, 162
ALGOL 60 6–7, 25, (42), 46, (57), 77, 84, (128), (150), 167
algorithm 168, 173
alphabet 14, 61, (102), 111
ambiguity 86
application 111
approximation 128
architecture 158–9
argument count 99, 123, 125
arithmetic trap 152
arithmetization 82, 144, (150)
assembly language 64, 130–1, 139, (141), 152–3
assignment statement 98
atrocious coding 169
axiom 111

base function 46
best program 170
binary code 135–6
black box 11
Blum, M. 177
bookkeeping 157, (165), 171

Booth, T. L. 44
bounded minimalization (103)
bounded quantification 85, 93, (103)
branch 162
Burroughs B5500 106

Cantor correspondence 95, 124
characteristic function 108
Church's thesis 55, 96–8, 108, (121), 140, 144, 167
   essential/inessential 97
clock pulse 11, 21
closure 46
   finite state languages 30
coding 82–3
compiler 133, 139–40, 147–8, (150–1), 169, (177)
   faithful 149, 168–9, 174
   self-compiling (150)
complete 119
complexity 157–8, 168
   abstract 169
   concrete 170
   interpreter (176)
component Turing machines 67, 75
composer 146
composition 46, 55, 71, 76
computable real number 128
computation 63, 132–3
   begins 63
   terminates 63
compute 65, 132, 155, 162
compute in time 172
concatenation 86–7, (104)

194 Index

constant (42)
  function 47
  substitution 49
contents 132, 154, 160
control card
  DEC PDP-10 (43)
  UNIVAC 1108 exec 8 (42)
Cook, S. A. 166, 177
copying 75
correctness 91
current state 61

data 158, (165)
Davis, M. 58, 106, 122
debugging 149
decimals 128
decimal arithmetic 130
declaration 88, 112
decomposition of machines 44
definition 131
design flaw 157
deterministic
  acceptance 22
  and nondeterministic acceptors 23, 26–7
  finite acceptor 22
diagonalization 51, 55, 95, 115
difficulty of compilation 149
digital computer 7, 11, 16, (57), 62, 67, 82, 130, 132, 152, 157–8, 167, 171
  multiplication 39
disk pack 131
division by two 52, (57), 136
double 131, 135
dovetail 109, 121

eccentric numerals 83
Elgot, C. C. 166
empty function 55, 121
empty string 14
enumeration 94, 144, 146
equivalence
  of deterministic and nondeterministic acceptors 26
  of finite state languages and regular sets 35
  problem for finite acceptors 39
error message 6
even numbers 108
execution time 171
existential quantifier 86
explicit transformation 48
exponentiation 49, 86

extend 112
extended transition function 15
extension 100, 112

factorial 46, (56)
Fermat's last theorem 51, (58)
finite acceptor 21–2
  examples 23–5
finite experiment 12
finite state string machine (43)
finite transducer 14, 18
  with start state 14
finite-state language 24, 28, 30, 35
  examples 24–5
flowchart 3
  universal 3
formalization 2, 13, 17, 131, 163
FORTRAN 5, 7, (42), 83, 88, 140
Friedberg numbering 149
Friedberg, R. M. 149, 151
function 46

general recursive function 52
generator 128, (128)
Gödel numbering 82, (143), 149
Gödel, K. 82
grammar 44

halt 162
halting problem 91, 115, 169
Hamlet, R. G. 122, 177
hardware/software distinction 159
Hartmanis, J. 166, 177
hierarchy 167, 173
Hopcroft, J. E. 44, 177

IBM 7090 160
ICECHIP (121)
ICE9CHIP (121)
identifier 25, 112
illegal operation 162
immediate instruction (165)
implementation language 82
index modification (164)
index register 130, 152–3, 158–9, 162, (164), 171
indexing 145
indigestion 132
indirect address (165)
infinite program 152
input grouping 12, 16, 18–9
input/output register 131–2

instantaneous description 61, 132, 155, 162
instruction 162
  labels 132, 155
  timings 171–2
intermediate storage 4, 167
  unlimited 5–6, 8, (9)
internal states 14, 19, 61
interpretation 146
interpreter 94, 146, 148–9, (150), 175, (176)
intuitively computable 96
irrational number 127, (128)
iterative programming 77–8

jump 162

K 115–9, 128
Kleene, S. C. 94, 106
Kleene closure 29, 33
Kleene normal form 59, 94, 96, 100
Kleene T-predicate 85, 90, 92, 144, 149, 169, 174

label 132, (142), (165–6)
  exit 132
  local 135, 138
  start 132
lambda notation 46
Landau, E. 58
language
  finite state 24, 27, 30, 35
  formal 44
  high level 7, 90, 144, 169, 171
  low level 63–4, 66, 80, 144, 169
  non-finite-state 36, 55, (164)
  non-procedural 63, 134
  regular 24
  subrecursive 167
  Turing 46, 60, 134, 139, (164), 167
length 14
list 109
loader 134, 154
location 155, 162
logic 110

machine-independent 170
macroinstruction 135–6, 152
marking 71
Mealy, G. H. 18
meaningfulness 91
measure function 169

memory 11, 18, 37, 152, 161
memory dump 82
memory location 160
Mendelson, E. 58, 151
Meyer, A. R. 58
microprogramming 152, 159
minimalization 55, (57), 78, 96, 100, (104)
  bounded 93, (103)
  restricted 52
  unrestricted 55
Minsky, M. L. 122, 129, 143
Moore, E. F. 18
  transducer 18–9, (41–2)
multiplication 4, 18, 38, 47, (103)
  by two 130

natural numbers 45, 108, 123
negation 86
nested parentheses 38
nondeterministic
  acceptance 23, 27
  finite acceptor 22
  finite transducer (43)
non-negative integers 45
non-recursive set 115, 119
non-recursively-enumerable set 116, 120
null string 15, 18
number (42)
numbering 145
number-theoretic function 45
numerical computation 65, 132, 155, 162

object-code semantics 140
object language 133, 147
one-bit words 155, (164)
operating system 131
operation code 152, 160, 162
optimization (142), 149
oracle (141)
output equivalence (42)

pairing function 124, (128), 133, 146–7
  inverse 124
parametrization 98, (105), 125, (142), 144, 146–7, (150)
partial recursive
  argument counts 125
  derivation 55, (57), 59, 79, 96
  function 46, 55, (57), 71, 74, 93, (105), 125, 134, 144, 173
  function enumeration 95
patentability (see program)

Index

peripheral equipment 134
plausibility argument 54–5
polynomial equations (129)
Poor Richard Turing machine 61–3
positional notation 128
positive computation 73, 79
Post canonical system 111
Post, E. L. 110, 113
Pour-el, M. B. 151
predicate 85
   function correspondence 86
preventive mathematics 44
priestly caste 7
primitive recursion 46, 55–6, 76
primitive recursive
   derivation 50–1
   derivation listing 51
   function 46–7, 50, (57), 167
procedure 2
   finite 2
   malfunction 4
   mechanical 5
processor state 162
production 111
program 5, 145
   modification 149
   patentability 168, 175, (177)
   self input 6
   self-modifying (9)
program counter 160–1
programmer's nightmare 170
programming language 55, 56, 59, 63, 80, 112, 116, 134, 144, 149, (176)
projection function 46, 70, 72
proof 110–2
proof preventive 70
proper subtraction 47
property 146, 174

quadruples 63, 87, 90
quality control 18

racial relations 24
RAM (see random-access machine)
random program 149
random-access machine 155, 157, 163, (164), (166), 171, (176–7)
random-access stored-program machine 161–2, (164–6), (176–7)
RASP (see random-access stored-program machine)
RASP program 162

rational number 127, (129)
real number 127
Reckhow, R. A. 177
recognition 21, 107–8
recursive
   derivation 53–4
   derivation listing 54
   function 52, (57), 95
   programming 77
   set 108, 119
recursively enumerable 108, 113
recursively listable 109
reduction 115–6
reference language 81
register 130, 132
register—contents set 154–6, 161, (164)
register machine 132, 134, 139, (141), 144, 149, 152, 156, (164)
regular
   expression 29
   language 24
   set 29–30, 35
relation (57)
remainder 135
reserved words 86, 89
reset button 11
Rice, H. G. 121–2
Rice's decision theorem 119, (121–2)
Ritchie, D. M. 58
Ritchie, R. W. 106
Robinson, A. 166
Rogers numbering 149
Rogers, H., Jr. 10, 106, 129, 148, 151
Rogers' translation theorem 148
Rosser, J. B. 10
royal road 133
run time 167, 169–70, 172

Salomaa, A. 44
scanned square 72
self-compiling compiler (150)
self-listing lister 6
semantic error 89
semantics 59, 63, 66, 81, 90, 100, 139, 144, 168–9, 174
   mapping 145
semi-infinite tape (102)
set 107
   non-recursive 115, 119
   non-recursively-enumerable 116, 120
set product 29, 32
shared code 153

Index

Shepherdson, J. C. 143
shifting 69, 72
six-digit constant (42)
slot machine 18
SNOBOL (101), 110, (121)
source language 132, 147
sparse matrix 156
special characters 45
speed-up 170
square root (176)
start state 14, 22
state diagram 15
step 109
straight-line program 158
string 14
string variable 111, (121)
Sturgis, H. E. 143
subrecursive (see language)
subroutine 67, 69, 80, 99
    Turing 75
successor function 46, 69, 71
symbol table 88–9, 91, 113
syntactic composition 99, (106), 125, (142), 144, 146, 149—50, (150)
syntax 59, 63, 66, 81, 86–9, 139, 144–5, 160, 165, (166)
    error 89
    semantics division 7, 91, 139, (141–2), 145, 149–50
S-m-n theorem (see parametrization)

table look-up 170
tag sorting 156
tape 61–2
technical trick 147
test-input programming language (10), (150)

theorem 111
total
    function 50, 54–5, (57), 95, 116
    recursive function 52
transition function 14, 61, 132
translation 147–8
trap 153
T-predicate (see Kleene)
Turing computable 65, 74, 93
Turing machine (see language)
    multitape 170, (176)
    -ness 81
Turing, A. M. 10, 46, 63, 110, 129
Turing's thesis 96

Ullman, J. D. 44
uncomputable real number 128
unique program 149–50
universal Turing machine 94, (104)
undecidable 115
unlimited register 130
unsolvable 116, (150)

value computed 93
virtual memory 130
von Neumann, J. 81, 158, 171
    vs. Gödel 81

weakest link 3
well-formed formula 110
word 14

yield 62–3, 132, 155, 163, (165)
Young, P. R. 122, 129

zero 45
    function 46, (56), 66, 162